The Atlantic Papers
Volume Two

The Atlantic Institute is a private international organization which promotes co-operation among the Atlantic nations and Japan in economic, political, social and cultural affairs. Its work extends not only to the relationships of those countries between themselves but also with those of the East and of the developing world.

1.

The Atlantic Papers

Volume Two

Published for The Atlantic Institute

Lexington Books
D.C. Heath and Company
Lexington, Massachusetts
Toronto   London

Table of Contents

Military Forces and Political Conflicts in the Mediterranean

Introduction
Curt Gasteyger

Of all oceans and seas the Mediterranean is probably the most puzzling. As the cradle of three major religions and of Western and Arab civilization it has seen the rise and fall of more empires and the fighting of more battles than any of the other seas. Its political and strategic importance is only matched by its role as a commercial artery between Orient and Occident. The relatively small size of the area is more than compensated for by the complexity of the problems, the discrepancies in economic development and the explosiveness of some of the conflicts that bedevil the littoral countries.

In the seventeen countries grouped around the Mediterranean (including Cyprus and Malta) live some 280 million people with a total of 2.8 million armed forces. Taken together, this represents a considerable military potential, which would compare well with any world power; but this is, of course, a simple addition of figures; it means little, if anything, since its components come from a highly heterogeneous group of countries, most of which have hardly more in common than the shores and waters of the Mediterranean Sea. They have different political backgrounds and are at varying stages of economic development. Albania at present is politically and ideologically closer to distant communist China than to her neighbour Yugoslavia. Israel's GNP is about two thirds that of the UAR, which has a population twelve times as large. The countries on the European coast—from Spain to Turkey—with a total population of well over 200 million and a GNP of 240 billion dollars, outweigh by far the Arab countries—from Syria to Morocco—with some 75 million people and a GNP of some 16 billion dollars.

Of the seventeen countries only five (France, Italy, Greece, Turkey, Spain) either belong to the Atlantic Alliance or have a bilateral treaty with the United States. Britain still maintains air bases in Cyprus, and base facilities in Malta, though their future seems uncertain. Albania has ceased to be even a nominal member of the Warsaw Pact by formally declaring her withdrawal from it in the wake of the Czech crisis in August 1968. The status of the eight remaining countries can be labelled as being of various kinds of non-alignment. It must, however, be added that for the time being the former "non-alignment" of Egypt and Syria has in reality been replaced by an almost total dependence on Soviet military and technical assistance.

Already this superficial survey of the different degrees of alignment and the still wider range of non-alignment, the imbalance of economic development

Dr. Curt Gasteyger is the Deputy Director of the Atlantic Institute, Paris.

between, first, the European and the Arab states and, second, between many individual countries, shows that the Mediterranean area is far from possessing a political or economic unity, and that the countries themselves are less likely to form a distinct community of interests than almost any other constellation of states, except perhaps the countries bordering the Indian Ocean.

Why, then, a study on the Mediterranean? When the Atlantic Institute decided, in conjunction with the Italian Institute of International Affairs, to organize two international conferences on the Mediterranean—the first on political-military aspects, the second on economic problems—it was well aware of the difficulties such an undertaking would present. There is hardly a common denominator for the wide range of problems which exists in the Mediterranean area, and hardly a common language in which to discuss them fruitfully. If the two Institutes nevertheless decided to go ahead with the project and invite participants from all the major Mediterranean countries as well as from Britain, the United States and Germany, they did so because of two major developments which, in fact, concern all the countries present in the area; the arrival of the Soviet Union as a naval and politico-economic power, which has led to a simultaneous presence of the two super-powers with its attendant risk of a direct confrontation between them; and the growing discrepancy in the economic development of the Arab states on the one side and the European countries on the other, generating a potentially explosive instability in the former and calling for a more active and co-ordinated development policy of the latter.

Both developments, actual or potential, seemed to justify a more extensive debate among experts from the countries concerned. Thus the conference on the politico-strategic situation in the Mediterranean was convened from June 19-21, 1969, at the Atlantic Institute in Paris. The second meeting, which will be devoted to the politico-economic problems is scheduled to take place in March 1970, under the auspices of the Italian Institute of International Affairs, Rome.

Some of the papers published in this issue were especially prepared for the first conference; they are reprinted here in a revised and updated version. Other papers were written by participants after the conference. They deal, of course, only with selected major aspects of the present politico-strategic situation in the Mediterranean; reasons of time and space unfortunately did not permit the inclusion of contributions on other aspects such as the position of France or Italy, important as these certainly are.*

The following papers turn upon the first central theme referred to above: the presence of the two super-powers in the Mediterranean, its effect on the security of the area and the reactions of the local countries to this presence. Paradoxically the arrival of these external powers has, more than anything else, given the Mediterranean area a semblance of cohesion and unity which, for the reasons explained above, hardly existed before. Thus, as John Campbell shows, until the 1960s the United States gave the Mediterranean a role in her global deterrent strategy; "it was the locus of military power that could be brought into play to

---

*The Institute much regrets that it was unable to include a contribution from an Arab country although it tried very hard to do so. For reasons of his own, not known to the Institute, the Arab author did not present the paper which had been agreed upon.

serve American or general Western interests in the recurrent crises of the Middle East; it was NATO's southern flank and the main avenue for military support of Greece and Turkey."

Today, the intrusion of Soviet warships into an area of hitherto unchallenged Western predominance has had a similar "uniting" effect. It is as if Moscow's roaming Mediterranean fleet had linked together this heterogeneous group of countries; suddenly it seems unthinkable that a crisis or conflict could occur in this area without the Soviet Union playing a more or less important role in it. Nobody can say whether this will in fact happen. The way the world looked at the possible political and strategic consequences of the recent coup in Libya shows, however, that such a possibility has entered the calculations of everybody who has a stake in developments in the area.

By its mere physical presence in the Mediterranean, the Soviet Union has increased her potential influence and widened the spectrum of possible action. Aside from the important part Moscow is likely to play in any new flare-up of the Arab-Israeli conflict, we can think of a number of possible developments looming on the Mediterranean horizon which the Soviet Union might well take advantage of to increase her influence: a Tunisia deprived of the dominating figure of President Bourguiba and sandwiched between the revolutionary regimes of Libya and Algeria; Morocco—isolated as the only remaining monarchy in North Africa; a Spain without Franco and a Yugoslavia after Tito or a Greece with or after the dictatorial regime of the Colonels.

The uncertainties of the political future are therefore manifold. It would be both naïve and short-sighted to ignore the opportunities they offer to a determined Soviet leadership. How far the Soviet Union could get without being confronted with more or less the same obstacles the West had run up against before her, is another question. It has been pointed out that the United States as a result of the Soviet fleet now being in the Eastern Mediterranean could no longer effect an intervention of the kind undertaken in Lebanon in 1958. This may be so. The same, however, is probably true of similar interventions that the Soviet Union might feel tempted to undertake: the "neutralizing" or even "paralysing" effect resulting from a simultaneous presence of the two super-powers in a given area, works both ways.

There are other limiting factors. A major one is, of course, the limited operational capacity of the Soviet Navy. First of all, its freedom of manoeuvre is restricted by the fact that the two accesses to the Mediterranean which are operational at present (i.e., the Bosporus and Gilbraltar) are controlled by NATO members; second, the Soviet fleet still lacks sufficient air cover mainly because it does not have one single combat-aircraft carrier; and, finally, as the paper by Renè Mertens demonstrates, Russian vessels have failed in most cases in the past to score a success over their often less well-equipped enemy.

These and a number of related factors, to which Mertens refers, should be kept in mind when the military value of the Soviet Mediterranean Fleet and its potential impact are being appraised. The conclusion of it all is that the political and psychological effect of this naval force is much greater in peace-time than its military value would be in times of conflict; it is no doubt better equipped to

5

prevent military actions by other countries than to enforce the political aims of its own.

Malcolm Mackintosh brings out this latter point very clearly. In his view Soviet policy in the Mediterranean is "to weaken and expel Western influence from an area which extends to the south of the Soviet frontiers, outflanks the south-eastern members of NATO, forms a land bridge to Africa and the Indian sub-continent, and cuts across traditional Western routes to the East, and potential Chinese routes to the West."

By establishing what is most likely to be a permanent presence in the Mediterranean and by heavily supporting a number of Arab states, the Soviet Union has scored substantial gains. This surprising initial success, however, is neither self-perpetuating nor without risks. There is a price to be paid for it. If the Soviet Union merely wants to gain influence by exploiting protracted conflicts, to expand her presence and promote her own interests without taking on more responsibilities within the area, then she may discover that in a region as diverse as the Middle East, and with partners as volatile as the Arabs, she will inherit the responsibilities without the influence. She is already learning, as Mackintosh points out, "the hard and unexpected lesson that recipients of economic aid do not necessarily express their gratitude in terms of political loyalty and obedience." Already today the Soviet Union is faced with what Arnold Hottinger calls a basic dilemma, from which she will find it very hard to extricate herself. Over the last ten years or so Moscow has invested vast amounts for economic aid and arms in Egypt and in other Arab countries. Thus far she has done so in return for little more than Arab goodwill and a certain degree of political influence the extent of which is difficult to measure. The first might easily turn into hostility if the second were to be used against what the Arabs consider to be their own interests. Thus, "to force Egypt and the other Arab states to a settlement in the Israeli dispute which, in Arab eyes, would seal their defeat, would almost certainly mean for the Russians that the previous sympathy towards the Soviet Union would change to indifference or resentment" (Hottinger).

The Soviet Union's freedom of action in the Mediterranean will therefore be restricted not only by the obvious limits to her naval activities, but also by a number of political and economic considerations. The Soviet Union may willy-nilly have to develop a sense of restraint and responsibility which both the permanent risk of a direct confrontation with the United States and her interest in the protection of her newly acquired positions in the Arab world will impose on her. This does not mean, as Mackintosh rightly points out, that she would like to see a Middle East and a Mediterranean devoid of tension. It is, after all, precisely this state of tension which helps to legitimize her presence and make Arab countries so dependent on her support. What Moscow is seeking, however, and prepared to contribute to, is "some degree of stability and control of the political forces in the area" (Mackintosh).

While the Soviet Union cannot hope—and, in fact, does not want—to eliminate Western influence completely, she is certainly determined to become a major, if not the predominant, power in this strategically and economically crucial area. In striving for this, she may be helped by two factors: first, by what we might call a growing discrepancy in the scope of the two super-powers' commitments to the area; and, second, by the absence of Western Europe as a political force in the Eastern Mediterranean, which would be strong enough to take the place of a gradually receding American presence and counterbalance a growing Russian one.

In this context Europeans might be well advised to read carefully the last paragraphs of Mr. Campbell's paper because they reflect a new and important trend in present American foreign policy: the desire to transfer gradually some responsibilities, which the United States has so far held, to local countries. If this is true for South-East Asia, there is no reason why it should not apply to the Mediterranean and the Middle East as well. These two areas will undoubtedly remain of great importance to the United States. They are, however, no longer of vital interest to her—Middle Eastern oil is no longer indispensable for her economically and the Mediterranean no longer decisive for her strategically. An indefinite American commitment to these areas, at its present extent, should therefore not be taken for granted.

Against this the Soviet Union has a number of persuasive reasons for not only establishing a permanent presence in these areas but for making it as solid and comprehensive as possible. Being a Middle Eastern power herself, she feels more immediately concerned about the political-strategic fate of this important land-bridge linking three continents, than her remote American rival; her interest in Middle Eastern oil is growing rapidly, and she may hope to get better and more direct access to the Persian Gulf and the Indian Ocean once the Suez Canal is reopened. In the words of a Soviet weekly,[1] the Middle East is a region in which there "are concentrated, as in a focus, international problems on whose solution hangs the fate not only of the Middle Eastern countries themselves, but of countries in Europe, Asia and Africa." It was not the Soviet aim, the paper continues, as Western propaganda asserted, to wrest this (i.e., Middle Eastern) oil and this strategic position from the West; the Soviet Union wanted only to replace a one-sided relationship with "many-sided international links."

This blunt statement leaves little doubt that the Soviet Union is determined to improve the existing balance of forces in the Middle East in her favour. So far her endeavour has met with little resistance from the West. France's recent reappearance in the Mediterranean suggests that she is more interested in picking up what Britain and the United States have had to relinquish than in containing the Soviet Union.

Equally, the political trend in many Mediterranean countries tends more towards "active neutralism" than the consolidation of defensive alliances. This trend is certainly noticeable on NATO's southern flank. The Mediterranean members have never really felt themselves an integral part of the central strategic balance which constitutes the military and political backbone of the Atlantic Alliance. This feeling is becoming stronger as the East-West *détente* progresses. It reflects a general weariness of military alliances and political alignments particularly if they are marked by a strong American preponderance. France's withdrawal from NATO gave new momentum to this trend. It is significant that

[1] *Za Rubezhom*, November 21, 1969 (quoted from *The New Middle East*, London, No. 16, January 1970, p. 10).

7

the Soviet appearance in the Mediterranean, which fifteen years ago would have caused alarm and concern, is now likely to accelerate rather than stop this process of cautious political reorientation among NATO's southern members. It is less a defensive reaction to the Soviet intrusion than a gradual adaptation to the shift in the balance of power which this intrusion symbolizes. Even Turkey, a most loyal ally, is trying to reduce her dependence on the United States by simultaneously improving her relations with the communist neighbours. Greece may well follow suit.

The movement towards a more balanced position between the super-powers does not, however, stop at the doorstep of the Arab world. Some Arab countries would certainly like to normalize their relations with the United States. They feel, however, inhibited in doing so by their heavy dependence on the Soviet Union on the one hand, and too close an association of the United States with Israel on the other. Contrary to what many communists proclaim and to what, strangely enough, the Spanish Government has called for, there is not going to be a neutralization *of* the Mediterranean by eliminating the presence of the two super-powers, but more neutralism *in* the Mediterranean because of this very presence. If this assumption is correct, Western policy will be faced with new and difficult tasks. Their solution will require a new and imaginative approach.

To be sure, purely military reactions, necessary as they may be, will not be adequate as the Soviet challenge becomes more subtle and diversified. Sooner or later, therefore, NATO as a collective security organization will have to be complemented by new forms of bilateral and multilateral co-operation in the political and economic fields. Besides Greece and Turkey, these could embrace other countries such as Yugoslavia, Malta and Cyprus, and possibly those Arab countries which wish to enter into a closer form of co-operation with the West in general or with Western Europe in particular.

It is here that the presence of a more united and outward-looking Europe would be most useful. Unfortunately, Europe is still far from that minimum degree of political coherence which would make her contribution really effective and significant. Many countries on the northern and southern shores of the Mediterranean that wish to reduce their one-sided dependence on the super-powers, would however hope for precisely such an increased European commitment. Rightly or wrongly—and probably too optimistically—they see in Europe the natural "interlocutor" from which they can expect a more sympathetic understanding of their external aspirations and a more active support for their internal development. No doubt the latter is a precondition of these countries' internal stability. It may in turn enhance their readiness to tackle the many unsolved conflicts and tensions that bedevil their mutual relations. It is hoped, therefore, that the conference on the political-economic development of the Mediterranean area will provide them with some answers.

The ideas presented in the contributions to this *ATLANTIC PAPER* are those of their authors. The Atlantic Institute is responsible only for their presentation to the public.

The United States and the Mediterranean

John C Campbell

For the United States, only in the past few years has the Mediterranean appeared in the guise of a problem in its own right, calling for a policy, a strategy, or action. It had always been a part of some other problem and some other policy. Until the 1960s the inland sea and parts of its littoral had a role in America's global deterrent strategy, notably as the home of the Sixth Fleet with its nuclear punch and of the Moroccan, Spanish and other bases of the Strategic Air Command; it was the locus of military power that could be brought into play to serve American or general Western interests in the recurrent crises of the Middle East; it was NATO's southern flank and the main avenue for military support of Greece and Turkey. The salient fact was that the dominance of America's military power, together with the forces of her NATO allies, was unchallenged. They could afford differences among themselves, as when Britain and France launched the Suez operation in 1956 and when General de Gaulle withdrew units of the French Mediterranean Fleet from NATO command in 1959. The Mediterranean was a sector of the defence of the West against the Soviet Union, but Soviet sea and air power, except in the form of an occasional submarine, was nowhere around.

Stalin, following his unsuccessful attempts in the early postwar years to break into the Mediterranean with his demands for footholds in the Dodecanese and in Libya and his strategy of subversion and pressure against Greece and Turkey, seemed to lose interest. But Khrushchev embarked on a political strategy of entrenching Soviet influence in a number of Arab states bordering on the Mediterranean, and in due course his successors brought into being what is now the Soviet Mediterranean Fleet. These developments took place just as American strategy was being reappraised, largely because of changes in the character and technology of weapons. Thus there was uncertainty over what American policy was and what it should be, and these two questions remain with us today. Before dealing with them directly, it may be instructive to look briefly into the past.

The Period of Western Predominance

The Eastern Mediterranean, from the time of the assumption by the United States in 1947 of responsibility for the security of Greece and Turkey, became

Mr. John C. Campbell is a Senior Research Fellow at the Council on Foreign Relations, New York.

central to the development of an American policy for the whole region of the Middle East. That policy went through several metamorphoses, but it always rested on the basic purpose of preventing the expansion of Soviet power. The maintenance of a considerable US military presence, the efforts to shore up an obviously declining British position, and the attempts to organize a regional security system were all ancillary to the basic purpose. During the decade in which the United States and Britain were quite free from serious Soviet challenge in pursuing this objective, their real problems were not military at all but came from the rise of an assertive Arab nationalism which, with notable success after the Egyptian revolution of 1952, resisted participation in Western defence alignments directed against the Soviet Union, pressed for reduction of British bases remaining on Arab soil, and took issue with the West on the question of Israel.

Western military dominance in the Mediterranean could not prevent Arab refusal to join a Middle East Defence Organization, the loss of Britain's huge base at Suez, the outbreak and continuance of the Algerian revolt against France, the failure to extend the Baghdad Pact to any Arab country except Iraq, or Abdel Nasser's turn to the Soviet bloc for arms. In 1956 came his defiance of the West through the seizure of the Suez Canal Company and the ultimate humiliation of Britain and France in the crisis of November. Nasser showed by blocking the canal that a local ruler could turn the West's "lifeline" through the Mediterranean from an ocean-linking highway into a dead-end street. It was no wonder that the Soviet Union's leaders took the occasion to move into the area when the Arab states most sharply at odds with the West showed themselves happy to issue invitations. The result was a situation in which the United States and her Western associates had to cope with a working alliance of Arab nationalism and Soviet power politics which seemed for a brief period to be carrying all before it.

The events of 1958, from the union of Syria and Egypt to the violent replacement of the pro-Western regime in Iraq by a mixed group of nationalists and communists, brought Western influence and prestige to the lowest point yet. All this took place, moreover, in the presence of overwhelming American and other Western power: huge air bases available for use by SAC's strategic bombers in Spain, Morocco, Libya, Turkey and Saudi Arabia; the powerful Sixth Fleet; US tactical air power and ground forces easily available from the European theatre; and to these should be added the British forces and bases at Gibraltar, Malta, Cyprus, Aden, and the Persian Gulf; the French at Bizerta and in Algeria; the forces of Italy, Greece and Turkey, all committed to NATO. At the height of the crisis of 1958 American forces did land in Lebanon, and British troops flew into Jordan to prevent the situation from getting entirely out of hand. But once they were there the major problem was to get them out again with some political results and no loss of face. If the events of that turbulent year demonstrated anything, it was the wide discrepancy between the balance of military force and the course of political events in the Middle East.

Those events showed also that a foreign physical presence in the form of naval and air bases could be a political liability in countries characterized by nationalist sensitivity. They were natural targets for agitation and pressure, a fact which, as the United States discovered, applied to her own bases as well as to those of the historic colonial powers of Europe. Americans might consider themselves anti-colonialist, but Arab nationalists did not see it quite that way. As the British slowly relinquished their bases in Egypt, Jordan, and Iraq and their protectorate over Kuwait, the United States had to weigh the consequences of staying in Morocco, Libya and Saudi Arabia, for even the friendly governments of those states had no desire to expose themselves to political attack at home for the sake of that friendship. And so the agreement for military use of Dhahran was allowed by Saudi Arabia to lapse in 1962, and the huge air based complex in Morocco was evacuated by the end of 1963. The only remaining US air base on Arab territory was Wheelus Field in Libya, which was of sufficient financial importance to the host country to keep it in being for some years.

The American withdrawal from these bases was cause for relief to American diplomats, who had enough crises on their hands without inviting more, but the general acquiescence of the Pentagon in this diminution of American power was more surprising. The key could be found in the effects of technological change on military geography.

No one base, of course, could be said to be crucial when there were others still available in the same region. Spain could serve as a substitute for Morocco. Turkey would still co-operate when nearby Arab countries would no longer do so. The fundamental change, however, came with new military capabilities which reduced the role of such bases in the maintenance of America's overall deterrent. Through refuelling techniques it became possible to increase the range of SAC's bombers, which no longer needed to be poised so close to the Soviet Union. More important was the entry of the ICBM and the Polaris missile into the armoury of strategic weapons. The shift to reliance on such weapons (although long-range bomber aircraft still had a place in the total pattern of deterrence) made it possible for American diplomacy in the Middle East to be free of nearly absolute "requirements" of a military nature which were nothing but political liabilities in those countries which were not and did not intend to be America's allies.

The question of bases and military presence can be confusing, however, unless the distinction is made between the requirements of global strategic deterrence (having nothing to do with the Middle East) and the requirements of containment, defence, alliance obligations, transit and communication, access to oil, and all the other aims and interests which lay at the roots of the policies which had brought the United States onto the Middle East scene in 1947 and kept her there. American warships in the Mediterranean had on board marines ready for landing as well as strategic weapons which could reach the Soviet Union.

Commitments to defend Greece and Turkey might have to be carried out right there, on the soil of those countries and the adjacent waters.

A military presence was of no great help unless suited to the dangers, opportunities and possibilities of the local situation: for defence against limited attack by an outside power, for coping with regional conflicts, for encouraging some states, discouraging others, and even intervening in case of crisis. Intervention in Lebanon in 1958, at the invitation of the government in office, was probably the most graphic illustration of the use of available military power to support a general political strategy. It achieved its purpose at least in part, but the use of such a blunt instrument in a delicate political situation has been questioned, and it is instructive to note that there has been no comparable military move since.

However one might argue about the uses and abuses of the predominant military power which the United States enjoyed in the Mediterranean in that period, it was comforting to Washington, to her NATO allies, and to friendly states on the littoral to know that it was there. The balance of military power was never far from the thoughts of those in responsible positions in any of the countries concerned, including the Soviet Union. With the Mediterranean Sea itself the preserve of American and NATO naval forces, hard-won Soviet political gains appeared to be at the mercy of the Western powers in any critical situation.

Khrushchev, in particular, apparently took to heart the lessons of some of his more adventurous political moves in areas far removed from the reach of Soviet military power. When his attempt to capitalize on the Congo affair in 1960 turned sour, he had to take account of the fact that in a showdown Western military force could be brought to bear on the situation and Soviet force could not. His attempt to put Soviet missiles in Cuba two years later brought on a crisis from which American military superiority in the area left him no way out except retreat or nuclear war. It was shortly after the Cuban crisis that the Soviet Government began its build-up of naval and other forces to increase the reach of its military power and give it a flexibility comparable to that of the United States. The most solid evidence of this expanding capability was the growth of Soviet naval forces in the Mediterranean, beginning slowly in 1964 and rapidly increasing in the next two or three years. As Admiral Gorshkov and others explained it, the Soviet Union intended to put her naval power on all the oceans and to provide her armed forces with the capacity to strike crushing blows to the imperialists on all the continents.

Those Soviet decisions were part of a global strategy, and the American reaction to them could be expected to be of comparable scope. One question was what, if anything, America should do to increase her own naval power. Another was whether the Soviet Union, with virtual parity in nuclear weapons, was planning a strategy of military and political challenges in various parts of the world to which America could not reply without grave risks of nuclear war. But if the general Soviet aims were global, the immediate challenge was in an area, the Mediterranean, where the Soviet Union had already made striking political gains and where periodic crisis was predictable.

Planners in Washington and at NATO headquarters had already begun to think about the implications when the Arab states and Israel provided a crisis in

12

1967 which could serve as a test case. The Six-Day War was remarkable in the manner of its origin, the rapidity of its operations, and the one-sidedness of its outcome. For our purpose here the most remarkable point was the fact that each of the two great powers made sure above all that the other knew it was not intervening in the fighting. There was a moment towards the end of the week's battles, as Israel kept on fighting in Syria and seemed poised for a possible push to Damascus, when Moscow spoke menacingly of taking direct action, but we do not and may never know how serious that threat was meant to be.

Any observer can draw his own conclusions from the events of 1967. Some accepted the general proposition that military intervention by one of the big powers in such a local conflict could be ruled out for the future because of the incalculable dangers it would involve. Yet others could argue that the United States did not take military action because she did not have to: Israel won the war handily and did not need help. Or that the Soviet Union did not intervene because she knew the United States had local superiority in the Eastern Mediterranean as she had had in the Caribbean in 1962. If the facts had been different (an Arab victory threatening the survival of Israel, or a more even balance of Soviet and American forces), perhaps the results would also have been different. At any rate, the Six-Day War pumped new fuel into the process of reappraisal going on in American thinking on what to do about the Mediterranean and the Middle East.

Facing the Soviet Challenge

It would be incorrect to refer to definite schools of thought on American strategy, but there were differences in approach and in conclusions which can be described in general terms. There were those who found the situation serious and even alarming: Soviet naval power in the Mediterranean which virtually neutralized, though it did not match, American power; ability of the Soviet fleet to use facilities in Egyptian, Syrian, and Algerian ports while vessels of the Sixth Fleet could no longer pay visits to former ports of call like Beirut and perhaps even Istanbul (due to anti-American rioting there); a disastrous decline of American influence in the Arab world, already in progress but vastly accelerated by the Six-Day War and the rapid Soviet action to rearm the radical Arab states and bind them even closer; the weakness of NATO's eastern anchor because of the Greek-Turkish dispute over Cyprus and Soviet efforts to exploit it; the success of Soviet diplomacy in making economic deals with Turkey and Iran and weakening their ties with the West; the possibility of Soviet military interventions to support friendly regimes or overthrow others; and increasing signs of Soviet activity in the Red Sea, the Horn of Africa, the Persian Gulf and the Indian Ocean where British positions were being given up and no Western power was filling the vacuum.

The proposed cures followed from the diagnosis. These should be a major build-up of American naval strength, especially in the Mediterranean; increased military aid to Turkey and Iran so that they would have the wherewithal and the confidence to stand firm; open support for those Arab states which were still moderate and pro-Western such as Morocco, Tunisia, Libya, Lebanon, Jordan, Saudi Arabia and Kuwait; firm maintenance of existing bases, rights and facilities for air and naval movement, communications, oil production and transport, and the like; and especially, because the Soviet offensive threatened to turn NATO's flank and envelop Western Europe from the south, a serious effort to persuade Britain, France and other European allies to play a greater part in protecting the common Western interests.

Those who did not accept the above analysis, at least not in its entirety tended to discount the estimate of Soviet strategy as overdrawn and the proposed countermeasures as not wholly responsive to the present and future situation. The reasoning was somewhat as follows: the Soviet Union's strategy is not carrying all before it in the Mediterranean and Middle East; despite her gains among the Arabs because of the Israel question, her client states are weak and by no means represent the wave of the future in the Arab world; Arab nationalism can be counted on to resist Soviet domination as it has resisted the West; the policies of Turkey and Iran in seeking better relations need not undermine their security or their fundamental ties with the West; the presence of the Soviet fleet in the Mediterranean is a natural result of the desire to exercise the attributes of a super-power, especially in waters much closer to home than they are to the United States, and does not really threaten Western naval superiority or the independence of littoral states; the Soviets know they cannot take over the Mediterranean area and use it against Western Europe; and finally, Soviet strategy is basically political and will avoid military ventures as not worth the risk.

Again, the views on policy flow from the analysis: no need for a crash build-up of the Sixth Fleet to greater strength, though a close watch should be kept on Soviet naval forces; promotion of naval, co-operation with European states bordering on the Mediterranean, within and outside NATO; strong efforts to bring about an Arab-Israel settlement in order to stop the drift of Arab policy towards hostility to the United States and co-operation with the Soviets; maintenance of good relations with the moderate and conservative Arab states but not to the exclusion of attempts to improve relations with the radical ones; continued reliance on Turkey and Iran as allies and sources of strength for the Western position in the region; emphasis on political means in carrying on competition with the Soviet Union; and attempts to open a channel to Moscow for discussion of such matters as an Arab-Israel settlement and the levels of armaments in the Middle East.

Drifting American Policy

To repeat, these are not schools of thought so much as trends in thinking, and no battle lines were drawn between them. American policy, in the late 1960s when these questions were to the fore, took shape from a multiplicity of diplomatic moves, bureaucratic compromises and budgetary battles rather than from any all-encompassing decision at the top to adopt a grand strategy of cold war or of political and diplomatic manoeuvre. Inevitably, American policy had

14

its cold-war aspect because the cold war was going on in the Mediterranean and Middle East even as it seemed to slacken elsewhere. Clearly, American policy was bound to have other aspects as well because the very nature of politics in the region, which had frustrated the single-minded American approach of the 1950s, made such an approach in the late 1960s patently absurd—not to speak of the politics of the United States and the fierce official and public concentration on Vietnam. It was not surprising that the drift of policy was in the direction of the second trend rather than the first.

"Drift" is the right word, for the place of the Mediterranean in US military strategy was defined by default, so to speak, in the absence of positive decisions to undertake a large expansion of forces there. The Sixth Fleet was kept at its existing strength despite the addition of new units (including a helicopter carrier) to its Soviet rival force and the uneasiness of the US Navy over the growing capabilities of that force. No changes were made in the small Mideast Force in the Arabian Sea-Persian Gulf area despite the British withdrawal from Aden and pending withdrawal from the Gulf and the unexpected sight of Soviet naval vessels plying those waters. US military aid to Turkey continued to decrease year by year in the knowledge of its unfavourable effects on Turkish-American relations, and the delivery of considerable quantities of modern arms to Iran was made possible only by that country's ability to pay for them.

These statements suggest a system of decision which insured that if a proposed measure were going to cost anything it would be automatically rejected. That is too crude a way to put it, for these matters were given serious attention. But with a regular military budget at record levels, the mounting extra costs of the Vietnam War, and the calls for economy issuing from the fiscal managers, it was predictable that vast new sums would not be devoted to a region where existing forces seemed to have the situation in hand.

As for aid to Turkey, there the President was restrained by the drastic congressional cuts in his total foreign aid programme. Yet in that case as well there was a decision on priorities; sufficient funds were not transferred from some other country's aid programme to give the Turks what they had been promised, although it was clear enough that Turkey, because of her control of the Bosporus and Dardanelles, might hold the key to the fate of Soviet naval power in the Mediterranean.

In judging how well America's military dispositions measure up to possible challenge, we might consider four contingencies: general war, local hostilities involving the great powers, conflicts between local contestants, and the general course of local and great-power competition in the absence of war.

In the event of general war the Soviet forces in the Mediterranean would be destroyed in a short time; whatever mission they had would be of a *kamikaze* character. In any case a general nuclear war, if one can picture it at all short of total holocaust, would hardly be much affected by what happened in the Mediterranean.

A limited war arising from a Soviet attack on, say, Turkey or Iran, to which the United States and others would respond locally with conventional arms, would also enable the Sixth Fleet to assert mastery over the rival naval forces, although much would depend on how much land-based air power the Soviets

15

could bring to bear. But there is an air of unreality in this kind of speculation. The chances that the Soviets would launch such an attack must be rated as slight, not only on the basis of history but also on any calculation of how long such a period of conventional war involving the big nuclear powers would last before they either agreed on some way to stop it or carried it up to the nuclear level. The contingency is one which the United States and her allies should not banish from their minds, for it demands that, as on Europe's central front, there be force in that area or easily available, in order to maintain deterrence at lower levels than that of strategic nuclear war; but hardly one for which radically new dispositions of armed forces are required. The main deterrent behind the forces of the ally attacked and mobile reserves which could be brought from elsewhere is still the Sixth Fleet and the great nuclear power behind it.

The possibility of local conflict—for example, between the Arabs and Israel, Iraq and Iran, or Greece and Turkey—poses more practical and also more varied and complex problems of planning and strategy. The task of highest priority would be to hold to a minimum any temptation to the Soviet Union to intervene militarily. Second would be helping to persuade the parties to stop fighting, perhaps joining with others in enforcing a UN order to cease fire or to return to the *status quo ante*. Third would be to meet emergency situations in which vital American interests or the lives of American citizens were endangered by the fighting.

All these instances would require the availability of armed forces adequate to the respective tasks. The first one would seem to require a superiority of American and allied over Soviet forces to get the full value of deterrence. That superiority now exists in the Mediterranean. East of Suez it exists in the small squadrons maintained by Britain and the United States in the Persian Gulf and the Indian Ocean. If the Suez Canal is reopened, the Soviet Union will almost certainly move to establish her own naval presence there, possibly using Aden as its main base. That is one reason why the United States has taken no initiative for the reopening of the canal.

Future Trends

It seems like folly to predict that the most likely contingencies to be faced in the Mediterranean area over the next few years will be those of peace-time, yet we may do so by stretching the definition of peace to include the situation that has existed since 1967—with its full quota of coups d'état, desert border skirmishes, civil violence, Fedayeen raids, and an active military front between Israel and the UAR. This is the environment, now considered normal in some parts of the area, in which American policy will have to prove itself amid interlocking struggles for political power involving both the big and the small powers against a background of crisis which is more or less continuous but stops short of war. American policy and strategy will therefore be primarily political, with the double aim of preventing war and preventing any major shift in the world balance, whether that balance is viewed in political or military terms. Fundamental to those purposes are a necessary minimum of control over the level of conflict between the Arabs and Israel; maintenance of present commitments to NATO countries and of relations of confidence and solidarity with them, including some tolerable regulation of the present awkward situation of Greece and of the Greece-Turkey-Cyprus imbroglio; support for the economic and social progress of *all* Mediterranean countries; maintenance of open channels of communication to all of them, hostile as well as friendly; and, in all probability, a measure of co-operation with the Soviet Union. This last point could be the key to success or failure in all the others, but such co-operation requires two willing partners.

The instruments for such a grand strategy are primarily political, economic, diplomatic. It is a legitimate question whether military power is relevant at all. Both the United States and the Soviet Union may have exaggerated ideas of how much influence their warships cruising in the Mediterranean will have, for example, on whether Yugoslavia turns to the left or Algeria turns to the right. But where alliance ties are strong, as they are within NATO, or where military positions are well entrenched, like those of the Soviet Union in Egypt or Syria, the military presence of both powers is obviously there to stay and cannot be simply wished away. The American and Soviet naval forces tend to balance and to deter each other in so far as political developments in the Mediterranean area are concerned, and perhaps that is not so different from the situation if neither were present at all. The suggestion put forward in countries as far apart in other things as Yugoslavia and Spain that both powers should withdraw their fleets and leave the Mediterranean to the Mediterranean countries has its attractions, but no possibility of realization whatsoever.

Our subject has been American policy and strategy but the Mediterranean is or should be of more direct concern to America's allies in Europe. Anyone familiar with the mood of America in the past few years may also question whether the United States will maintain past levels of interest, commitment and leadership in this region. The increased sense of the limitations of America's resources and of her ability to control or even measurably affect the course of events in distant lands is colouring official as well as public thinking. The feeling that "Europe should do more," which is already discernible in American policy on NATO defence in Europe, may find its logical extension in the Mediterranean and the Middle East.

The Arab-Israel war in 1967 and the Czechoslovakian crisis in 1968 both focussed attention on the dangers flowing from the visible evidence of Soviet military strength and, in the latter case, of Soviet willingness to use it. Hence the flurry of activity at NATO meetings on the subject of what to do in the Mediterranean, the declaration that any Soviet intervention affecting the situation in the Mediterranean area "would create an international crisis with grave consequences," and the decisions to improve the effectiveness and co-ordination of allied surveillance there and to create an allied naval force (which the United States, Britain, Italy and Turkey joined).

Not earth-shaking decisions in a military sense, these were signs of common

17

concerns and common policies not much in evidence in recent years. For Europe's own future, it may be a significant beginning towards assumption by Europe of a larger share in safeguarding interests which are more directly European than American, such as access to oil, freedom of navigation and commerce in Mediterranean waters and on to the east, and the reconstruction of historic ties, now badly battered but still indispensable, between the civilizations which grew up along the shores of the inland sea.

Soviet Mediterranean Policy

Malcolm Mackintosh

Before analysing Soviet policy towards the Mediterranean and the Middle East, it may be worth while drawing attention to a few general points connected with Soviet foreign policy and its decision-making process. Soviet foreign policy is decided by the Politburo, which does not include either the Foreign or the Defence Minister, whose advice, therefore, is dealt with in their absence. The first priority of Soviet foreign policy is to avoid a military confrontation with the United States or NATO which could lead to a nuclear war; survival of the Soviet Union as a state and as a super-power is an essential requirement which transcends all other political or ideological priorities for the Soviet leaders. Nevertheless, within this framework, the present leaders of the Soviet Union are convinced that she has the right as a super-power to expand her political, economic and military influence wherever possible in the world, without endangering the security of not only the Soviet homeland, but areas like Eastern Europe which are of vital importance to the Soviet Union. The Soviet leaders, like their pre-revolutionary predecessors, also feel an urge to come to terms with the principal rival to make deals on spheres of influence, and to eliminate the risks of military conflict. The Soviet Union sees some value in using the United Nations' machinery mainly to increase Great Power influence, and therefore potential control, in areas of dangerous crisis. All these trends are visible in Soviet policy towards the Middle East and the Mediterranean.

Political and Military Objectives

Soviet policy in this area can conveniently be divided into its military and political aspects. Strategically the Soviet Union faces the naval and air-strike forces of the United States and NATO in the Mediterranean, specifically the United States Sixth Fleet, and one of the high priority tasks of the Soviet Mediterranean Squadron is to carry out peace-time surveillance of the Sixth Fleet, and to be prepared, in the event of war, to sink as many Western ships as possible before facing destruction itself. In the case of vessels capable of launching nuclear strikes against the Soviet Union, the Mediterranean Squadron would try to attack these in the area of launch in order to reduce the damage their strikes would cause in the USSR. The main weakness of the Soviet Navy's strategic position in the Mediterranean is that it is cut off from its home bases by

Mr. Malcolm Mackintosh is Consultant on Soviet Affairs to the Institute for Strategic Studies, London.

the Straits, controlled by Turkey, and that the Straits of Gibraltar are also dominated by a NATO Power; moreover, the closure of the Suez Canal has eliminated another exit from this almost closed sea. The Mediterranean Squadron also lacks effective air cover and air strike power. The Soviet naval air force is land-based, and although Soviet reconnaissance aircraft are believed to be based in the United Arab Republic, and the Squadron is joined from time to time by a helicopter ship (whose main task appears to be anti-submarine warfare) these elements of air power cannot make up for the absence of mobile and effective air cover and air-strike capabilities.

The peace-time, politico-military task of the Soviet fleet is, in the words of the Soviet Navy's Commander-in-Chief: "to support Soviet foreign policy on the high seas." Soviet policy in the area may be summarized as designed to weaken and expel Western influence from an area which tends to the south of the Soviet frontiers, outflanks the south-eastern countries of NATO, forms a land bridge to Africa and the Indian sub-continent, and cuts across traditional Western routes to the East, and potential Chinese routes to the West. In the short to medium term, Soviet policy probably aims at building up Soviet political, economic and military influence in as many countries bordering on the eastern shores of the Mediterranean as will grant the Soviet Union diplomatic, trade or other politico-military access. In the process the Soviet Union will try to weaken Western influence wherever she can, by means of political and propaganda activity, subversion, and the manipulation of political forces in the area. The methods adopted by the Soviet Union to increase her influence initially involve offers of trade and, in some cases, economic and military aid, backed by wide-ranging diplomatic activity; and it is here that the peace-time role of the Soviet Navy is of particular relevance. For those countries in the area which have a Mediterranean coastline, the Navy may "show the flag," pay visits to main ports, and leave an impression that the Soviet Union is in the Mediterranean and Middle East to stay, and is capable of deploying powerful modern ships with which to back up her political presence. Clearly the Soviet Union now understands the advantages to be gained by exploiting the freedom of the seas in supporting an active foreign policy.

When political and other conditions are favourable, the Soviet Union is prepared to send military advisers to countries in the area, and to take over the training of their armed forces, especially where advanced electronic equipment and weapons systems (as in air defence) are involved. The Russians must hope that extensive non-military aid programmes, and the involvement of Soviet technicians and training officers in the day-to-day running of the national armed forces should make the particular country increasingly dependent on the Soviet Union and responsive to Soviet demands. These demands normally take the form of requests to support Soviet foreign policy initiatives (for example in the United Nations), but in certain limited circumstances they may involve Soviet interference in the country's internal affairs. At the same time, while paying due attention to Soviet politico-military aims in the Mediterranean and the Middle East, it should not be forgotten that the Russians genuinely want to increase their trade with the area for normal commercial reasons as part of the expansion of their world-wide trade.

In accordance with these general aims and methods in the Mediterranean and the Middle East, the Soviet Union first made an "economic assault" on selected countries in the area in the late 1950s, having come down firmly on the Arab side in the main dispute—that between Israel and her Arab neighbours. The reasons for the switch in Soviet support from Israel (in 1948) to the Arab countries (in 1955) included the Soviet conviction that Israel was culturally and financially a Western state, with indissoluble ties to the United States; a traditional desire to be on the side with numerical superiority (which is, incidentally, one of the reasons for the often obsessive Soviet reaction to China in the course of the Sino-Soviet dispute); and a belief that an expansion of Soviet influence in the Arab countries was feasible because of politico- and socio-economic conditions in the Arab countries themselves. Moreover, on strategic grounds, the Arab areas offered a chance to undermine the 1954 Baghdad Pact, and eliminate the Western military presence throughout the area.

The development of Soviet influence has proceeded largely on an opportunist basis, although it would probably be true to say that the Russians kept their eye firmly on the UAR as the most promising country for the expansion of their influence. The military defeats of the UAR in 1956 and in 1967 gave the Russians increased opportunities to intensify their influence and spread it more widely, particularly in the military sphere, and the Soviet Government has continued to emphasize to the UAR that if Soviet advice and aid (and all that goes with it) is rejected, the UAR has no one else to whom she can turn. But the Russians have by now had enough experience of the area not to try to push ahead towards their political goals too fast; in the UAR they have established an extremely strong politico-military and economic presence, and they find the UAR Government normally, but not inevitably, responsive to their will. But the Russians probably find Iraq, Syria and Algeria unpredictable and difficult to influence, in spite of their acceptance of Soviet economic and military aid; the last two are quite frequently recipients of "flag-showing" visits by the Soviet Navy. No doubt the Soviet Union finds encouragement in the coups d'état which took place in the Sudan and Libya in 1969, especially since the latter may open up further Arab ports on the Mediterranean coastline for possible "flag-showing" visits and displays of the Soviet naval presence in that area.

While the most effective progress in expanding Soviet influence has occurred in the UAR, Syria, Iraq and Algeria, the Soviet Union has been active politically, diplomatically and economically in many other countries of the area, including those which are members of Western alliances or are culturally and economically associated with the West. The Soviet Union has improved her relations with both Iran and Turkey (taking to some extent the Turkish side in the dispute with Greece over Cyprus), and has delivered some Soviet arms to the Cyprus Government, as well as undertaking a good deal of diplomatic activity probably designed to persuade Cyprus to dispense with the British Sovereign Base Areas on the island. The Soviet Union has shown considerable commercial and some political interest in Malta, and would like to expand her political influence in Valetta. The Soviet Union supports the Spanish case on Gibraltar. Potential interest of the Soviet Union in her "lost" ally, Albania, should not be forgotten; for although the Albanians have followed an anti-Soviet and pro-Chinese course since 1960, the Soviet Union has probably never lost sight of the possibility that a change of regime (perhaps Soviet-inspired) could make Albanian ports once more accessible to the Soviet Naval Squadron in the Mediterranean.

Soviet policy in the short and medium term, therefore, in the Mediterranean and the Middle East is a many-sided activity whose general aim is to weaken Western influence in the area and to replace it by Soviet influence. In the longer term, the Russians would probably like to have sufficient influence in the area to be able to control the policies of its major governments, decide between tension and stability in local disputes, tie national foreign and economic policies to those of the Soviet Union, and "vet" access to the area by Western commercial and political organizations. Except for these very broad aims, it is unlikely that the Soviet leaders are working to a master-plan with a carefully worked out timetable. Soviet policies are part of a probing exercise, an experimental operation in which successes are reinforced and failures (including high risk policies) are abandoned.

New Trends in Soviet Policy

In the course of this probing exercise, two new and important trends in Soviet policy have appeared. First, the Russians have learned the hard and unexpected lesson that recipients of economic and military aid do not necessarily express their gratitude in terms of political loyalty and obedience—in other words, that aid does not imply control. They have discovered that Arab nationalism does not always operate in their favour, and occasionally even clashes with the official and orthodox Communist doctrine issuing from Moscow. Second, having acquired the degree of influence that they now possess, the Russians have had to develop policies for protecting their interests, as well as aiming to destroy or at least reduce other people's interests and influence. The protection of vested interests means some degree of stability and control of the political forces in the area; and this is one of the things the Russians now seek. They are not interested in a Middle East and a Mediterranean which are devoid of tension, for much of their probing exercises depend on a degree of political tension, for example, between Israel and her Arab neighbours. But they want a state of crisis control in which they can most successfully pursue the policy of expelling Western influence from the area; and as one stage in this process they characteristically turn towards the Western powers, first to try to ensure that the military tension is lowered to manageable proportions, but also to see whether four-power collaboration to bring some sort of order into the situation could set useful precedents for future treatment of crisis areas by means of a great power "directoire." The Soviet Union is probably fairly pessimistic about the prospects for such collaboration in the short term, but may regard it as a worthwhile probe in itself. Another possibility is that the Soviet Union might come to consider the advantages of "sealing-off" the Middle East, or placing it in "quarantine," so that whatever conflicts might break out, these would not escalate outside the area.

The Soviet Union appears to be worried about the consequences of growing

22

Fedayeen activity, not because she is opposed to terrorism, but because of the Fedayeen's lack of susceptibility to outside control and because their effort is not directed against the Soviet Union's main target, the West. Israel is not the Soviet Union's main enemy in the Middle East. The Soviet Union could live with an Israeli state and even collaborate with it if its political life became less identified with the West, and became more of a non-aligned, self-contained Middle Eastern state. Moreover, in Soviet eyes, some of the Fedayeen organizations might develop extreme right-wing characteristics, and this is one of the reasons why the Russians may not want to become too closely involved with the movement at this stage in Middle East affairs.

Soviet overall policy is, therefore, still largely one of experiment and probe. Experiment means change, and in the Mediterranean and the Middle East the Soviet Union's view of her interests can also change. Russia's policies towards Israel, Iran, Turkey and Cyprus, for example, have all changed in the last 20 years (in the case of Iran and Turkey, in the last five years) and it would be unwise to rule out altogether the possibility of further changes. It is true that in the Soviet Mediterranean Squadron the Russians have brought into being a highly professional instrument whose use they will continue to develop and perfect. But not all the other instruments tried out by the Soviet Union in the area have proved as reliable, and the Russians, while patient and prepared to wait, are not inclined to reinforce failure indefinitely.

The Arab States on the Eastern Mediterranean

Arnold Hottinger

The political situation in the Arab countries on the eastern Mediterranean is conditioned by one overwhelming factor: their defeat in the Six-Day War. From this has resulted Israeli occupation of Egyptian, Syrian and Jordanian territory, continuing tension along the new armistice lines, Fedayeen activity and politics, and the need for the governments of the stricken countries to recover their lost territories.

Arab Politics and Israel

Palestine has not always loomed as large in the politics of the region, even though it has always been a factor of aggravation and irritation since it first emerged as a problem. In the years preceding the Six-Day War, the main political cleavage in the Arab region seemed to be between the so-called progressive and the conservative Arab regimes. The Israel question—never entirely forgotten—appeared to have receded into the background. Problems of development, of Arab unity, of state-managed socialism versus private capitalism, of the choice of alliance (with the Socialist bloc, a neutralist Third World grouping or the West) had gained the centre of the stage.

But nearly all those problems proved difficult to solve. Indeed one may say that their very permanence and insolubility caused the Israel question again to assume primary importance in Arab politics. It was at first something of a gradual redirection. The Syrian Baathists encouraged infiltration into Israel well before the war, and after the accession of the Jedid group early in 1966 formulated a policy whose main plank was "popular war against Israel." The Egyptian regime was drawn step by step into menacing gestures towards Israel until the war broke out, largely as a consequence of the Syrian policies and the actions of the infiltrators. Had their socialist policies at home been entirely successful, probably neither regime would have found it necessary to let itself be involved in a new confrontation with Israel, at least not before it had developed greater strength. It was to a large extent the partial failure of their "progressive" policies—Egypt's in the Yemen and in building competitive modern industries, Syria's in collaborating with other Arab countries and bringing about the

Dr Arnold Hottinger, is Correspondent on the Middle East and the Iberian Peninsula for the *Neue Zürcher Zeitung* in Madrid.

promised Arab unity—which drove both countries into a trial of strength with Israel.

However, this was the past; today there is little doubt that the Israel issue dominates politics completely. The governments concerned are aware that in the long run they have really only one chance of surviving the defeat: to make up for it within a reasonable time by gaining back what they lost in the last war, plus, if possible, some bigger advantage, however slight. If they do not accomplish this within a reasonable time, perhaps three to five years, in all probability they will be overthrown, and they are aware of the fact. This is the basic situation that the Syrian and Egyptian governments have to take into account. It makes clear that they have really no choice but to concentrate all their resources and all political action on this one question.

Relations with the Soviet Union and with the West are conditioned by this fact, as are all other questions. As the main arms supplier and the main source of diplomatic and financial support the Soviet Union is indispensable in the confrontation with Israel. (Syria's development and financial aid comes practically only from the Soviet Union and Eastern Europe; for Egypt—and Jordan—there is also the budgetary aid of the Arab oil countries.)

Changing Attitudes of the USSR

The Soviet Union during the first two years following the war made it clear that she did not desire a new full-scale war. In her estimation, the Arabs—who were being trained to a considerable extent by Soviet advisers—were not ready for it. On the other hand Arab impatience caused considerable criticism of the Russians; many officers and civilians felt that the Arab armies, particularly the Syrian and the Egyptian who relied entirely on Soviet equipment, had not been supplied with the offensive armament they really needed to start a new war against Israel or at least threaten her plausibly.

But in the course of summer 1969 the mood began to change. Abdel Nasser declared that a new stage in the confrontation had been reached. He named it "the war of attrition." Small-scale activities on the Suez front were stepped up and sufficient success stories of a military nature were printed every day in the Egyptian press to keep most civilians happy.

At the same time a strict separation of army and civilians was maintained so as to avoid any military news other than official communiqués reaching the cities. In this way it was possible to reduce the impatience for action and the criticism of military leaders expressed by civilians, especially students.

The image of the Soviet Union in Arab eyes benefited from this change. But the Soviet diplomats had to pay a price. The Egyptians in their new belligerent mood were less disposed than ever to listen to peace-making proposals such as the Soviet Union and the United States tentatively agreed upon in the course of the summer. From all that is known it appears that the Soviet Union accepted the Egyptian position and did not try to press Cairo too hard towards a compromise peace.

Foreign Minister Gromyko paid a dramatic visit to Cairo, but returned without having influenced President Nasser. There were signs of strain in the following months. Visits of Nasser and of other dignitaries of the regime to Moscow were postponed. Some of the more pro-communist Cairo leaders lost their positions.

But there were no open outbreaks of disagreement, partly because Egypt was too dependent on Soviet support to be able to afford an open quarrel, partly because of the elastic attitude of Soviet diplomacy which continued to give support to the official Egyptian aims of "liberating" the territories occupied by the Israelis and implementing the UN resolution of November 1967, even though, in private, Russian diplomats and emissaries seem to have attempted—in vain—to obtain Egyptian approval for a certain elasticity in implementing the UN resolution.

Egypt

It is in Egypt that the dangers which confront Soviet policy in the Middle East can be most clearly seen. Developments there have gone further than in the other Arab countries. Syria stands back somewhat from the confrontation with Israel, contenting herself with verbal declarations and with help to the Fedayeen as long as they consent to use neighbouring Lebanon and Jordan as the main starting points for their infiltration. Lebanon is involved with her own particular problems which are conditioned by the special bi-polar nature of the country. However, Egypt finds herself in the forefront of the struggle against Israel because her leader, Abdel Nasser, can only save his prestige among the Arabs if he manages to "eliminate the consequences of the aggression" of the Six-Day War.

This he has promised to his people and is bound to attempt. It means the return to the *status quo ante* June 5, 1967. It does not mean a compromise peace in which Egypt would have to make concessions of any significance to the Israeli position.

For Egypt, then, the question centres on regaining the occupied territories without making any concessions to Israel which could be sufficiently visible to the Egyptian population to justify the feeling that the Six-Day War meant a defeat and not just a temporary setback. If this feeling became established, the present regime would have only a small chance of surviving. As long as it can hold out hope that ultimately the results of the war can be reversed, the Government has a good chance of remaining in power.

It appears that the Russians have, after some discussion, at least provisionally accepted the point of view of the Egyptian regime. They are now defending it in their discussions with the US and in the four-power meetings. Russian wavering on the question of how far to underwrite the Egyptian point of view and how far to use pressure to induce in the Egyptians a more pliant attitude can be explained as tactics in the context of their dealings with the Americans on big power concerns.

To sum up the pendular movement of Soviet diplomacy after the Six-Day War, it can be said that during the first two years after the war Russia seemed ready to exert a certain restraining influence on Cairo. This was during the time of the re-equipping and retraining of the Egyptian army. Moscow had consequently to accept a certain amount of Arab criticism and resentment, which sometimes came close to jeopardizing the favoured position that her previous and continuing investment had been earning for her.

The turning point appears to have been Gromyko's visit to Cairo in summer 1969 after which the Soviets showed greater regard for the Arab point of view, at least publicly, and went much further in subscribing to it. This endorsement of greater Arab belligerency preserved the Soviet investment in terms of goodwill, but encouraged the drift towards a new war.

Syrian Internal Rivalries

In the case of Syria the debate about Soviet aid, offensive arms and criticism of the soft Soviet attitude has become associated with the larger issue of the power struggle between two factions of the ruling Baath party. This is being waged around two poles: General Salah Jedid, former Chief of Staff, who at present holds the title of Assistant Secretary-General to the Syrian Baath Party, and General Hafez al-Asad who is Minister of Defence, Army Commander and Commander of the Air Force. Jedid had dominated Syrian politics between January 1966 and spring 1969. He was repeatedly challenged by al-Asad. The latest round has led to the suicide of one and the removal of several more of the main supporters of the old strong man. His opponents, army men close to al-Asad, have charged him with the responsibility for the defeat by Israel and an isolationist policy which has led Syria away from collaboration with other Arab countries, thus weakening her capacity to stand up to Israel and forcing her into excessive dependence on the Soviet Union.

The power struggle between the two has been shelved for the moment, but it is probably not over. It led, in spring 1969, to the visit of the Chief of Staff Mustafa Tallas, al-Asad's closest supporter, to Peking. This, however, appears to have brought little result as the Chinese were not able or willing to deliver the kind of weapons the Syrians desired, principally ground-to-ground rockets.

The al-Asad group has also approached Iraq, where a rival faction of the Baath, the so-called national Baath is governing. These overtures came to nothing because of Baath inter-party rivalries. In the end al-Asad was forced to rely on Soviet support nearly as exclusively as Jedid had done. This fact also explains why Jedid was allowed to continue as Assistant Party Secretary, even though al-Asad appears to have concentrated most of the military power on his side: the Russians had made it clear, while the power struggle was still in progress, that Jedid was their man.

Lebanon

In the past Lebanon's governments have been friendly towards the United States, Beirut being open as a port of call for the Sixth Fleet. American action in

1958, although coming late in the day, was said to have been aimed at maintaining Lebanon as a haven of individual freedom and liberal enterprise.

But the country has been under a cloud since spring 1969. Its great problem is the Palestine refugees who have been awakened to the concept of revolutionary activity by the Fedayeen. The Fedayeen organizations claim the right to use Lebanese territory as a base for their infiltrations into Israel. In order to achieve this aim they make use of the bi-polar nature of the country which is divided into two fundamental tendencies of nearly equal strength: pro-Western groups, mainly Christian, and pro-Arab communities, mainly Muslim. The Muslims who are also the poorer group, sympathize strongly with the Fedayeen and are willing to permit them to use Lebanese territory as bases for their exploits against Israel, regardless of the danger of Israeli reprisals.

The Christians on the whole would prefer Lebanon to remain aloof from the war against Israel. Furthermore Lebanon's small army, a considerable political factor ever since the former army commander, General Chéhab, became president in 1958, is aware of the danger Israeli reprisals present for the army and the country. It has therefore in the past attempted to restrain Fedayeen activity in Lebanon.

However, the Fedayeen used their radio located in Cairo to call on the Lebanese people and the Palestinian refugees in the camps and cities to demonstrate against so-called army persecution of the Fedayeen. This led to riots in spring 1969 and to the resignation of the Government. No new government could be formed as long as the Fedayeen question remained unsettled. With the tacit consent of the Lebanese army authorities, some Fedayeen groups consisting mainly of Fatah and Sa'iqa factions penetrated a remote corner of Lebanon in the summer of 1969 and stationed themselves on the western slopes of the Hermon range, close to the Syrian border and the Israeli-occupied Golan Heights.

In the second half of October fights broke out between the infiltrators and the Lebanese army. These conflicts originated in the southern part of the country close to the old Israeli border when the Fedayeen attempted to infiltrate across it into the regions of Galilee (which had been settled by Israelis) and the army acted to stop them. Again appeals to the refugees and the population were made over the radio. Left-wing and pro-Muslim elements caused trouble in Tripoli; Lebanese border posts were attacked from Syria, officially by Fedayeen but certainly with the approval of the Syrian authorities. Syria closed her borders with Lebanon and moved troop units close to them. Fedayeen attacked in several border regions, but their main thrust came from the Syrian frontier on the western side of the Hermon range down the Hasbani Valley. It was clearly aimed at opening up an all-weather path from Syria across the southern Bekaa to the previous strongholds of the infiltrators on the Hermon slopes and down towards the south and the Lebanese-Israeli frontier. But it failed to achieve its military aim: the army stopped the Fedayeen half way down the Hasbani Valley when they attempted to take the police post of the town of Rashaya.

After this setback the Fatah spokesman, Yaser Arafat, agreed to conversations with the commander of the Lebanese army, Emile Bustani, under the

28

auspices of Abdel Nasser and other Egyptian mediators. An agreement was reached, the exact contents of which remain secret. However, it is known that several provisions allow the Fedayeen to cross Lebanon for their actions against Israel. They are said to have agreed not to maintain permanent camps in south Lebanon and to recognize the sovereignty of Lebanon as long as they are in her territory; also they are said to have promised not to shoot across the Lebanese border into Israel but to start their attacks only from inside Israel. The details of the agreements remain to be worked out. There is little doubt, however, that the Israelis will retaliate against Lebanon if they are attacked by infiltrators coming from that country. It seems likely that under these circumstances new difficulties will arise and Lebanon will not easily settle down to her old position of a pro-Arab but essentially uninvolved spectator in the Arab-Israeli conflict.

This new situation clearly contains possibilities for Russian political gains. One point has already been gained: it seems unlikely that the Sixth Fleet will be welcomed in the now troubled waters of Lebanon. In the long run it is not impossible that the parliamentary institutions and the traditional freedoms enjoyed in Lebanon might be eroded and forced to give way to some more authoritarian regime. Such a "progressive" regime would doubtless be more exposed to Soviet political influence than the present one.

Soviet Naval Policies

Given such a delicate situation in the Arab countries, the Soviet Union has so far refrained from making excessive demands for collaboration—military, economic, even diplomatic—which might serve only to increase the danger of Arab resentment. This applies also to naval policies. It would not be good policy to demand naval bases, submarine shelters or similar permanent facilities in Syria or Egypt now.

In Latakia visiting naval units have already had the experience of being received very coolly because they happened to call while the struggle between Jedid and al-Asad was in full swing and no leading politician wanted to compromise himself by being too openly cordial to the Soviet visitors.

Egypt, more necessarily dependent on Soviet help than Syria, can be handled more firmly. But there also, permanent bases and big naval installations would soon serve the arguments of elements who are already saying that the masters of Egypt seem to have handed considerable power to Russia, and appear not to get in return what they really want: the elimination of the consequences of the aggression (of the Six-Day War).

In fact, the Russians have avoided installing themselves with visible permanency in Syria or Egypt. They have obtained facilities for repairs and replenishments in Alexandria and Port Said. It seems they have some technicians working for their own navy (apart from naval counsellors for the Egyptians) living in Alexandria. There is a floating dock which was towed there from the Black Sea. But this seems to be about the sum total of Russian installations.

What there is can be easily justified on the grounds of having to help the Egyptians to resist the Israeli menace on the Suez Canal and in the Mediterranean. At the present time a greater presence would probably be unnecessary. As long as the canal stays closed the Eastern Mediterranean is another *cul de sac* for the Russians. If the canal should ever open, conditions might change since the Soviet Union does have a definite interest in the Red Sea—as a highway towards the Indian Ocean, or to prevent the Chinese from acquiring staging posts along that same route towards the Mediterranean.

With regard to Syria and Egypt, one would expect naval policy under these circumstances to aim at conserving what has been gained so far without breaking the back of the camel by adding too much weight. That would mean to keep up friendly relations, pay visits, assist in the build-up against the Israelis (and help at the same time to prevent an uncontrollable escalation of the war), work to ward off any sudden internal changes of regime, pay visits to Syria when the circumstances seem right and give the Jedid group in Damascus whatever political support can be accorded.

The Soviet Dilemma

This brings us back to a basic dilemma the Soviet Union is faced with in the Eastern Mediterranean.

Given Nasser's position (and to a considerable degree that of the other Arab leaders) and the apparently strong will of the Israeli leadership not to return to the territorial status existing before the war—certainly not without considerable political concessions and assurances from the Arab side—the Soviet Union has only two choices, either to persuade the Arabs to reach a realistic settlement with Israel, or to uphold the Arab point of view and to risk a drift towards a new Middle East war.

The situation is being complicated by the fact that by now she has to protect a considerable investment in Egypt and in the other Arab states. She has invested quite sizeable amounts in economic aid and in arms in return for Arab goodwill whose political fruits are seen today in terms of growing Soviet influence in the Eastern Mediterranean and the Red Sea. But goodwill is a commodity that might easily evaporate or even change into resentment if it is not constantly fed and cared for.

To force Egypt and the other Arab states to a settlement in the Israel dispute, which in Arab eyes would seal their defeat, would almost certainly mean for the Russians that the previous sympathy towards the Soviet Union would change to indifference or resentment. Such a change in attitude could come about easily, for after a settlement the Arabs would no longer depend on Soviet help as urgently as they do while the confrontation with Israel lasts. On the other hand to back the Arabs in their intransigent stance and to defend their interpretation of the UN resolution of November 1967, means to back the already clearly visible trend towards another Middle East war, and with it a possible further defeat for the Arab armies and their Russian war material. This is not in the interest of the Soviet Union, at least as long as the Soviet experts are not convinced that Israel will this time lose the war, or at least not win it again in a few quick blows. Even the hypothetical disappearance of Israel as a state, the war aim of the guerillas, would not be in the Soviet interest, as Israel and the Arab resentment against her have been the main vehicle of Russian penetration so far, and promise to serve as such in the future as long as the state of Israel exists.

In fact the Russians have never called for the disappearance of Israel. They have in the past permitted themselves a certain amount of criticism of the Fedayeen who do so, calling them unreasonable and unrealistic. But they have in recent months abstained from such criticism, no doubt in the general context of their increased readiness to accept the Arab point of view, and perhaps also in consideration of the growing popularity of the Fedayeen among the Arabs and the possibility that the guerillas might collaborate increasingly with China if Moscow continues to spurn them.

If any predictions for the future can be made it seems quite likely that the Soviet Union will attempt to avoid both extremes of the dilemma with which she is confronted—a new outbreak of the war or losing the goodwill of the Arabs—by endeavouring to pursue a course of alternately restraining the Arabs from all-out war and backing their demands and approving their war-like noises. This would be attempted perhaps in the hope of frightening the Americans and the rest of the world into greater concessions at the expense of Israel, but principally to save Arab goodwill while avoiding a new outbreak of war.

What lies beyond such future developments cannot be prophesied now. It will depend on the outcome of that future Middle East war—hypothetical but quite probable. To judge from precedent and from what is known of technical training and preparedness on the two sides, it can only be said that the odds of the Arabs winning this time do not appear to be particularly great, even though a new Israeli victory could easily be more costly than the last one was. The Russians in that case would have to decide whether to repeat the process of rearming the Arabs once more and to start another round, or whether this time to follow a different course.

If Russia pressures the Arabs into a settlement she risks losing Arab sympathy and increases the chances for the eventual downfall, probably by military coup, of the governments who—in Arab eyes—have admitted defeat by dealing with Israel.

If Russia does uphold the Arab cause against Israel and the United States, she encourages the Arab leaders to draw closer to a new war, to the point where such a conflict becomes unavoidable and, like the Six-Day War, begins by itself without any one of the participants, and certainly none of the great powers, really desiring it.

The experience of the last two years seems to suggest that the Soviet Union will favour the second rather than the first alternative. Nobody can say beforehand whether she would be willing to permit the Arabs to go to war once more, thus again risking Soviet arms and exposing Soviet prestige for an undertaking of questionable outcome. It has been seen, however, that the Soviet Union's diplomacy is inclined to weaken when confronted with serious and resolute objections from her Arab clients, such as the Egyptians must have expressed in the course of summer 1969 when Soviet-American agreement seemed close and the Russians attempted briefly to obtain Egyptian consent.

This can be understood if the size of the Russian investment is considered, from the Aswan High Dam to the (not very successful) contribution to industrialization of Egypt and the other Arab nations and to the different arms deals. This position would be lost should the Arabs turn against the Soviet Union. And this would probably happen as soon as they become convinced that she was not backing them strongly enough to achieve an ultimate victory over Israel.

These considerations must strongly influence internal Soviet policy decisions since political careers and reputations are in part determined by foreign successes and failures. Enough is known about internal Soviet discussions immediately after the Six-Day War regarding the opportunity to re-equip Egypt to make it quite probable that another Arab defeat would have consequences for the political standing of the leading supporters of an activist Arab policy in the Soviet Union herself.

However, to accept the Arab point of view more or less completely also has its dangers for the Soviet Union. It might lead eventually to another Arab defeat and to the extremely dangerous choice for the Kremlin leaders of either helping them actively, i.e., with volunteers or pilots (risking possible US involvement on the opposite side), or else taking the blame for having again let down their allies.

Possibly because the danger of another outbreak of all-out war seemed remote, the USSR has so far preferred to back the Arabs and to attempt to obtain a settlement which would be hard to realize but would have the virtue of being agreeable to her Arab political clients. It is probable that when the brink of war has been reached once more, Soviet diplomacy will attempt to restrain the Arabs. But it is not probable that it will be more effective in that task than in the past, particularly as the Arabs this time are likely to endeavour to take advantage of the element of surprise which so far has worked in favour of the Israeli side.

The Naval Forces
in the Mediterranean
René Mertens

Talking about the Mediterranean nowadays means almost automatically talking about the recent emergence of the Soviet fleet and its impact on the balance of forces in that area. Since June 1967 the Soviet naval presence has rapidly and substantially increased. Its concomitant political and propagandistic overtones have induced public opinion to overrate considerably the military effectiveness of the Soviet Navy and hence its impact on the security of the West in general and the Mediterranean area in particular.

It therefore seems appropriate to begin the general evaluation of the naval forces in the Mediterranean with a brief examination of the Soviet Navy's past performance, its present strength and weaknesses and its potentialities for future actions.

The Soviet Navy

Today the Soviet Navy owns as many as 3000 warships. Most of them are fully commissioned, but about 60 per cent are of small size and limited fighting value. They serve mainly for coastal defence along Soviet-controlled shores and on such inland waters as the Amur, the Danube and the Caspian Sea. All these small craft would only be useful if an enemy intended to operate with naval forces in the Baltic, the Black Sea or similar restricted theatres. Experiences in the Second World War have shown, however, that even a numerically superior Soviet flotilla was not able to deal effectively with the naval forces of the Axis powers.

Likewise, it cannot be taken for granted that the more modern equipment of the Soviet Navy necessarily assures its operational superiority. Past experience has shown again that on several occasions the more modern, faster and better armed Russian vessels failed to score a success over their enemy. Soviet inability to use modern naval forces was shown in the war against Germany from 1941 to 1945, when the Soviet surface forces lost one battleship, one cruiser and about 40 flotilla leaders, destroyers, torpedo boats and large escort vessels as well as over 250 other surface warships without sinking *with gun fire* one single sea-going war or merchant ship of the Axis powers. Only mines and torpedoes from Soviet submarines, aircraft and motor torpedo boats claimed some victims.

The obvious conclusion is that the number of warships is not necessarily the

Mr. René Mertens is a naval historian from Basle.

decisive factor in sea warfare. Nevertheless, this is all too easily overlooked in discussions on the build-up of the Soviet Navy and, in particular, its swelling numerical strength in the Mediterranean.

One of the main weaknesses of the Soviet Navy so far has been that it does not have one single combat-aircraft carrier (as against 20 in NATO). The reasons for this are manifold and are based more on ideological and technical factors than on purely strategic grounds. Today the Soviet Union has at least two small helicopter carriers. They are, however, serving mainly as anti-submarine and landing-support vessels. Here, too, the Western powers have a tenfold superiority.

Therefore the Soviet Navy faces the problem of how to fight hostile surface forces without carrier-borne aircraft and without a chance to come within gunnery-striking distance of the enemy. The Soviets did not attempt to improve their guns (which are inferior in number and calibres) or their gunnery in general (in which they do not any longer believe), but turned towards rockets. Besides surface-to-air missiles (SAM) of inferior capacity compared to similar American, British and French weapons, the Soviets also developed special missiles against surface warships (SSM), and in this field they were leading for some time. *Sark* and *Serb* missiles credited with ranges of between 1600 and 2000 kilometres and which may carry nuclear warheads are to be found aboard certain Soviet destroyers and submarines, but they are mainly strategic weapons to be fired against coastal and inland targets, as are the *Shaddock* missiles with a range of less than 400 kilometres, which are carried by some submarines. The use of these long-distance missiles against naval forces at sea would only be of interest if such fleets remained concentrated, but this would hardly be the case. Furthermore, the Soviets still have to solve the problem of how to locate exactly these enemy task forces and how to guide their missiles to such targets. Realizing how difficult it would be to destroy small moving targets spread over several hundred square kilometres with such long-distance missiles, the Soviets also constructed tactical weapons, the *Strela* and the *Styx*, with ranges between approximately 25 and under 200 kilometres and probably capable of carrying small nuclear warheads or ordinary explosives.[1]

The Western navies have in the meantime produced similar if not superior models thus compensating the temporary advantage of the Soviet Union in this field. Consequently, the main problem of the Soviet Navy remains: namely, how to approach an enemy task force or convoy closely enough without being spotted and sunk before reaching a firing position. The US Sixth Fleet is able to undertake air reconnaissance over distances of up to 2000 kilometres and to attack enemy vessels by air at distances of about 1000 kilometres. It can therefore spot and hit Soviet surface vessels long before they can fire their tactical missiles. The land-based Soviet naval air force will be of little help in such actions far away from Soviet-controlled shores, but might be able to provide some sort of umbrella for Soviet naval forces operating in the Baltic, the Black Sea and elsewhere near the Soviet coasts. But a future war will not be

[1]Four of these *Styx*-type rockets fired by Soviet-built, Egyptian-manned OSA and *Komar*-class launchers sank the old Israeli destroyer *Elath* in October 1967.

decided by operations in the Baltic, the Black Sea or the waters adjacent to China; in order to win a major confrontation, the Soviet Union must be able to exercise full control of the Atlantic, Pacific, the Indian Ocean and the Mediterranean. This would mean above all wiping out not only the US Navy, but also all other NATO fleets plus the air forces of all these countries—a task well beyond the capacities of the Soviet armed forces. It ought to be added that, so far, the Soviet Navy has had no experience in world-wide wartime long-distance operations of modern naval and air forces. Equally, it seems fair to say that its supply techniques and the co-operation between naval forces and land-based air forces are inferior to the standards of Western navies.

Soviet interest in the Mediterranean is of long standing. After the Second World War the Soviet Union tried to acquire a permanent foothold there, first in Yugoslavia (until 1948), then in Albania (until 1961), and since about 1956 also in Egypt and Syria. The Egyptian and Syrian navies are being equipped with Soviet-built warships, and a number of Egyptians and Syrians have been undergoing naval training in the Soviet Union and Poland. In spite of this close co-operation the Soviet Navy refrained from any action during the Six-Day War, and the vastly superior Arab naval forces remained idle in port.

One of the major reasons for the Soviet reserve and the inactivity of the Arab navies was the overwhelming superiority of the Israeli Air Force. The Soviets did not have any aircraft in the Mediterranean, and the Arabs had almost none left after the first Israeli strikes. As wars in the Middle East tend to be very short but vehement, naval forces of the belligerents do not have the time to make their weight felt. Wars are over before a blockade would produce any effects. This is one of the reasons which led the Israelis to neglect somewhat their naval forces. Their reasoning is that as long as they have the air supremacy they can prevent hostile naval operations against and off their coasts, and if one day they should lose this air supremacy they will lose the war anyhow, with or without a strong navy. This consideration seems sound if applied to all-out wars like the one of 1967, but in case of prolonged "limited wars" like the one that has been developing for almost two years along the Suez Canal and the Sinai coasts, Israel will need a minimum of light naval forces to patrol and conduct commando-type raids.

Since the Six-Day War of 1967 the Soviet Navy has maintained a rather strong naval squadron in the Mediterranean. Its strength varies between about 20 and 60 warships of all types, including cruisers, helicopters, carriers, destroyer escorts, submarines and auxiliaries. About half of the available strength is composed of naval auxiliaries and supply vessels. This naval force has above all a political task, namely to show the flag and to prevent by its presence Israeli raids against Egyptian and Syrian ports. Thus far this undertaking has been successful. Soviet naval forces also paid courtesy visits to Algeria, Morocco, Yugoslavia and France, but have not ventured so far to call at such sensitive ports as Tripoli and Beirut. Soviet plans to open the Suez Canal by a show of force have, at least for the time being, been postponed, and Soviet warships have so far not participated in Egyptian actions along the Suez Canal or south of Suez. In the Red Sea a few Soviet warships frequently cruise in Yemenite waters, but have to date refrained from coming northwards towards the Gulf of Suez, where most of the Israeli-Egyptian fighting takes place.

The Soviet Union realizes that a confrontation with Israel cannot succeed without adequate air cover and that this protection cannot yet be provided by Arab air forces. It is true that certain air formations on Arab soil have at least mixed Arab-Soviet crews, among them some bomber and long-distance reconnaissance squadrons, but this is not sufficient to make them fully operational. The weak points are always the maintenance problem, communications and protection of the airfields. As long as the Soviets cannot take over completely at least certain airfields in Egypt and Syria, they do not consider it safe to send in larger formations of their own air force. On the other hand, the Arabs feel that the Soviet presence is already heavy-handed enough and do not wish to yield still more of their national sovereignty and dignity. The Soviets realize that only a complete take-over of the Arab states would permit them to build up a truly efficient, completely Soviet-manned air-defence system, and they know, too, that such a political solution will not be forthcoming in the near future. Furthermore, Israel would probably destroy again the existing Arab installations before the Soviets could take them over and improve them enough to prevent such actions.

Without a strong, Russian-manned air force of several hundred planes the Soviet Union cannot hope to protect her Mediterranean naval forces for any length of time against strikes by NATO forces. The Mediterranean is so small that surface naval forces have no chance to escape observation from the air, and with the vastly superior air and naval forces at the disposition of NATO, all the Soviet vessels can do in case of a general war is either to ask for internment in Yugoslavia, or to scuttle their ships in some Arab ports, or else fight a battle lost in advance. Of course some Soviet warships might launch their nuclear missiles before being interned, scuttled or sunk, but the destruction of one or several towns and ports in Western Europe would not prevent the NATO forces from sinking the Soviet ships.

Finally, the loss of the air and sea bases formerly belonging to France, Italy and Britain in North Africa—Mers-el-Kébir, Bizerta, Tripoli, Tobruk and Alexandria—is a nuisance in peace-time because the Soviet Navy can use them. In the case of a general war these bases would, however, become untenable for the weaker belligerent. They are therefore of limited interest to the Soviet Union, and the Arabs are too weak to defend them against a resolute attack. In the case of a nuclear war, fixed bases will probably become death traps. Mers-el-Kébir and Bizerta are far from invulnerable to nuclear attack. Militarily speaking de Gaulle, however, committed a serious mistake when he handed Mers-el-Kébir and Bizerta back prematurely to Algeria and Tunisia. Some small strong points are still under Western control, like the Spanish Presidios along the Moroccan coast and the airfield Bou Sfer near Mers-el-Kébir. These bases permit at least a better surveillance of the Western Mediterranean area.

We may therefore draw the conclusion that the military value of Soviet naval forces in the Mediterranean in times of open conflict will be very limited indeed. On the other hand, there is no doubt that in peace time their political and

36

psychological effect, irrespective of the fluctuations in their numerical strength and composition, is and will remain considerable.

The US Sixth Fleet

Without going into details about the strength and distribution of this fleet it can be said that it represents the West's main asset in the Mediterranean. Among the 50 to 60 warships belonging to the Sixth Fleet are two or three attack aircraft carriers, with between 150 and 235 combat planes, which in co-operation with the shore-based aircraft of the other NATO powers dominate the Mediterranean, while those missile-carrying nuclear-powered subs that are assigned to the Mediterranean could reach targets deep inside the USSR. The high mobility and tremendous striking power of this naval force, which does not depend upon fixed bases and ports, make it the spearhead of the NATO forces.

The overwhelming American superiority would, however, only be effective in the case of a general war against the Soviet Union, and cannot be applied to the current game of "flag-showing" and political and economic pressure in which the Soviet Navy is engaged. To the naïve native's eye a Soviet missile cruiser is at least as impressive as an American aircraft carrier, but he is less impressed by the Soviet sailors, who are seldom allowed ashore and have no money to spend.

The American supply lines stretch westwards through the Gibraltar Straits and are relatively immune from Soviet interference. Some US warships carry ship-to-air missiles, but none has so far an efficient ship-to-ship missile, while several large Soviet surface vessels and numerous inshore patrol boats are equipped with effective ship-to-ship missiles. The Americans rely upon their aircraft to destroy distant enemy vessels, and on their guns for dealing with vessels within gun-range. The Soviets, on their side aware of the complete failure of Russian naval gunfire in 1904-05, 1914-17 and 1941-45, set their hopes upon missiles. They succeeded in sinking the Israeli destroyer *Elath*, although under almost ideal target-practice conditions. However, the American long-distance ballistic missiles are far more numerous and efficient than such Soviet weapons.

The British Navy

The British Navy still controls some of the best naval and air bases in the Mediterranean, such as Gibraltar and Malta, and exercises some rights on Cyprus. However, it hardly maintains enough local forces to defend these places. Until 1968 only a few frigates and minesweepers were permanently in the Mediterranean; land forces consisted of one battalion at Gibraltar, two at Malta, two at Cyprus, and even smaller units in Libya. In January 1969, when the NATO Defence Ministers agreed to create a special naval force in the Mediterranean to counter-balance the Soviet squadron there, Britian offered to add two more frigates and one guided-missile destroyer. But even this small "task force" seems not to be a standing one, but "on call" only. Also the assault ship *Fearless* has been assigned to the Mediterranean, and the cruiser *Blake* may go there if and when repairs in England are completed. The Royal Air Force maintains a nuclear bomber striking force and a fighter squadron in Cyprus, and reconnaissance aircraft are operating from Malta and Gibraltar, but for the time being the British land, sea and air forces in the Mediterranean are hardly sufficient to garrison the remaining British possessions. Britain could and should send at least one attack aircraft carrier and a light aircraft carrier to the Mediterranean, together with some additional surface warships and submarines.

France

Owing to de Gaulle's policies, the bulk of the French Navy, including the two modern aircraft carriers and most of the modern destroyers, frigates and submarines, left the Mediterranean some years ago for Brest on the Atlantic. The French naval forces in the Mediterranean, now a dozen frigates, some escorts, submarines and training vessels, should be brought up to about two thirds of all available French warships, including the two attack aircraft carriers. It is to be hoped that the departure of de Gaulle will permit such a redeployment. It would allow France again to play a role second to none in the Mediterranean. France should give higher priority to preventing Algeria from falling even more under Soviet domination. Since strong naval forces can serve as an instrument of political persuasion, a stronger French Mediterranean Fleet would contribute to this effect.

Italy

Over the past 15 years the Italian Navy has undertaken a considerable programme and has built some very efficient warships, several of which are equipped with missile-launchers, for which the Italians do not yet have any nuclear warheads. With this exception the Italian Navy alone is numerically stronger and in a far better strategic situation than the Soviet Mediterranean squadron. Italy remains, however, vulnerable to (nuclear) attacks against her long shores and many coastal towns, and for lack of any naval striking force (naval air combat planes or missiles with nuclear warheads) Italy depends on the US Sixth Fleet for destroying more distant Soviet warships which might launch missiles against Italian targets.

Greece

The Greek Navy is mainly an escort force, lacking any punch to deal with the more modern Soviet warships, but as the Greek geopolitical position is of great strategic importance, the West should have considerable interest in reinforcing the Greek armed forces. The Soviet Union would doubtless like to bring about a change of government in Greece by political pressure.

Turkey

The bulk of the Turkish Navy, ten older destroyers and ten obsolete submarines with conventional armament are of course hopelessly outgunned by the more modern, powerful and sophisticated Soviet warships, both in the Black Sea and the Mediterranean. Its role will therefore mainly consist in support of the defence of the Turkish Straits. As the geopolitical and strategic importance of the Turkish Straits in the event of war cannot be overestimated, NATO and Turkey might wish to accelerate the modernization of the Turkish Navy and to station a symbolic NATO task force there, which could visit the Black Sea each time a Soviet warship enters the Mediterranean as a psychologically important gesture.

Spain

The Spanish Navy is above all an escort force, the bulk of which should be concentrated in the Mediterranean. The striking potential is still almost non-existent because most of the existing warships and combat planes are of conventional type and considerable age. Spain's main contribution towards the West's defence consists of her geopolitical situation and some bases on lend-lease to the US Navy and Air Force. The Balearic Islands and the few remaining Presidios and the Alboran Islands off the Moroccan coast are of special interest to the defence of the western approaches to the Straits of Gibraltar.

Altogether the NATO powers and Spain have as many as 1500 land-based combat aircraft available in the Mediterranean area, plus approximately 200 shore-based naval aircraft, to which must be added about 200 US Navy combat planes aboard the aircraft carriers of the Sixth Fleet. Another 200 combat planes could be added by ordering two French and at least one British attack aircraft carrier to the Mediterranean.

Israel

Although Israel is not a member of NATO it might be assumed that in the event of a general war Israel would be obliged to enter the conflict on the side of the West, while probably nobody would come to the assistance of Israel if she were attacked once more by her Arab neighbours. Israel has only a small but efficient coastal defence and "cloak-and-dagger" navy with almost no long-distance striking power. The Israeli Air Force might, however, prove to be once more a very dangerous foe in the event of war in the Middle East. It seems hardly probable that the Soviet Navy would dare to operate within range of the Israeli fighter-bombers, which means that Port Said and Alexandria could not be used with any degree of safety.

39

Syria

The Syrian Navy is composed mostly of Soviet-built motor torpedo boats and a few missile-launching boats, while the Soviet Navy frequently uses the port of Latakia. The efficiency of the Syrian warships remains very low due to bad seamanship, lack of spares and insufficient training. Syria's turn to Peking has, of course, weakened the strategic and political situation of the Soviets and the Soviet fleet in the Eastern Mediterranean. But as regards China, her naval capacity is far too limited to allow her any powerful presence in the Mediterranean. Politically, however, Syria's attempted "defection" shows how little Moscow can in fact rely on its Arab allies.

The United Arab Republic

Since 1955, the Soviet Union has made great efforts to strengthen the Egyptian Navy, handing over four destroyers, more than a dozen submarines and a large number of motor torpedo boats and missile-launching ships. Numerous Egyptian sailors were trained in the USSR, and came home disappointed. Neither in 1956 nor in 1967 did the Egyptian Navy show any fight, and although numerically far superior to the Israeli Navy, the Egyptian naval forces have little chance of military success as long as the Israeli Air Force remains operational. The strength of the combined Soviet and Arab naval forces in the Mediterranean depends in the event of a conflict upon airpower, and although there are about 1000 Soviet-built Arab combat planes available in Algeria, Egypt, Syria and Iraq, the fighting spirit and efficiency of these air forces have been at a low level so far. It is possible that in a war Soviet pilots would take over at least some of these Soviet-built planes. Already Soviet TU-16 reconnaissance bombers fly with Egyptian markings and mixed crews over the Mediterranean and shadow the Sixth Fleet.

The Remaining Countries

The non-aligned Mediterranean powers, MOROCCO, TUNISIA, LIBYA, LEBANON and CYPRUS possess only very weak naval forces, and although Libya has acquired some very modern patrol boats from the UK, none of these countries would be able to resist any form of NATO or Soviet naval pressure.

YUGOSLAVIA deploys a navy purely for coastal defence with no offshore striking power. Strategically the Yugoslavian coast is dominated by Italy, and the Adriatic Sea would be, as in 1914-18, a trap rather than a refuge. This would not change very much even if Albania returned to the Warsaw Pact, because the Albanian coast is insufficiently developed and the hinterland provides almost no resources.

Notwithstanding the long-lasting ideological conflict between Tito and the Soviet leaders, Yugoslavia recently received some modern Soviet-built motor torpedo boats and missile-launching boats. Some of these deliveries took place

40

even after Tito had criticized the Soviet intervention in Czechoslovakia. As always, Tito's attitude is not clear, but it seems that he would like to see both the American and Soviet warships leave the Mediterranean. Despite these feelings, during and after the June 1967 Arab-Israeli was he permitted the Soviet Air Force to fly over Yugoslavia to the Mediterranean and to Egypt, and so contributed towards the build-up of a small but active Soviet air force in the Middle East.

ALBANIA'S small navy is of Soviet origin. Since the break with the Soviet Union in 1961 it suffers from an almost complete lack of spares, so that the few submarines, motor torpedo boats and patrol craft that still exist are hardly operational. Also Albania's Chinese benefactor can only provide limited assistance in this field. Even as a strategic objective Albania is only of small interest to both NATO and the USSR, at least since the Soviet Navy was ousted ingloriously in 1961. The often-mentioned "red Gibraltar of the Adriatic," the small island of Sasseno is in reality of little military value. Rumours about the installation of Chinese ballistic missiles are for the time being hardly more than pure propaganda. The Albanian communist system survives only because nobody has so far openly attacked it, but it is not impossible that the Soviet Navy might one day be used to bring about or to support a revolt against the pro-Chinese rulers of this country.

ALGERIA received several Soviet-built motor torpedo boats and missile-launching boats, and Algerian crews are being trained in the USSR for additional vessels, while Soviet warships and aircraft occasionally use Algerian ports and airfields.

Main Naval Forces in the Mediterranean

		Attack aircraft carriers	Escort/helicopter carriers	Cruisers	Missile cruisers	Destroyers, frigates	Missile destroyers, frigates	Coastal escorts, sub-chasers, patrol craft, escort minesweepers	Minesweepers	Submarines w/torpedoes	Missile submarines conventional or nuclear propulsion	Landing craft	Landing ships	Auxiliaries	MTB/MGB	Rocket patrol boats	Intelligence trawlers
NATO																	
	USA	2		2	1	20	4		4	4	1		3	20			
A	Britain																
	Italy				4	19	2	25	61	10			60	3	75	17		
	Greece					12		12	14	2		55	15	35	7		
B	Turkey					10		22	22	10		18		22	27		
C	France	2	1	2		41		22	99	18	1	10	5	140			
D	Spain			1		25		20	25	4		29		54	3		
E	USSR		1		4	10		10	4	13	3	8		30			8 **Max**
				1	1	6	2	4	2	6	?	4		12			4 **Min**
	Syria							3	2	?		?		?	15	10	
F	UAR					12		11	6/9	16 ?		19		?	45	20	
G	Israel					2		5		4		7 ?		10 ?	16 ?	5	

Naval Forces of Other Countries

		Destroyers, frigates	Submarines	Coastal escorts, patrol craft	MTB/MGB	Minelayers, minesweepers	Others
H	Morocco	1		3			
I	Algeria			2	19	1	
	Tunisia			2			
J	Libya	1		1	3	2	7/11
	Lebanon			5			1
K	Albania		3	20 ?	14	8	15
	Cyprus			20 ?			
	Yugoslavia	5	5	20	100 ?	38	32

A
A small naval squadron and maritime reconnaissance aircraft from the Western Fleet.

B
The bulk of the Turkish Navy is in the Black Sea and not available for operations in the Mediterranean. Figure for 22 minesweepers includes 6 minelayers.

C
The bulk of the French Navy has been outside of the Mediterranean for several years. At present, one cruiser, 12 destroyers and frigates, approximately half of France's submarines, 20 minesweepers, plus numerous other small craft and auxiliaries are in the Mediterranean. Politically and psychologically the NATO position could be considerably improved by the presence of French attack aircraft carriers which are now based at Brest. France left NATO but in 1968 resumed participation in NATO Mediterranean manoeuvres.

D
Part of the Spanish Navy—33 per cent to 50 per cent—is normally not in the Mediterranean. Five year defence agreement was reached between United States and Spain, March 1969.

E
The overall total of Soviet vessels in the Mediterranean was probably never above 65.
The lowest figure recorded since June 1967 was about 25 vessels after 15 October 1969. Some fluctuations are due to short visits of Soviet warships from the Baltic and Arctic Fleets. Normally the strength of the Soviet squadron in the Mediterranean fluctuates between 30 and 60 vessels of which approximately half are supply ships.

F
About 20-30 Egyptian naval craft are in the Red Sea, mostly small vessels of limited fighting value, several of which have been lost.
Some of the vessels listed as Egyptian or Syrian may still be in Soviet hands, and the contrary also may be true, i.e., some Soviet ships may have been handed over to the Arabs.

G
Part of the Israeli Navy, including about half of the small craft, is in the Red Sea.
The two Israel destroyers are relegated to harbour duties and are no longer of any fighting value.

H
Part of the Moroccan naval forces are outside of the Mediterranean.

I
Additional deliveries of Soviet-built warships are expected, including sub-chasers and probably submarines.

J
Some of the very sophisticated, fast patrol craft built in Britain are already suffering from neglect and inadequate maintenance.

K
Most of the Soviet-built submarines, subchasers, MTB and other craft are handicapped for lack of spare parts. Some Chinese-built patrol craft may have been acquired recently.

Europe and Technology :
A Political View

René Foch

'We move backwards into the future'   PAUL VALÉRY

List of Abbreviations

ABAP	Association of Belgian Companies for the Breguet Atlantic (Aircraft Construction).
BAC	British Aircraft Corporation.
BSEL	Bristol Siddeley Engines Limited.
CEA	Commissariat à l'Energie Atomique
CECA	Communauté Européenne de Charbon et d'Acier.
CECLES/	Organisation européenne pour la mise au point et la construction de lanceurs d'engins spatiaux.
CEEA	Commission Européenne d'Energie Atomique.
ISPRA	(Italian) Four national components comprising the 'Centre Com-
PETTEN	(Dutch) mun de Recherches de la Communauté'.
GEEL	(Belgian)
KARLSRUHE	(German)
CEPT	Conférence Européenne des Postes et Télécommunications.
CERN	Centre Européen de Recherche Nucléaire.
CERS/ESRO	Centre Européen de Recherches Spatiales (European Space Research Organization).
CETS	Conférence Européenne sur les Télécommunications/Satellites.
CNEN	Comitato Nazionale Energia Nucleare.
CNES	Centre National des Etudes Spatiales.
COMSAT	Communications Satellite (American firm).
CSE	Conférence Spatiale Européenne.
ELDO	European Launcher Development Organization.
GfK	Gesellschaft fur Kernforschung (Association for Nuclear Research).
INTELSAT	International Telecommunications Satellite.
LAS	ESRO stellar satellite (satellite astronomique).
MATRA	French missile/rocket firm.
MRCA	Multi-Role Combat Aircraft.
NAMMO	NATO Multi-Role Combat Aircraft Management Organization (Tripartite research organization established for Jaguar and Martel project).
NFK	Neues Kampfflugzeug (proposed European aircraft to replace the American F-104).
SNECMA	Société Nationale d'Etude et de Construction de Moteurs d'Avions.
TO/RCN	Reactor Centrum Nederland.
TRANSALL	First two joint European aircraft construction projects.
BREGUET	
UEO/WEU	Union Européenne Occidentale/Western European Union.
USAEC	United States Atomic Energy Commission.
VFW	Vereinigte Flugtechnische Werke.

Introduction

Christopher Layton

Men get the technology and the politics they deserve. Europe's present confused and inadequate efforts to pool its resources in advanced technology have been a fair reflection of its lack of will to unite and of lack of awareness that others, plus inertia, are shaping Europe's future.

No one can claim it is a satisfactory situation, or one that need persist. The necessities of Continental scale have already forced European countries to work together in space, aircraft and nuclear research; are drawing them together in fields such as computers and nuclear fuel; and will do the same in great new areas of human endeavour such as the exploration of the ocean depths and the protection of our environment. Yet the methods chosen have been 'co-operative' programmes between nation states which fall apart with depressing regularity under the pressure of national interests, and *ad hoc* projects escalating in cost through divergent industrial interests; in the major fields of advanced technology there is not even a common public market; there are few European companies capable of matching their global rivals.

René Foch's useful study starts by caustically analysing the failure of existing European efforts to co-operate under the banners of the nation states. He draws on his long experience with Euratom. He goes on to suggest the elements of a strategy for the future.

M. Foch first lays down certain crucial conditions for the success of an overall European policy for science and technology: one is so important, and so rarely understood, that the readers' attention must be drawn to it. This is the need for a common attitude towards the United States and other external powers. Whether the subject is the search for a common policy on nuclear fuel enrichment, or a common space policy, there is no doubt that different national attitudes towards the United States and different relationships with it have been endlessly divisive for Europe, and that a common European policy towards the US is a condition of success. One might add that it is also a condition of an effective transatlantic partnership (look, for instance, at the negotiations on a European share in the post-Apollo programme), even though a single European voice may speak in forceful terms. A European policy for technology cannot be considered in isolation from the United States, still the powerhouse of the world's advanced technology.

47

At the heart of M. Foch's paper are his suggestions for the development of effective institutions and procedures to bring Europe's fragmentary national and collaborative programmes within a common strategy. Two aims of these proposals stand out. One is the need to bring national technology programmes, as well as joint projects, within a common policy. It is sheer waste to set up ambitious European laboratories or programmes, if national programmes compete fiercely with them for resources. The second aim is to develop what he calls an effective Machinery of Choice – procedures for the systematic allocation of resources to technological objectives which have been the subject of full political debate.

His ideas are timely. The new European Commission in Brussels has a sharper cutting edge, and is awake to the need for a more efficient and systematic policy for European technology, and for a reappraisal of objectives to include such new fields as pollution. The work of the Aigrain Committee is expanding and may soon move on from talk to action; its present organization cannot be considered either a durable or adequate framework for a European science and technology policy.

Above all, the negotiations to enlarge the Community open the possibility of a systematic reorganization of Europe's ramifying scientific and technological organizations within an overall policy. Once a coherent policy emerges there can be serious political debate at European level on what we use technology for. The slavish imitation of American priorities, the sense that technology is out of control and creating a society and a world we do not want, can only be overcome when Europe has effective institutional machinery for managing and controlling the technology it does in common and subjecting it to public opinion.

The present negotiations for British membership of the European Community suffer from the sense that Britain is joining an archaic Community concerned only with beef and butter. Foch's study is fuel for the debate on the much more important industrial tasks of the 1970s.

If some of his ideas are realized, the enlarged Community should, by 1980, be spending as much, or more, of its common budget on the new industries as it does on the farms. That would dramatically change the outlook for the British, who could expect to receive far larger benefits from the common budget than they do today, with its emphasis on agriculture. A substantial Community budget for science and technology should not merely be good for European industry, but help to solve the key problem in Britain's negotiations to join.

His long experience of working in the Communities equips René Foch well to explore these new perspectives. It has not inhibited him from speaking out.

René Foch is an international civil servant, but the views he expresses here are purely personal and should not be interpreted as the views of the Organization to which he belongs.

'To control coal and steel is to control Europe'. So Hitler said during the last war, and in 1950 those who sought to make a new Europe duly began with coal and steel, at a time when coal was still the continent's chief source of energy and a country's industrial power was measured by its steel production. Today, twenty years later, we must agree with Silvain Wickham when he says that 'the Ruhr coalfields and the Lorraine deposits of iron ore no longer play any part in European industrial integration, except perhaps to slow it up'.[1]

Relations between the EEC and the signatories of the Yaoundé Convention certainly represent a European contribution to the development of the Third World; they also mean that Europe as a whole is helping two member states of the Community to bear the increasing burden of development aid to their former colonies.

As to the common agricultural policy, it has been calculated that the Council of Ministers of the EEC has spent 70 per cent of its time on this subject, although agriculture represents only 7 per cent of the Community's total GNP and the number of farmers is steadily declining.

Thus it appears, paradoxically, that the main effort of European integration has been directed towards the old-fashioned sectors of the economy. The fields of activity inherited from the past are those in which European states have been least reluctant to delegate sovereignty and most ready to accept imaginative forms of integration and supranational institutions. Moreover, while an embryonic federal government has been created to deal with surplus stocks of coal and butter, the European states are trying, one after the other, to recapture an elusive sovereignty by launching ambitious national programmes of advanced technology. When they fail to bring these off single-handed and are obliged to resort to collaboration, their first thought is to hold a diplomatic conference to determine the ways and means of conducting large European enterprises. The results of this are significant.

The recent memorandum on industrial policy by the EEC Commission contained the following diagnosis:

'It is no exaggeration to say that as far as the products of advanced technology are concerned there is no real Common Market – neither free trade within the area, nor protection from outside. This state of affairs

[1]Sylvain Wickham, *L'Espace Industriel Européen*, Paris 1969, p. 63.

is all the more serious since the advanced technological industries are precisely those which it is very difficult if not impossible to develop, especially in the early stages, without the support of a large, unfettered and reasonably protected home market. In Europe these industries suffer from permanent discrimination as compared with traditional ones, which have benefited to the full from the Common Market and the freeing of international trade. Aid to key industries on a national basis has helped to bring about this compartmentalization, but is not sufficient to outweigh its ill-effects. So we should not be surprised to find that the United States' competitive lead over Europe in this sphere is steadily growing, at the same time as the American government is doing its best to limit imports of European steel, textiles and chemicals. If this process is not reversed the Western Europeans will find that, without their realizing or at all events intending it, they have become specialists in traditional products while forfeiting their long-term opportunities of growth and technological independence'.

The same memorandum quotes figures to illustrate the overwhelming and growing American superiority in the advanced industrial field: 'In the huge area of electric, electronic and electro-mechanical products the total turnover of the six biggest American firms in 1968 was nearly $29 billion, or more than double that of the nine principal EEC firms ($12·6 billion). Each of the six American firms accounted for over $2·5 billion, and General Electric alone for over $8 billion, while only three of the Europeans exceeded $2 billion, including Montecatini-Edison whose activities extend far beyond the electronic sphere. The five leading Japanese firms alone did nearly $8 billion worth of business.

'As regards nuclear power stations of 100 MWe or over, four American firms have built or contracted to build 93 with a total power of 75,000 MWe – including 74 for General Electric and Westinghouse, totalling 61,000 MWe – while ten or a dozen EEC firms have only 22 stations with a total power of about 10,000 MWe.

'As regards data processing our figures are not very precise, but it would seem that in 1968 the total sales of EEC industries, excluding American-owned subsidiaries, were under $130 m, while American companies totalled $8·75 billion – i.e. 67 times as much, or 25 times if the figures for Britain are added to those of the EEC.

'There is also grave imbalance in the field of aerospace, where in 1967 American firms did more than 13 times as much business as those of the EEC, which in this field is very little ahead of Britain'.

Thus, while Europe is holding its own in traditional industry, the Americans show a clear superiority in the industries which belong to the second industrial revolution and which are those showing the fastest growth rates: in 1967 US exports of computers went up by 58 per cent, and those of the aviation and telecommunication industries by 34 and 30 per cent respectively.[1]

---

[1]François Closets, *En Danger de Progrès*, Paris 1970, p. 77.

The object of this essay is to describe Europe's attempts to react, to analyse the reasons for its setbacks and to outline the institutions it must have in order to hold its own in the fields of industry to which the future belongs.

The role of OECD

While such a book as *The American Challenge*[1] had a spectacular effect in awakening European opinion to the widening gap between American and European technology, the credit for first drawing attention to the problem belongs to the OECD (Organization for Economic Co-operation and Development), whose first step was to draw up internationally comparable statistics of the amounts devoted to research and development (R & D) by its different member countries.

The following passage is taken from a General Report on Gaps in Technology drawn up for the third Ministerial Meeting on Science, held at Paris in March 1968:

'In 1964, the United States devoted 3·4 per cent of GNP to R & D, the economically-advanced OECD countries together 1·5 per cent, the EEC 1·3 per cent, Canada 1·1 per cent and Japan 1·4 per cent . . . .

'Measured at current official exchange rates, the United States devoted four and a half times as much public money to R & D as industrialized Western Europe, and eight times as much as the EEC. For privately financed R & D these differences are cut by about 50 per cent in the case of Western Europe and Canada.

'The American government expenditure on R & D is, however, highly concentrated in defence, space and nuclear energy programmes in which private industry is the principal performer. For example, 56 per cent of total R & D expenditure in the United States in 1963–64 was concentrated in these three areas. The corresponding figure for Britain was 40 per cent, France 43 per cent and Sweden 31 per cent. This being the case, it is clear that civilian economic benefits of R & D have depended to a large extent on "fall-out" and "spin-off" effects'.

On this essential point M. Théo Lefèvre, one of the experts appointed by the OECD to study science policy in the United States, wrote as follows:

'Opinions differ considerably as to the extent of scientific "fall-out". It is partly a question of definition. In some industries the importance of direct fall-out cannot be overestimated. Thus it has been of great benefit in electronics, advanced chemistry and scientific and technical equipment, if only by the amortization of the first production series, making later ones commercially profitable (for instance computers). But it would seem that direct fall-out has had little effect on consumption industries. As to indirect fall-out, the repercussions of major projects have been

[1]Jean-Jacques Servan-Schreiber, *The American Challenge*, 1968; French original *Le Défi américain*, Paris 1967.

much greater, though they are hard to quantify. Such projects have created a general movement and have helped to form a certain scientific climate: it is good business, as well as a duty, to carry on research or to encourage and finance it. If the American businessman is "scientific-minded", "research-minded", ready to take risks and aware of the future, this is undoubtedly due in large measure to the big projects which act as a spur to expansion in all fields'.

Following what has been called the naive period of the technological gap, when attention was chiefly drawn to the difference between the amounts spent on R & D on either side of the Atlantic, there soon came a more critical phase during which the causes of the gap were sought in various fields connected with the process of technical innovation, particularly education. But, while in no way underrating the part played by American universities, which derive strength both from their diversity and from their integration into a single system, it was soon found that first impressions had to be qualified.

'The proportion of men and women who have completed advanced studies is higher among the working population of the US than in other countries, but when it comes to those holding science or technological degrees the American lead is much less pronounced. Both in relative and in absolute terms, Europe's effort in technological training is in advance of the United States. However, in the US holders of advanced degrees are more likely to become managers than in Europe, so that American private industry possesses cadres with better scientific training'.

Attention was then directed towards the 'management gap', but it soon became clear that it was artificial to emphasize this aspect. 'Business strategy is the essential link in the chain of events leading to the commercial exploitation of new forms of knowledge. It is the factor which increasingly determines the pursuit of lines of research which result in new products or processes offering a prospect of commercial success. From this point of view it is doubtful whether the "technological gap" and the "managerial gap" should be treated as opposing concepts. The essence of the problem lies in the integration of technological skill with the process of decision at management level, in the light of market conditions and expected competition'.

Thus the OECD has played, and continues to play, a decisive part in arousing European awareness of the widening technological gap and encouraging the study of ways and means of reducing it.[1] Even so, its contribution has in large measure been complementary and subsequent to the efforts of several European governments to grapple with the problem.

[1]The above paragraphs are concerned only with recalling this fact, and do not attempt to survey the whole activity of the OECD in the political, scientific and technical fields. They do not, for example, cover the Organization's essential role, past and present, in formulating a policy concerning environmental problems.

National reactions

Realizing that their own private enterprises were in no position to develop the new industries, and that American firms had only succeeded in doing so thanks to large government-financed programmes, Britain and France embarked on national programmes copied from America. The consequences of the war prevented Germany and Italy from doing likewise, and lack of resources ruled it out for other European countries.

Britain in the fifties thought that in this way she could make up for the loss of an empire by means of a systematic, government-inspired effort to attain leadership in certain fields of advanced technology. The French, a few years later, made a similar bid, and it is remarkable how far their industrial strategy conformed to the choices earlier exercised by the British, at a time when the drawbacks of this policy were already clear to the more discerning.

The British and French, by comparison with the Americans, devoted a similar proportion of their R & D budget to the sectors of national defence and atomic and space research. But in both countries the total expenditure on R & D was below that of the United States as a proportion of GNP; moreover, the latter's GNP was vastly higher than that of Britain or France. Consequently the British and French national programmes soon ran up against the inexorable law of scale, obliging the two nations of Europe which set most store by their sovereignty to co-operate with each other.

At the present time Germany is striving to regain a position of leadership in research, and shows signs of wanting to emulate the national ambitions of Britain and France in space and nuclear development, aviation and computers. The size of its firms, the enterprise of German businessmen and their readiness to collaborate with the United States are manifest advantages, and the Federal Republic's nuclear industry already appears formidable. Nevertheless, when it comes to transforming individual efforts into a large-scale industrial breakthrough, we may wonder whether the factor of size which explains some of the more notable British and French setbacks will not bring home to German industry in like manner the limitations of going it alone.

Apart from these national reactions, European governments have responded to the challenge by various attempts at co-operation which may be classed under three heads, starting with the simplest: bilateral, as in the aviation industry; multilateral, leading to inter-governmental institutions as in the field of space research; the community style, as in Euratom.

Bilateral co-operation in the aviation industry

It was in this sector that the European governments first recognized the limits of their national possibilities. The figures speak for themselves: the aircraft industry in Britain, France and Germany respectively employs 247,000, 103,000 and 43,000 people, while the American industry employs 1,400,000. The first joint European projects, both on a Franco-German basis, were the transport aircraft Transall and the Breguet Atlantique.

Transall was first conceived in 1957, and agreement was reached on development in 1959. In 1964 it was decided to produce 110 of these aircraft in Germany and 50 in France. Costs of development were shared equally between the two countries, and those of production in the same ratio as orders (11:5). The project was managed by a joint working committee of the French firm Nord-Aviation and the German VFW and HFB (Hamburger Flugzeugbau). The aircraft, which is of a fairly traditional type, was not exported outside the two countries, but a French expert estimated that its final cost was 25 per cent lower than if it had been constructed on a purely national basis.

The Breguet Atlantique was designed to meet a NATO requirement for naval reconnaissance and anti-submarine detection. A consortium was set up to manufacture it, consisting of Breguet (responsible for technical leadership), ABAP (Belgian), the Dutch firm Fokker, and Sud-Aviation. Only a small number of aircraft were finally produced: 80 for France and 20 for the German Federal Republic. The British and Americans, who had taken part in the NATO competition, continued to use their own aircraft. None the less the Breguet Atlantique was technically successful, and the cost per unit to France was 25 per cent lower than it would have been on a national basis.

Although the British government took part in neither of these ventures, British industry profited to a considerable extent, as both types of aircraft used Rolls-Royce engines manufactured under licence. But it was not until the sixties that British industry made up its mind to collaborate with the Continent, in the first instance with France. This was the origin of the famous Concorde project, which we shall describe in some detail in view of its scale and the working methods involved.[1]

The Concorde

After long negotiations the Concorde programme was finalized in an Anglo-French treaty of 29 November 1962. The construction of a supersonic airliner was entrusted to four companies: the British Aircraft Corporation (BAC) and Sud-Aviation for the airframe, Bristol Siddeley Engines (BSE) and the Société Nationale d'Etudes et de Construction de Moteurs d'Avions (SNECMA) for the engines. The programme was divided into two phases:

(a) The development phase, i.e. the whole range of studies, manufacture and tests necessary in order to secure permission from the

[1]On the basis of a report by Jacques Forestier to a colloquium on *International Scientific Co-operation and the European Problem*, Aix-en-Provence 1967.

competent authorities to use Concorde for passenger transport. The total cost of this phase was estimated in 1967 at 7 m francs untaxed and it is expected to run until 1973, the customers during this period being the two governments.[1]

(b) The production phase, i.e. manufacture for the purpose of commercial use by airline companies. The turnover corresponding to the sale of 100 aircraft and spare parts was estimated in 1967 (before France's devaluation) at over 20 m francs; in this phase, the customers will be the airline companies.

INTERGOVERNMENTAL COLLABORATION

The agreement of 1962 laid down the principle of strict equality between the two parties in both phases and in all respects, including volume of work, management responsibility, expenditure and receipts.

DEVELOPMENT PHASE

Under the initial agreement the two governments assumed liability for the expenses of this phase, the financing to be carried out by national contracts between the respective government authorities and each of the four companies. The effects of this contractual system were that: (a) Each contract was drawn up on the customary national basis, so that the English and French ones differ to some extent in the method of calculating expenditure and incidental costs. (b) The parties to each contract have concluded sub-contracts with firms in each other's country. (c) Wherever these expenses may finally fall, there is no reason to assume that the cost borne by the two governments will be equal at the end of the operation.

Discussions have been going on for the past five years to decide on the final arrangements for balancing the accounts. The French seem prepared to accept a certain final imbalance provided the expenses borne by each government correspond to work done in its country, while the British are more in favour of an exact sharing of the burden. The French proposal is not supported by the letter of the agreement, but it would have the advantage of getting round the difficulties arising out of different methods of calculating expenses.

Two further problems are still being discussed between the governments: the final sharing between them of the ownership of Concorde products, and the sharing of expenses for the work done on the project in the respective government establishments. These have so far been left out of account, as the way in which the establishments are financed makes it particularly hard to compare the expenses arising directly out of the Concorde project.

[1]In 1970, 10 mld francs (£752 m or $1,818 m).

It has been agreed in principle that the governments will recover at least part of the expenses incurred by them in the development phase by means of royalties on sales in the second phase. But the amount of these and the basis on which they should be shared is still the subject of discussion.

CO-OPERATION BETWEEN THE COMPANIES

During the year prior to the signature of the treaty, agreements on the sharing of work and technical responsibilities had been reached between BAC and Sud-Aviation for the airframe and BSE and SNECMA for the engines. These agreements were ratified by the treaty itself. They involved the setting up of similar organizations for the airframe and engines respectively. Each company retained its independence, but the management of the Concorde project was entrusted to a joint Committee of Directors comprising a chairman, a vice-chairman and a number of directors for technical matters, production, finance, etc. Each member of the Committee had a deputy of the other nationality: the chairmanship was held alternately by the chairman and vice-chairman at two-yearly intervals.

As regards the use of patents held or taken out by each of the four companies, both agreements were based on the principle that these would be made freely available to the other party.

The two prototypes were flown for the first time in 1969. The French and British engineers will no doubt succeed in solving the outstanding technical problems, but the real question that no one can yet answer is that of the Concorde's economic future: will it be like that of the Comet or the Caravelle ? At all events, for better or worse it has brought about a close association between the two chief aircraft industries in Europe. At present the Concorde project, by the ambitiousness of its aims and the volume of resources involved, is the most striking example of international co-operation along the lines recommended by the Plowden Report of 1965 on the British aircraft industry.

This Report pointed out that the American market accounted for 75 per cent of world military and space purchases and at least 50 per cent of civil aircraft purchases, which automatically gave it a huge advantage over the British industry. In 1955–61 the United States produced on the average 530 military aircraft of a given type compared with Britain's 177, and four and a half times more transport aircraft of a given type than Britain. The Report recommended that Britain should give up the idea of developing projects of any importance on a national basis and should co-operate fully with other European countries on a series of military and civil projects, so as to build up a European industry which could look the Americans in the face. This Report became the keystone of European co-operation in the field of aircraft construction.

The Martel and Jaguar projects

The lessons learnt by France and Britain from their large-scale co-operation on Concorde led to two other joint projects, Martel and Jaguar.

Martel is an air-launched guided missile developed jointly by Hawker Siddeley and Engins Matra. Development costs have been split equally between the two countries ($140 m each) and exports are to be shared in the same way. Production is split according to orders in the two countries, Britain purchasing eight times as many as France.

The Jaguar project is more advanced both technically and from the organization point of view. This aircraft was originally a Breguet conception, but its performance has been raised in co-operation with BAC. Development costs are estimated at about £100 m, shared between France and Britain, and it is hoped to sell several hundred of the aircraft at about £600,000 apiece. At the Government level there is a management committee of four British and four French members: at industry level joint Anglo-French companies manufacture airframe and engine.

These three examples of Anglo-French co-operation prove that the combined industries of the two countries are technically able to carry out projects on the international – i.e. the American – scale; but they also show that commercially the Franco-British market is too small, like the Franco-German one in the case of Transall and the Breguet Atlantique. Without a European-scale market, technically successful projects are likely to come to grief commercially. But as things are today one cannot expect Italy and Germany – especially the latter, whose reborn aircraft industry is closely linked with the United States – to buy European instead of American aeroplanes if they have not had a share in construction. Consequently plans have been set on foot for multilateral as opposed to bilateral co-operation. Two of these are worth attention here: the Variable Geometry (VG) aircraft and the Airbus project.

The Variable Geometry aircraft

When this project was mooted the British were looking for a successor to the F-111's that they were planning to buy from the United States, while the French wanted a high performance aircraft for the 1970s. By co-operating with the Germans it was hoped to provide an eventual replacement for the F-104 which was being produced under licence. The market in question would be over a thousand aeroplanes. Franco-British conversations made fair progress, and in January 1967 a preliminary agreement was signed; it was, however, denounced by the French government some months later, the chief reason apparently being that the RAF wanted a strike reconnaissance aircraft of considerable range while the French chiefly wanted a fast interceptor for European conditions only. Meanwhile, the Dassault company put into the air a VG prototype of its own.

After the agreement was denounced, the British sought to co-operate with the Germans and Italians. A long history lay behind this. The members of the 'F-104 club' – West Germany, Italy, Belgium, the Netherlands, Norway and Canada – had originally decided on a joint study for a new aircraft to replace the F-104 used by their defence forces. When the British decided not to buy F-111's, and after their plan to co-operate with the French had failed, they turned towards the other Continentals and took part in the study of the new machine. Under their influence the original plan, which was simple and inexpensive, turned into a much more elaborate enterprise, the Multi-Role Combat Aircraft (MRCA); but as costs grew the number of participants dwindled to three – Britain, Germany and Italy – working through a single preparatory body known as NAMMO (NATO MRCA Management Organization). The final plan is apparently for a 20-ton twin-jet two-seater aircraft capable of flying at twice the speed of sound. Owing to rising costs, the number it is intended to manufacture has been much reduced. Meanwhile the French government and the Dassault company are suggesting to countries alarmed by the rising cost of the MRCA that they should co-operate instead with France to produce a simpler and less expensive VG aircraft than the Mirage G8.

The Airbus proposal

In 1965 the British Minister of Aviation suggested to the French, and then the Germans, who had been thinking on similar lines, that the three countries should jointly develop an aircraft on much more traditional lines than the Concorde for intra-European traffic in the seventies and eighties, where with the rapid expansion of the market there was need of a larger machine than the Caravelle, Trident or Boeing 727. At the instance of the West Germans, attention was first given to plans for a 300-seater aircraft with a special Rolls-Royce engine, the HB207. However, in view of possible competition from various American aircraft and the time and expense involved in developing a 150-ton aircraft with new engines, a less ambitious solution was adopted at French suggestion, namely the A300B which, in its standard version, was to be a 250-seater, short and medium range aeroplane with large fuel tanks.

The British Government by this time had decided to withdraw from the project owing to its increasing cost, and it seems that they may instead finance a British project, the BAC-311. The French and Germans are going ahead with the Airbus, and its first flight is scheduled for 1972. It will be equipped with General Electric jet engines or with Rolls-Royce ones, a choice which would let the British in at the commercial stage. The British company, Hawker Siddeley, keeps a modest part in the airframe work.

A symmetry may be observed between the two last-mentioned

projects: MRCA including the British and Germans and perhaps the Italians, but not the French, while Airbus includes the French and German Governments, but not the British. All in all, European co-operation in aircraft construction has not gone far beyond the bilateral stage. It is true that, in addition to the full-dress agreements described above, there are numerous sub-contracts to facilitate entry into a given market (e.g. the Dassault-Belgian agreements) or to avoid creating an industrial potential which might afterwards remain unused. Thus there are sub-contracts for the Mercure in Holland and Italy, and agreements for the maintenance of Boeing 747s. Broadly speaking, such agreements are designed to use existing industrial structures but not to rationalize them. As for the intergovernmental projects, they represent combinations of different partners for specific objectives but fall short of true integration, which is essential if we are to achieve rapidity of decision, avoid overlap, make the most of our resources and generally compete with American industry.

The choices made also lend themselves to criticism: the Airbus idea may be well enough tailored to Europe's needs and possibilities, but can this be said of the Concorde venture ? Having decided to devote such large sums to technical advance in the field of transport, would it not have been more useful to develop an electric automobile, thus reducing urban air pollution, or up-to-date methods of mass surface transport instead of a de luxe aircraft for the few ? Even if it was right to spend the money on maintaining and developing existing air potential, was it the wisest course to enter the supersonic race, with its attendant risk of causing intolerable nuisances ? The choice actually made seems, to say the least, more a matter of technical extrapolation or prestige than of rational development. The same, of course, might be said of the American space programme – or the Pyramids!

Apart from all this, how could the European aircraft industries be expected to unite when the governments did nothing to unify the market ? The chief customers for aircraft are national defence forces and the airline companies. We shall come back to defence later. In civil aviation it seemed at one time that the Common Market would have its counterpart in Air Union: the airlines of the Six – except for Luxair, and KLM which withdrew later – succeeded in 1959 in working out draft terms of association. The governments intervened in October of that year, and took five years to bury the plan.[1]

However, it may be supposed that sooner or later the economic integration of Europe, followed by its political union, will bring about a unified system of civil aviation. This will have consequences both within and beyond united Europe. Within the Community thus extended to air transport, national airlines with their internal monopolies will be replaced by a competitive system which will be to the benefit of all but will have to be regulated by a body similar to the United States Civil Aeronautics

[1] See the article signed Aventin in the *Lloyd Anversois* for August 1969.

Board. Outside the Community, the effect should be to bring about fair terms of competition between European and American airlines. Such routes as London–Paris–Rome would become fifth freedom routes for American carriers, and it would be easier for Europeans to secure in exchange cabotage rights within the United States. As things are at present, every citizen of the Common Market countries may cross the Atlantic under his own national colours, but the plane in which he flies will always be American.

Multilateral co-operation in space

As compared with aviation, co-operation in space research is further advanced from the institutional point of view, being organized multi-laterally.

In 1960 Britain, recognizing in the light of American and Soviet advances that its Blue Streak missile was useless for defence purposes, proposed to other European countries that it should be made the basis of a joint satellite launching programme. Britain was to provide the first stage rocket, France the second, Germany the third; Italy the first series of experimental satellites, Belgium the ground control stations, Holland the telemetry systems and Australia (which had a prior agreement with Britain) the launching site at Woomera.

These seven countries formed in 1962 the European Space Vehicle Launcher Development Organization, better known as ELDO. From the institutional point of view it was in practice an intergovernmental organization of the traditional kind, operating for practical purposes on the unanimity principle, since an important country could not be over-ruled on any matter of significance, including the annual budget. It was, in short, an application to advanced technology of the doctrine of *l'Europe des patries*. Incidentally, the question of what the European launcher was to put into orbit was not settled.

About this time the scientists who had created the European Organization for Nuclear Research (French initials CERN) set about founding ESRO, the European Space Research Organization, which began operations in 1964. Its object was purely scientific, namely to construct satellites for research purposes and place them in orbit by means of national, American or ELDO rockets.

The new organization was formed by ten countries: the Six, except Luxembourg, plus Britain, Denmark, Spain, Sweden and Switzerland. Once again it was an inter-governmental organization, but of a more advanced type than ELDO. Instead of separate national efforts united by diplomacy, an attempt was made to create joint installations working to a common end. Contracts for the purpose were farmed out to industry on a competitive basis.

In 1963 a third body was set up, the European Conference on Satellite Communications (CETS), which was concerned with applications satellites. The European countries wanted to define their attitude and if possible agree on a common line with regard to the Intelsat negotiations for a world organization of satellite telecommunications. They wished to strengthen their collective position by creating a communications satellite of their own and to study jointly other uses of satellites such as meteorology and air navigation. The new body had a larger membership than its predecessors, comprising, besides the European members of ESRO and ELDO, Austria, Eire, Monaco, Norway, Portugal and the Vatican City.[1] Australia on the other hand, is not a member of CETS.

Thus Europe possessed three separate bodies concerned with space: one to build rockets, one for research satellites and a third for applications satellites. The problems created by this profusion of enterprise were expressed in very moderate terms by M. Bourely:[2]

'To begin with, the purposes for which ESRO, ELDO and CETS were set up are different in each case. The first was the work of scientists, the second mainly of European countries wishing to promote their launching industries. As for the third, its main purpose was that the postal administrations of different countries might work out a common line concerning satellite communication problems, which did not fall within the traditional scope of the European Conference on Posts and Telecommunications (CEPT). On account of this diversity of origin, some countries are represented in the three bodies by delegates from different government departments. The scale of participation by different countries varies considerably, as does the method of financing projects in the respective bodies.

'The gravest disadvantage, however, is that there is no regular provision for co-operation among the three bodies, or between them and other European organs of technical co-operation. Thus we have the paradox that ESRO can and does use non-European launchers to put its large scientific satellites into orbit, while ELDO is developing a launching rocket without the certainty that it will meet the needs of any user. Finally, while CETS proposes to create a European communications satellite, there is in theory no guarantee that ESRO or ELDO will have any part in constructing or launching it'.

Thus realization slowly dawned that the lack of a joint, co-ordinated European space programme meant duplication in the national and international fields and prevented the nations concerned from making the best use of their human and material resources. By way of remedy a proposal was put forward at ELDO's first ministerial conference in 1966 for the establishment of a European Space Conference (CSE). In other words, a fourth space organization was to be set up to co-ordinate the other three, and an advisory committee was appointed to suggest a coherent programme. Its report, known as the Causse Plan from the

[1]Greece has taken part in its work from time to time.
[2]'L'Europe à la recherche d'une politique spatiale' in the *Revue française du droit aérien*, No. 1, 1970.

name of its chairman, was submitted in January 1968.[1]

Throughout 1968–9 the European space organizations staggered from one crisis to another. We need not go into the details here: the essential conflict was between two points of view represented by the British and French respectively. The British held that it was unnecessary for Europe to go all out for an independent launching capacity since this would probably be available on acceptable terms from the United States; they also thought the Intelsat agreements could be renegotiated on terms satisfactory to Europe. The French, on the other hand, thought it essential for Europe to have its own launchers and communications satellites, if only to be in a strong position in the Intelsat negotiations and to put an end to the virtual monopoly of the American Comsat company. The Germans, Dutch and Belgians agreed with the French view and declared themselves ready to go ahead alone with the Europa II rocket which was to place in orbit the satellite Symphonie, a joint development by France, Germany and Belgium.[2]

[1]The Causse Plan was based on three main ideas:

1 Launching programmes must be dependent on satellite programmes but must not become too expensive. The ELDO budget should therefore be kept at its present level of $90 m p.a. till 1975, while the ESRO budget of $50 m should be progressively raised to about $150 m by 1972, comprising $100 m for its basic activity of space research and $47 m for applications satellites.

2 ESRO's research satellite programmes should not unduly prejudge the level of European technology but should be completed by a programme of applications satellites which will in due course give Europe a real chance of participating in Intelsat programmes, and which are the only satellites that are economically profitable in the medium term.

3 The existing European bodies – ESRO, ELDO and CETS – should be regrouped and restructured to enable them to carry out the proposed new programme. This was in three parts:

a As regards research satellites, the Committee was not much in favour of ESRO's project for a Large Astronomical Satellite (LAS), which would cost $180m and called for highly sophisticated development techniques.

b As regards applications satellites, Europe should in 1969 set about creating a first experimental television satellite weighing 190 kilograms, to be followed in 1975 by a 500 kilogram TV distribution satellite and later by a 2 ton satellite which could relay programmes directly to individual receivers. Less ambitious plans were also recommended, such as a meteorological or air navigation satellite.

c As regards launchers, the Committee recommended the development of two new 'generations', Europa III and Europa IV, designed to launch 500 kilogram and 2 ton satellites. These would use as their first stage the British Blue Streak rocket at present in use for the development of Europa I and Europa II. For the final stages oxygen and liquid hydrogen should be used, at least in the first instance. The British apparently had a strong preference for electric propulsion: they are studying the possibilities of this, but it will not be developed before 1980.

As soon as this programme was formulated, it became clear that it would not receive the necessary unanimous support from the bigger countries

[2]Germany and France had signed an agreement in June 1967 to develop this satellite and construct two flight models, to be launched from the space centre in French Guiana and put into geostationary orbit above the Atlantic by Europa II or similar-type rockets. Symphonie would thus cover Europe, the Middle East, three-quarters of Africa, South and Central America, the eastern seaboard of the United States and Canada and the southern part of Greenland. The two models are now expected to be launched at the end of 1972.

62

Thus the 'group of four' are carrying out the programme originally launched on Britain's initiative with Italian co-operation. The Italian position gave rise to a separate crisis within ELDO, since Italy was not prepared to share in the financing of an enlarged programme: the plans were therefore cut down, and some important work which had been assigned to Italy was cancelled. Italy was thus the chief country affected by the need to economize, which was intensified by the cut in the British contribution. Many months of negotiation were needed to resolve this second crisis, consequent on the first.

At the time of writing, the future of European space programmes is as uncertain as ever, and a new American development has thrown fresh doubt on the desirability of an independent European launcher programme.

Following the success of the Apollo project, the Americans are headed for a technical revolution in space matters. Instead of self-contained operations like sending astronauts to the moon and back, the plan seems to be for a complex development with the object of putting into low terrestrial orbit, first of all space stations and subsequently actual bases on which astronauts could remain for a long while. The stations would not be launched by rockets but by manned vehicles which would take off like rockets and land like aircraft, each being capable of about a hundred flights. Supplementary launchers known as space-shuttles would make it possible to get from the stations into geostationary or lunar orbit or on to the moon's surface: these would be chemically-propelled rockets, not intended to return to earth. Studies are also being made of nuclear-propelled rockets for interplanetary journeys.

When this system is in being it will greatly reduce the cost of putting a kilogram of material into orbit. At present this is $2,000 with an American rocket, and much more with a European one; the object is to bring it down to $200. Thus the cost of satellite programmes will be drastically reduced: an elaborate system will be functioning in 15 or 20 years from now, and the Americans have invited the European countries to help set it up.[1]

Will the Europeans accept the invitation, or will they be content to pay for the use of the new system? Once the US programme gets going it will involve an annual expense of $2,000 m, from which we may judge how large the European contribution would have to be if it is to count for anything. On the other hand it is clear that work on space shuttle-craft may revolutionize tomorrow's aviation problems, and that in general the uses of space are going to increase more and more. This being so, it is tempting to negotiate for the unrestricted right to use existing American launchers in return for European participation in the post-Apollo programme. It must not, however, be a mere question of sub-contracting. Europe should be given responsibility for a self-contained part of the programme, for instance the space-shuttle, for which

[1]As well as the Canadians, Australians and Japanese.

a hydrogen propulsion system is envisaged, similar to that on which studies have begun for the Europa III rocket.

From the technical point of view these various plans will take 15–20 years to carry out, so that the timing would not conflict with existing European programmes; but has Europe the financial means and the desire to continue with these and simultaneously take part in the post-Apollo programme ? And are the Americans prepared, in return for such participation, to guarantee the launching of European applications satellites, or what assurances would they require in exchange ? The fourth space conference, held at Brussels in July 1970, entrusted M. Théo Lefèvre with the task of exploration and negotiation, this being perhaps, as Dominique Verguèse puts it, the conference's 'most important resolution for the future'.[1] Europe's space programme will in large measure depend on the outcome of his discussions.

Another important step taken by the conference was to set up a working group to draft a Convention whereby ELDO and ESRO would be replaced by a 'European Space Research and Development Organization', a clear improvement on the existing situation. It is in fact extraordinary that the idea of a single space organization was not taken for granted from the outset. However, as the proposed new organization is to be an inter-governmental one, it is hard to see how it can reconcile the need for stability and continuity with the sovereignty of its members and their right to withdraw as and when they see fit.

A still graver difficulty is that ELDO and ESRO more or less officially recognized in 1966 the doctrine of a 'fair return', i.e. the right of each member country to recover, in the form of contracts, sums approximately equal to its total financial contribution. Thus the new organization for the whole field of space research and development would be fettered in advance by the 'fair return' principle, which is the exact contrary of a Common Market based on geographical specialization. Would the Americans ever have reached the moon if NASA had had to distribute contracts among the fifty states of the Union in proportion to the federal taxes paid by their citizens ? And can we imagine Europe taking part in the American space programme until it possesses institutions comparable to those of the United States in terms of efficiency and the power to take decisions quickly ? This is far from being the case at present, and there is every reason to fear that the new organization, despite the skill of its technicians and however great the spirit of co-operation at the top, will run into the same sort of difficulties as Euratom, which started out with a sizeable budget and a much more coherent institutional framework.

Community co-operation in the nuclear field

The story of Euratom is to a large extent one of failure; but in studying

---

[1]See *Le Monde*, 25 July 1970: 'L'Europe hésite encore à s'engager dans un programme spatial à long terme'.

the evolution of living species it is instructive to consider forms that have not survived as well as those that have. In considering what the Six were aiming at when they set up Euratom, and why the experiment failed, we must distinguish accidental causes from deep-seated ones, and incidental obstacles from planning errors which should not be repeated.

When the idea of Euratom was launched about 1956 it was a highly modern conception, far in advance of its time. The 'technological gap' and the 'American challenge' were not yet household words, but the men who devised Euratom were very conscious of the reality behind these slogans. They realized, too, that the scale of the problems was such that ordinary inter-governmental co-operation was quite insufficient to deal with them; and they saw clearly that research, important though it was, was not an end in itself and that the true object was to create a European industry.

Two of the six members of the EEC already had a nuclear programme and infrastructure of their own: Belgium, which with American help had embarked at an early stage on a modest but significant research and training programme, and France, which had a large national programme under the powerful Commissariat à l'Energie Atomique. The other four countries had as yet no research worth speaking of.

The drafters of the Euratom treaty soon realized that it would not be possible to cover the whole nuclear effort of the six powers, particularly in view of France's budding military programme. Consequently Euratom was designed from the start to co-ordinate and supplement national programmes, its chief instrument for this purpose being its own R & D programme. Under the treaty, research programmes and corresponding budgets were envisaged for maximum periods of five years.

Two five-year programmes have been carried out since Euratom was set up in January 1958. The first, for 1958–62, provided for the creation of basic structures for the Community at a cost of about $200 m. The Joint Research Centre was set up at this time, and co-operation with national institutions was set on foot in such matters as thermonuclear fusion, fast reactors and naval propulsion. Staff was recruited, policies were worked out as regards patents, security and commerce, and relations were established with the chief atomic powers.

The second five-year programme, for 1963–67, followed immediately on the first, with a budget more than twice as high, about $450 m. Its main principles were: to leave it to national enterprise to develop techniques that had already been tested or were about to be; to play a creative role in the middle term in sectors which appeared promising but had been neglected in national programmes – particular mention should be made here of the Orgel project, which since 1960 has been at the core of the Euratom Commission's own research programme; to combine and co-ordinate long-term Community interests, i.e. projects too large to be profitable on a national basis, such as fast-neutron reactors and nuclear fusion.

Euratom had most success in developing new and fruitful methods of work during its first years of existence. The first problem which confronted it was the multiplicity of national atomic research centres. At the same time as the Six were negotiating and signing a treaty which committed them to a large-scale joint effort, and still more between the time of signature and the entry into force of the new arrangements, the governments made haste to equip themselves with national centres so as to be in a strong position *vis-à-vis* their European partners.

The rivalry between Community and national programmes which came into view at this early stage continued to afflict Euratom throughout its existence. Not for the last time, member states acted on the principle that a national effort must necessarily precede or accompany co-operation on a European basis. The principle is a false one, since it implies that every European state has an equal right to develop every form of advanced technology within its own borders, which is the reverse of the regional specialization that characterizes a true Common Market. There was moreover the practical danger that the competition between six national programmes and a seventh European one would mean starving the latter, as in fact happened.

The immediate effect was to endow Europe with a superfluity of atomic research centres, more in fact than the United States possessed at that time! Naturally they were for the most part little more than token establishments – there was enough money to build them, but not to run them properly. Rather than add one more to their number, Euratom tried to reduce the confusion by taking one or more national centres under its wing, on a complete or partial basis. The Joint Research Centre thus covered four establishments: Ispra in Italy, Petten in Holland, part of Geel in Belgium and part of Karlsruhe in Germany. By the time 'cruising speed' was attained during the second five-year period, these four establishments accounted for half Euratom's research credits or about $45 m per annum – less than a tenth of the total for the six national programmes.

The other half of Euratom's research budget was spent in the form of contracts, which may be divided into three types. The first are 'direct contracts', whereby work is carried out for Euratom by public or private institutions of the Community. Under the second type ('contracts of participation') Euratom contributes money and staff for the construction of power reactors by Community enterprises, the return consisting of a measure of working experience which is placed at the disposal of the whole Community. The third, most important type are 'contracts of association', under which Euratom takes part in national projects by contributing on an average 40 per cent of the funds and seconding staff to multinational teams. The whole project is administered by joint management committees comprising representatives of Euratom and of the public or private contractor. A good deal of Euratom's research has been or is being carried out in this way, although the treaty did not

66

expressly provide for contracts of this type.

This procedure has been one of Euratom's most fruitful developments, though it was modified at an early stage by pressure from member governments. The original idea was to have only one association in the Community for each major development project, so that all would benefit from the initiative of a single member country, while the latter would receive Community help in the shape of funds and men, while duplication would be avoided. Soon, however, all the members saw advantages in the scheme for themselves and insisted on having their own contracts of association in each key field, e.g. for fast reactors. Even so, it was possible to maintain effective communication between the different programmes and even to organize exchanges of information on this basis with the American fast reactor programme.

Euratom's second main task was in fact to assist the spread of knowledge within the Community. This presented a problem from the outset. In theory it might have been supposed that the member states would agree to pool their knowledge without reserve, but this would clearly have led to a one-sided position. A centrally-administered country like France, where nuclear research and electricity production are state-controlled through the Commissariat à l'Energie Atomique and Electricité de France, would have been bound by an undertaking that would have meant little or nothing to Germany, where nuclear development is a matter for private industry. Consequently it was decided, broadly speaking, to limit the communication of know-how to that obtained through the Community programme as opposed to national ones.

Another of Euratom's essential tasks, linked with that of promoting the nuclear industry, consisted of furnishing that industry with nuclear materials. The Euratom Supply Agency was set up under the treaty to ensure that all Community users were regularly and equitably supplied with the necessary ores and nuclear fuel. While interfering as little as possible with the free play of the market, except where the treaty expressly requires it, the Agency looks after the whole range of transactions relating to the supply of special fissile materials to the Community. Thanks to the Agency's negotiating power *vis-à-vis* the supplier countries, principally the US and UK, it has been able to get better terms for nuclear fuel supplies than any of the member states individually.

The supply for civil purposes of materials which were also capable of military use raised the question of controls to prevent any possible military use of these materials. When the Treaty of Rome was under discussion it was thought that the Euratom treaty might be, so to speak, a first regional model of the non-proliferation agreement, whereby the member states would renounce the right to manufacture nuclear weapons as Germany had just done in the WEU treaty. By this sacrifice of sovereignty by states other than Germany, all members of the Community would have had equal rights and Europe would have set the world an example of nuclear disarmament.

However, the then French government did not consider itself entitled to give up national sovereignty in such an important domain, and a compromise was reached. The Euratom treaty left member states free to produce nuclear weapons if they wished and to develop a military programme alongside Euratom's peaceful one. Strict controls were set up to ensure that material intended for peaceful purposes was not put to improper use.

Since Germany, by a declaration annexed to the WEU treaty, had undertaken to confine its nuclear activity to peaceful uses, this meant in practice that the entire German nuclear programme would be under the multilateral control of Euratom, as would that of any other member state that did not wish to start a military programme.

The French, who at this time were laying the foundations of their military programme, agreed to accept the same controls as the rest of the Community as regards peaceful uses, so that in this respect the member states' laboratories and plants were all on the same footing. Since the WEU controls have remained a dead letter in practice and those of the Non-Proliferation Treaty are not yet in being, the Euratom control is the only one guaranteeing the German government's undertaking not to manufacture nuclear weapons on its territory.

This is an important political fact which is too little realized: thanks to multilateral control, a German nuclear industry has taken shape within the Community without causing any alarm on the part of its members. From the German point of view there is no injury to the Federal Republic's dignity or its equality of rights, since its fellow-members are subject to exactly the same controls as far as peaceful uses are concerned. As regards external relations, the existence of the controls and the system copied from the United States whereby fissile materials are the property of the Community enables the latter to treat with the American government on a less unequal footing: the latter waives the controls that it previously exercised over American fissile materials supplied to European countries, thus implicitly recognizing the value and efficiency of Euratom controls.

However, in the minds of some of its designers Euratom was not only a means of enabling Europe to run a nuclear programme entirely of its own, but was equally intended to bring about a large-scale transfer of materials, equipment, information and know-how from the more advanced countries, especially the United States. Those who thought on these lines pointed out that it would be an extraordinary coincidence if natural-uranium reactors – the only type the Europeans could build, having no enriched uranium – turned out to be the most profitable economically. Therefore one of the Community's aims should be to enable its members to diversify their efforts and experiment with the more complicated types of enriched-uranium reactors developed in the United States.

Accordingly Euratom lost no time in turning to the United States, with whom an important agreement was signed on 8 November 1958.

68

This laid down two specific objectives: a *joint programme for power reactors*, which led to the building within the Community of three large reactors of a type tested in the US, with a total capacity of some 700 MWe, and simultaneously a *joint research and development programme* in regard to the boiling-water and pressurized-water reactors constructed under the power programme. This American-European collaboration was first mooted at the time when the Suez Canal crisis brought home to Europe the precariousness of its oil supplies. The six foreign ministers instructed three 'wise men' (Louis Armand, Franz Etzel and F. Giordani) to estimate 'the quantity of atomic energy that might be produced within a short time in the six countries, and the steps that would be necessary to this end'. Their report, published in May 1957, estimated that a nuclear capacity of 15,000 MWe would have to be created by the end of 1967 to stabilize European fuel imports.

This goal was by no means reached, but such was the context in which Euratom negotiated its agreement with the United States. The joint programme gave the Europeans an opportunity to acquaint themselves with the American technique of enriched-uranium reactors, while the Americans were able to try out their reactors on an industrial scale in Europe, where conventional energy was considerably dearer than in the US and nuclear power should therefore become competitive within a shorter time. Two joint committees composed half of Americans and half of Euratom officials, were set up to manage the joint programme and make recommendations to the Euratom Commission and the USAEC, thus giving a concrete example of partnership in action.

The field of American-type reactors is perhaps that in which Euratom has been most successful, enabling some European firms to master the technique and build reactors at a very small cost in royalties to the American firms which pioneered them. But the operation took place in far from satisfactory conditions: for ten years the French government favoured the graphite-gas system as against Euratom's preference for American light-water techniques. The latter was right, as is shown by the fact that the French eventually gave up their system while German industry scored successes with light water. But as the French took so long to be convinced, it was Germany and not Europe as a whole which reaped the benefit from the Euratom-sponsored operation.

The system of joint committees with Europeans and Americans on an equal footing, adopted for collaboration with the USAEC, proved its value in many other fields. There is no doubt that Euratom made an important, perhaps a decisive contribution to the flow of technology by giving Europe access to American techniques. The countries and firms which took advantage of these arrangements have not had cause to regret it: Siemens, for example, which at first operated under licence from Westinghouse, is now a competitor with the latter in third-country markets.

In addition to the 1958 agreement and its subsequent amendments, Euratom concluded a co-operation agreement with the USAEC in regard to fast-neutron reactors. The fast reactors programme was the chief feature of the Community's second five-year research period, the sum of 82·5 m u.a.[1] being allotted to it under the programme. If we add the contributions from the five associates – CEA, GfK, CNEN, the Belgian government and TO/RCN – we arrive at a total of some 230 m u.a. spent on fast-reactor development within the Community in 1963–67. USAEC expenditure during this period was of the order of $200 m, so that it would have been possible for the two to collaborate on a more or less equal basis. Moreover, the Americans let it be known that as long as collaboration continued they were prepared to supply Euratom with the large quantities of plutonium required for its programme. In this way an international plutonium market started to come into being.

However, since the end of its second five-year plan Euratom has gone from one crisis and one interim budget to another. The European summit at The Hague seemed to presage the end of this period of crises: while voting yet another interim budget for Euratom, the governments indicated their intention of restructuring the Joint Research Centre to take account of the evolution of nuclear problems within the Community and also to enable the Centre to carry out non-nuclear research. In addition they intended to launch a new plan on a fresh basis, covering a period of years.

How is Euratom's achievement to be summed up ? The single Commission set up to replace the three Community Executives and carry out the European treaties reported as follows to the Council on 9 October 1968:

'The treaty setting up the European Atomic Energy Commission was intended to create conditions for the development of a strong nuclear industry. Ten years later, we must admit that very little progress has been made towards this end. Certainly Euratom's own activities have often been fruitful within the limits imposed on them. But the Community has not in general succeeded in co-ordinating the activities of its members, still less uniting them into a coherent whole.

'The dispersion of research and development programmes in the Community has prevented the effective creation of a nuclear Common Market. Members have reserved credits and government orders for their national industries. Orders placed by firms producing electricity have always gone exclusively to constructors of their own nationality. In consequence, the development of the nuclear industries in the Community has not been able to benefit from the abolition of customs duties and quotas since the Euratom treaty came into force. This state of affairs has led to the present crisis, which affects not only Euratom but the whole field of nuclear development in the Community.

'It cannot be said that the Six member countries have allotted insufficient sums for nuclear research. On the contrary, it is a striking fact that the total amount spent by their governments, individually and through

[1]u.a. = Units of account (equivalent to $1.)

the Community, on peaceful research has been nearly as great as that spent by the United States, which means a higher proportion of the GNP. This comparison, of course, does not take account of the American government's efforts going back to the time of the second world war, or the large sums spent in the United States on private research. But it is none the less saddening to observe the poor result of Europe's financial effort in the industrial and commercial fields.

'In spite of the much higher cost of conventional energy in Europe, the number of nuclear power stations in course of construction, on order or projected in the Community is no more than sixteen, representing some 6,500 MWe, as compared with 87 in the United States representing 70,000 MWe. From the industrial point of view it should be added that these 87 stations are being or will be built by four or five firms, whereas the 16 European ones are being or will be built by a dozen firms. The total volume of orders placed in the Community is less than that placed with any one of the American firms'.

It has to be asked why, despite the size of the funds involved, the results have been so unsatisfactory. In the first place, Euratom was unlucky from the economic as well as the political point of view. It was set up at what appeared to be a time of power shortage, when the Anglo-French action over Suez and the closure of the Canal threatened all Europe with fuel restrictions. As it turned out, however, the crisis had the indirect effect of lowering conventional fuel prices and thus prolonging the interval before nuclear power could be competitive.

Following the 'European' pattern originally inspired by the Fourth French Republic, Euratom is no doubt the most supranational of the three Community treaties. But, impinging as it does on sensitive areas of sovereignty and national defence, it received little support from the member state that was furthest ahead in the peaceful use of atomic energy. Thus it has been said that, while the Coal and Steel treaty was economically out of date, Euratom was politically before its time.

Functioning in an economic situation for which it had not been devised and in a different political climate from that of its birth, Euratom soon found itself in the position of a commando cut off from the troops that should have supported it. These, however, were accidental circumstances: the two main causes of Euratom's failure lay elsewhere.

Until recently its six members disagreed as to the best course of technical progress: five of them wanted to build enriched-uranium reactors while the sixth, until a short while ago, held out for natural uranium.

More important still, Euratom, operating on a single sector of research only, was hampered from an early stage by the 'fair return' principle, each country expecting to receive through contracts an amount at least equal to its own contribution. This idea, if not the actual formula, seems in fact to have come up for the first time in connection with Euratom's research budget.

Covering as it did only one area of the economy, Euratom could only have become a success if it had led to the formation of an overall research policy and an industrial policy embracing all sectors of advanced technology.

National and multilateral programmes

At this point we should study more closely the relation between multilateral and national programmes.

The case of CERN – a European effort carried on for a long period to the exclusion of any national competitor – is an exceptional one, due to the scale of equipment involved and its cost, which was clearly out of all proportion to the amount that even the richest of the European states were prepared to spend on high-energy physics.

At the same time, CERN's very success has encouraged the formation of national teams and programmes; this goes some way to explain the political crisis now threatening the Centre, which was long regarded as Europe's highest achievement in scientific co-operation. It appears, however, that this crisis may now be in process of solution.

Even when the idea of co-operation is accepted, what may be called the 'position of strength' complex often comes into play: a member state tries to manoeuvre itself into a starting position from which it can dominate future international bodies or at least turn their work to its own account. As a rule the other countries, as far as they are able, follow suit without delay.

Some examples of this have been given from the history of Euratom. Others might be cited from the space field, for example, where the French national effort for a time undoubtedly gave French industry a privileged position in ESRO. Exactly the same is true on a larger scale as regards American industry and Intelsat. This is in the nature of things, and is an inevitable drawback to systems combining national and international efforts. The relation between the two varies considerably according as the country concerned is large or small by European standards. If it is small, the national effort is reduced to its lowest terms, or disappears entirely as with Luxembourg, and the country's contribution to the common effort is larger than its national programme. But in a country like France or Germany, with a large national programme, the contribution to the joint effort represents only a fraction of this.

As a result, the two types of country differ in their attitude towards the multilateral programme. The former have a clear interest in the success of an enterprise which largely takes the place of a national effort as far as they are concerned, while countries which concentrate most of their resources at home tend to judge the multilateral effort in terms of its effect on their national plan.

The existence of both a joint programme and a series of national ones, with the different national authorities helping to determine the common programme, also has a specific effect on the allocation of tasks. The various countries include in their own programmes the easiest projects from the technical point of view, or those which appear most promising, and assign the less promising, more difficult or adventurous projects to the international authority. Thus for example, in regard to heavy-water reactors, France, Germany and Italy, having each decided on a plan for such a reactor, cooled respectively by gas, heavy water and steam, entrusted Euratom with the task of studying the less promising method of cooling by organic liquid. After $150 m had been invested in this system with perfect technical success, it was found that no one was interested!

No one, on the other hand, seeks to encroach on the work of Euratom's Bureau for Nuclear Measurements, which belongs rather to the public sector, or its long-term research on thermonuclear fusion, which offers no immediate commercial prospects. Similarly in the field of fast reactors, where all the member countries were using sodium as a coolant, it was decided nevertheless to exchange information within OECD on a gas-cooled variant in case the sodium method gave rise to any surprises. As long as the work is divided up on this basis, it is a miracle that joint programmes more or less bear comparison with national ones from the point of view of technical success.

If in addition financial difficulties present themselves, the situation soon becomes intolerable. Logically, if the funds available to a country for nuclear or space research grow less, it should cut down expenses on its national programme and devote a larger proportion of its funds to the joint project, which will benefit everybody. But in terms of political reality there is generally a competition between the national and international programmes for the limited funds available, and the latter is most likely to be cut back for the simple reason that it is drawn up by the people who administer the national programmes.

This harmful competition can be observed in most of the key sectors. In aviation, the British and French in May 1965 made plans for the joint production of a variable geometry aircraft, but they were nullified when M. Dassault put his Mirage G into the air. In the nuclear field, Euratom's history is that of a long conflict between the advocates of enriched uranium and the French CEA which argued for natural uranium.

As regards space, General Aubinière, the director-general of the Centre National d'Etudes Spatiales (CNES), discussing different alternatives for French space policy, observes[1] that: 'To abandon our national space effort altogether and concentrate on a European programme would be the worst solution of all. In view of the expanding national programmes of other European countries, our industry would lose its present lead and we should merely be financing foreign industry'.

[1] In Le Monde, 6 February 1970.

This does not seem to be the view of M. Laigle, representing the staff side of the CNES, who writes:[1] 'The staff is convinced that its effort only makes sense on a scale wider than that of the nation. It is clear that the European organization CERS-ESRO – which has launched four satellites in the same time as CNES and at a comparable cost, and which is taking on engineers who have resigned from CNES – has become an institution of standing and efficiency. Perhaps the answer is simply that, in the nature of things, CNES is incapable of being objective enough to define its own objectives and to understand the policy of what it seems to regard as a rival body'.

All these unfortunate developments are due to the choice of institutions rather than to any lack of goodwill, and the moral to be drawn from them is to avoid in future as far as possible hybrid situations in which national and multilateral programmes coexist, not always peacefully, in the same sector.

Another strong argument against national R & D programmes is that they reinforce the alarming tendency in all European countries for national firms to attain a quasi-monopolistic position.

It is well known that the first effect of the Common Market was not, as might have been hoped, to promote the formation of multinational European firms, but to bring American ones on the scene. What is less well known is that the second effect of the Common Market was to encourage concentration and mergers between firms of the same nationality, thus giving rise to what may be called 'nation-wide companies'. For example, Pechiney controls 80 per cent of French aluminium production, Fiat a still higher percentage of Italian automobile production; the Kraftwerk-Union (KWU) dominates the German nuclear industry, and the French government is doing its best to establish a similar dominant group in the nuclear field.

The economic objections to this have long been noted,[2] and they seem especially great in key sectors.[3] The political objections are no less great, for the effect of national concentration is to put the brake on economic evolution. The monopolistic firms, confined within the limits of relatively small nations, are faced with increasingly tough competition from American firms with a far larger base. Thus the process of merger cannot stop short when the stage of 'nation-wide' firms' is reached; but a marriage between two such firms, and still more the absorption of one of them by another, becomes in the fullest sense an 'affair of state'. It is far from clear that the technique of marriage negotiations which has played such a part in European history can be applied with the same success to the formation of multilateral firms.

[1]In *Le Monde*, 17 February 1970.
[2]Cf. Louis Armand in *Le Figaro*, 25 July 1966.
[3]Cf. Roger Priouret in *L'Express*, 13 July 1970.

The need for a global approach

The various types of collaboration – bilateral as in aviation, multilateral as in space exploration or on a Community basis as in Euratom – all suffer from the same trouble, calling for the same remedies. As regards ELDO the clearest diagnosis was given by M. Théo Lefèvre, chairman of the Conference of Ministers, in a report of October 1968.[1]

[1]'We know too that Europe will not succeed in recapturing its position on the world market for advanced products, a market which is already escaping from its control to a disturbing extent, on the basis of industrial structures and research programmes which would remain on the national scale.

'It is obviously this which has impelled us towards scientific and technological co-operation and this is why we cannot throw in our hand even in the midst of apparently insurmountable difficulties such as those we have to solve here.

'Do I need to recall the fact that the American success results not only from governmental research and development programmes, but also from the support of public procurement, the size of enterprises and the unity of a large market which accords full value to innovation?

'It so happens that the co-operation we have organized hitherto has been limited to research and development. The programmes have not been slanted towards the actual needs of our nations but rather towards technical or scientific performance for its own sake. They have not contributed to the establishment in Europe of consortia of enterprises or unified industrial structures capable of withstanding competition with American industry. Lastly, the marketing of the advanced materials resulting from our programmes has not been backed up by a public procurement policy which is likely to create a genuinely unified market.

'In these conditions, the lack of prospects of economic profitability now joins with the lack of precision in the goals to create doubt and discouragement among the participators.

'I share the opinion of several of those whom I have consulted that an industrial policy cannot be carried out by the multiple organizations for co-operation, specialized by sector and by subject, which we have created, because it is often the same enterprises and the same consortia which will make spacecraft or aircraft, nuclear power stations or electronic appliances, owing to the fundamental unity of advanced technology and the interdependence of its types of production.

'My conviction is therefore – like theirs – that technological co-operation will be able to survive and develop in Europe only if we plan the organs and methods of this co-operation in such a way that it effectively serves the industrial progress of this continent and each participating country is given an assurance that it will have its share of the economic fruits of its contribution.

'This involves two suppositions: that we should introduce more unity into the programmes, institutions and budgets for research and that we should extend joint responsibility beyond the research and development stage to the stage of production and marketing.

'Taking these premises as a point of departure, we think that technological co-operation, in order to meet the present situation of Europe, should be based on the following principles:

a It would extend to the major subjects of advanced technology, such as space, nuclear energy, data-processing and computers, aviation, transport and telecommunications.

b It would be based on the establishment of industrial consortia which would enjoy, on the one hand, the support of research and development contracts and, on the other, that of public orders co-ordinated among our governments.

c It would ensure that each country has its fair share in the new jobs, flows of business and stimuli to progress which will result from the joint action, this fair share applying to the programmes as a whole and not to each of them in particular, a proviso which assumes that our efforts should be established on a continuous and durable basis.'

Seeing, however, that the problem is a global one, a sectional organization like ELDO or Euratom could hardly provide the basis for an overall policy such as that suggested in the Lefèvre report. The Commission of the European Communities, which was given general responsibility in economic matters, was in a better position to achieve this. Its recent memorandum on the Community's industrial policy stresses the special problems involved in the promotion of advanced technology industries, i.e. those concerned with producing materials the development of which is so expensive that it cannot be envisaged without initial government support.

For the present this means nuclear equipment, high-power computers, large aircraft and equipment for space research and its applications. In these fields, and soon perhaps in some others like telecommunications, there is an industrial threshold below which production is condemned to being permanently uneconomic. Moreover, neither national funds nor the size of the national market afford a sufficient basis for the industries in question.

The inadequate development of Community enterprise in these sectors is due not only to the insufficiency of the national framework but also to the inefficient methods that have hitherto prevailed in these industries. Joint programmes of technological development have been negotiated *ad hoc* between different partners on each occasion, and do not add up to a coherent strategy. Their objective is limited to the development of a prototype by means of temporary collaboration between firms of different countries, instead of creating industrial structures integrated on a long-term basis. The result is that the money spent in Europe does much less than in the United States to increase the power and size of companies.

As far as products of advanced technology are concerned, the Common Market might as well not exist. Governmental or semi-governmental agencies, and often the chief private customers as well, confine their orders to the national industry even if they are not forced to do so by law. The consequent narrowing of the market is all the more felt as the number of countries involved is small. Failing an overall strategy, there is thus an insurmountable contradiction between the quest for efficiency which demands that there be fewer participants, and the need for a sufficiently large market, guaranteed in advance, which requires that the number of participants be increased.

Finally the West European countries, including members of the EEC, endeavour to defend their interests towards major partners outside Europe in a piecemeal and therefore inefficient fashion, often scoring successes at one another's expense.

From all this it is clear that the method of occasional co-operation without an overall plan must be replaced by a concentrated and concerted effort if industrial efficiency is to be achieved. This applies equally to development, trade and relations with non-European countries. The programme should include contracts for development on a Community basis, financed from the Community's own resources, invitations to tender being restricted as far as possible to firms which are prepared to embark on a process of permanent restructuring and are kept in a state of competition with one another.

As regards broadening the market, the only way of gradually modifying the behaviour of large public and private buyers of advanced technology goods would seem to consist in a concerted effort at Community level in regard to materials for which the Common Market does not function appropriately. The arrangements would take different forms according to the nature of the materials and customers; they might range from a single purchasing contract to a mere confrontation of intentions without commitment. The overall results would be periodically reviewed by the Community institutions. In the same way as for development contracts, the object would be to balance national interests on an overall basis and not by sectors.

Finally, co-operation with important associates outside Europe should at least be co-ordinated among the Six at Community level. It could only be to their advantage to try to reach a common attitude towards major powers outside the Community, especially the United States, but also the Soviet Union, Japan and perhaps one day China, not in a defensive spirit but in order to co-operate with them on a more equal basis and therefore more profitably.

Such are the main lines of the Commission's memorandum on the Community's industrial policy in the field of advanced technology. It will be seen that the Commission deliberately refrains from defining the institutions which might best give effect to its recommendations. We propose now to outline what these institutions might be, and also to indicate some conditions that must be fulfilled before they can operate.

Some conditions for success

CONDITION I

The policy adopted must embrace the whole field of advanced technology. As M. Théo Lefèvre pointed out in his report on ELDO, the same firms operate in various parts of the technological field: General Electric, for example, is concerned with nuclear equipment, aviation, space and computers. AEG and Siemens entered into partnership first in the nuclear field and now in computers, while the Dassault aircraft company has launched out into electronics.

Moreover, it should be noted that the same firms work on both military and peaceful applications. The pressurized water reactors built by Westinghouse derive from those which equip nuclear-propelled American submarines. As everyone knows, the biggest computers were used first to analyse the results of nuclear tests and afterwards by NASA. Rolls-Royce make engines for the RAF and also for BOAC. There is no need to go on multiplying examples, but the moral is important: for political and technical reasons it may be decided to have separate institutions for military and peaceful purposes, but the big decisions must take account of both at once, since the industrial structures are identical.

CONDITION II

The policy adopted must not be limited to co-operative activities but must cover national ventures as well as those of the Community. The European Commission went a considerable way towards recognizing this in a Note to the Council which it approved in June 1970.[1]

[1]This Note says *inter alia:*
'Up to the present, transnational technological collaboration has remained limited to certain fields or isolated projects. What has been lacking is a general view from the Community standpoint, and a broadly-based balance of interests between different fields or independent co-operative ventures. The difficulty of comparing the advantages and disadvantages of different projects, and the demand for a "fair return" on each one taken singly, have so far prevented the adoption of a coherent policy in this field.
'The Commission considers that the time has come to take a decisive step towards this double objective, i.e. the gradual working out of an overall view and an all-round balance of interests. It therefore recommends that the governments of member countries should undertake to consult one another systematically on all projects of a certain size and all financial measures which may play a decisive part in the development of a given sector. These consultations should apply to projects at the planning stage or to action contemplated, whether on the national scale or involving co-operation with one or more other countries.'

CONDITION III

Once the decision has been taken to carry out a project on a Community basis, it should be financed from the Community's own funds. After all, if the Europeans have accepted the idea of Community resources in the form of a European tax to subsidize areas of the economy that are in decline, it is reasonable to hope that the same formula may be used to promote tomorrow's industries while avoiding as far as possible the 'fair return' problem.

It is necessary to say 'as far as possible', since even in the United States, where major research is financed from the federal budget, it has not been possible altogether to eliminate inter-state competition for federal funds. But if a sufficient number of different projects were launched on a Community basis and with Community funds it would be much easier to reconcile the demands of efficiency which require that orders be given to the most capable industries, with the political necessity for a certain distribution of funds.

CONDITION IV: British entry into the Community.

Theoretically it may no doubt be said that the Six, with their present resources in manpower and finance, need feel no apprehensions of any kind, and that while British entry is desirable it is by no means a *sine qua non.*

In practice, however, the British contribution is essential as regards both quantity and quality. This is clear if one thinks of Britain's nuclear experience, her achievement in the computer field and the strength of her aircraft industry. Conversely, there is the difficulty of financing a particle accelerator or carrying out a space programme without the contribution of a country that accounts for a quarter of Europe's total potential. Hence the numerous bilateral and other arrangements by which the Continentals have tried to make good Britain's absence: the Dragon reactor, the tripartite agreement on the gas centrifuge process, Concorde, the MRCA, etc.

However, isolated projects of this kind are subject to the limitations and disadvantages discussed above. Only Britain's entry into the Community will enable the latter to pursue an effective policy in the field of advanced technology.

At the same time certain over-simplified mental pictures must be avoided, one of which is the naturally complementary relationship between Britain which is over-equipped and the Community which is less developed in these fields. As the Commission pointed out in September 1967, 'it would be a mistake to think that the overall complementarity, referred to above, between Britain and the Community would of its own accord lead to a satisfactory division of labour from the economic and political points of view'.

Another over-simple idea which will not hold water is that of a contribution which Britain might make in the context of the admission negotiations, a sort of dowry in return for which the terms of the marriage contract might be altered in her favour. For the British government could hardly make a present to its fellow-governments of knowledge possessed by British businessmen who own the relevant patents or hold exclusive licences. Nor could the European governments themselves make any use of this knowledge, which is only of value to the firms that know how to use it and can do so on an exclusive basis.

The problems involved are in fact those of relations between industrial groups and not between governments. Certainly there are some steps the British government could take that would have symbolic value, e.g. if it decided to take part in building CERN's next particle accelerator, or to go some way to meet the Continental viewpoint in space matters. Such gestures would be an earnest of Britain's state of mind, but could hardly enter into the negotiations themselves. The problems of technological co-operation are different in character and magnitude from those involved in the admission negotiations, and each of them has its own time-schedule which hardly coincides with any that the negotiations are likely to follow.

On the other hand, once the negotiations are concluded there is no doubt that the participation in Community institutions of the British government with its great experience of technology, and British firms with their technical equipment, should give full impetus to the industrial policy on which the Community has now embarked. In particular we may hope to see frequent associations and mergers between British and Continental firms.

Last but not least, Britain has no doubt more experience, adverse as well as favourable, in advanced technology than any other European country, and we may expect from her a large intellectual contribution to Community development in this field. Less devoted to institutions than the French, less convinced than the Germans of the absolute merits of free competition, the British seem likely to favour a middle way, fully recognizing the key importance of large firms but prepared to influence them by discreet operation of institutions whose role is to act as catalysts, to obtain the venture capital which they require and to facilitate regroupings as is done by the Industrial Reorganization Corporation (IRC).[1]

In this problem, as in all others, we are faced with the difference between national points of view which is Europe's handicap but also its strength. We may in any case agree with Christopher Layton that any advance by the Six in the technological field which meant that a larger share of the Community budget was spent on R & D and a smaller one on the common agricultural policy would facilitate Britain's admission in so far as she might reasonably expect to receive a substantial part of these funds.

CONDITION V

Finally – and the importance attached to this may surprise some people – we must take a good look at the specific problem of relations with the United States. It is misguided and impracticable to work out a policy for Europe in today's fields of advanced technology and then to set about organizing co-operation with the US. This would be a rational approach in many fields but not in the ones under consideration, for a number of reasons that are worth analysing.

The first of these is America's lead in most of the sectors in question. When the Europeans decide to leave a particular sector to American research and industry, to collaborate or compete with the Americans or to look for a niche that they have left unoccupied, in all these cases their decision is usually taken with direct reference to the American position. The second reason is that American firms have, as is well known, penetrated Europe more particularly in some of the sectors we are concerned with, so that for example European exchanges of electronic components largely reflect the division of labour between different European subsidiaries of IBM.

Thirdly, the American market is a primary target for European firms. Olivetti's exports to the United States are as important to it as are its exports to the Common Market countries. As regards short and medium-range turbo-jet aircraft, European industry has sold 89 within the Common Market but nearly as many (79) to the US; for the turbo-prop aircraft the figures are 68 and 84.

For these specific reasons, as well as the general dynamism and attractive force of American civilization, the relationship between a technological Europe and the United States cannot be a simple matter

[1]Cf. Christopher Layton's ideas in his book: *European Advanced Technology: A Programme for Integration*, London 1969.

of co-operation between two different systems. In most cases, the choice and development of a project by the Europeans must depend on how it fits in with similar projects and activities by the Americans.

Space exploration offers a striking example. France is the only European country to have launched research satellites by its own means, all others having been launched by American rockets. As regards applications satellites, the question is whether Europe will enjoy the unrestricted use of American launching potential or will have to have its own rockets to avoid depending on Comsat's *de facto* monopoly. But at the very time when Europe has been taking steps in the technical and diplomatic fields to secure the possibility of launching its own applications satellites, fresh prospects are opened up by the American offer of a share in the post-Apollo programme. Existing European programmes may be indirectly affected by this. In space matters, as in many others, independence is a relative concept, and the problem for Europe and the United States is to organize interdependence on terms acceptable to both parties.

The same lesson applies to isotope separation. For defence reasons, first Britain and then France made the considerable technical and financial effort necessary to provide themselves with gaseous diffusion plants for the separation of uranium isotopes. Later, still independently of American aid, the British, Dutch and Germans, after first separately studying the gas centrifuge process as an alternative, decided to combine their efforts in a large-scale trial of the gas centrifuge method. The French for their part have proposed to their Common Market partners that they should together build a large European separation plant using the French method of diffusion.

The European Commission has recommended that both techniques should be studied so as to make an informed choice, which might consist in using both processes. But Washington holds one of the keys in this matter, both technically and economically. In the first place the American government, realizing that the monopoly it held for so long is already broken, is studying the possibility of making over to Europe, against suitable compensation, American know-how regarding gaseous diffusion, which of course would diminish the value of the French proposals. Secondly, the Americans are at present ensuring, by means of long-term commitments, the supply of fuel to enriched-uranium reactors built in the Western world, and are even considering whether to construct a fourth American separation plant to meet the growing domestic and foreign demand.

If, as would be reasonable, Europe decides to put an end to the American monopoly by building large-capacity plants and not merely experimental ones, it would be in its interest to do so in an orderly manner by negotiating with Washington as regards not only the processes involved but also the new potential to be installed, the date from which it should start operating, the technical specifications of the U 235 to be produced etc. Some may object that if the Russians and now the

Chinese have set up separation plants and a space programme, there is no reason why Europe with its much greater resources should not do the same. But this is the wrong way to look at the problem. It is not a question of ability but of motivation. The Soviet Union and China made the effort because they were determined to ensure their national defence. Among European powers, Britain and France made the same choice without having the resources of a continent to draw on. Europe itself has the resources but not the political will to use them, a fact deplored by some and approved by others.

For the purpose of this study we are only concerned to emphasize that a certain consensus among Europeans on the question of relations with the United States is a necessary preliminary to the definition of any European policy whatever. We have seen this in each separate case: one of the causes of Euratom's failure was that five members of the Community chose the American line of technology and France a different one. One of Europe's troubles in space development is that the British think it would be possible to use American launchers on acceptable terms, whereas the Group of Four hold that Europe must have its own launching capacity. Such being the position in individual sectors, it is all the more true that in defence, which is at present of overriding importance throughout the field of advanced technology,[1] any policy adopted by Europe must be the outcome of a certain idea or philosophy of relations with the United States.

Appropriate institutions

Assuming that these preconditions have been met, the next question is to devise appropriate institutions. While those of the Common Market have worked satisfactorily for commerce and agriculture, it must be admitted that they are not suited to meet the demands of a technological policy. As the enlargement of the Community is in prospect it is proposed at the same time to plan for the extension of its functions and, the political framework having proved its flexibility, to outline the joint institutions that will be required if full advantage is to be taken of the new situation.

Programming Committee

The essential feature would be a Programming Committee to provide European states with the machinery for joint decision which they at present lack. Its membership would consist of the senior officials responsible for national technological programmes in each of the Community countries. Under the guidance of the competent member of the European Commission, the Committee's task would be to compare national

[1]"In France in 1967 "armament credits" covered 60 per cent of the electronic and 70 per cent of the aerospace industries, about 55 per cent of CEA outgoings.' General Fourquet in the *Revue de Défense Nationale*, May 1970.

programmes so as to arrive by degrees at a single programme designed to mobilize the entire resources of the Community for its collective purposes.

For this purpose, as explained above, the Programming Committee would study proposals for co-operation in different fields so as to arrive at a sensible balance of effort. Member states would be required to inform it of their own plans in excess of a certain level of expense to be fixed by the Council of Ministers. It would be understood that large-scale projects should normally be undertaken on a European basis, and any member state forming such a project should first invite the partici-pation of the Community or any of its members. This applies to all projects for which public financial support is envisaged, including basic research (e.g. CERN), applied research (e.g. Euratom) or technology (e.g. the Concorde). Private firms which hope for subsidies for their most important investment plans would have to submit them to the Committee.

The value of the Committee's work would largely depend on the quality of the information at its disposal. One of the tasks of the competent organs of the Commission would be to supply the necessary documenta-tion. The Committee should take advice from all appropriate quarters and organize 'hearings' for the purpose of consulting researchers and businessmen, not excluding Americans and others from outside the Community.

The Programming Committee would also be aided by advisory com-mittees, to be set up on either a vertical (specialized) or a horizontal (general competence) basis. Thus for basic research it would be desir-able to set up an inter-disciplinary Scientific Committee including all the chief European scientists. Such a body might play a some-what similar role to the Soviet Academy of Sciences. Its members would play a valuable part in enabling the Programming Committee to discuss on an informed basis the allocation of funds to, e.g., high-particle physics or molecular biology, the creation of great European laboratories or the subsidizing of national laboratories acknowledged to be of excep-tional importance.

In the same way, the competent member of the Commission should have at his disposal all the necessary advice and be legally and financially empowered to consult experts of his choice. Under his direction the members of the Programming Committee, aided by the advice they receive and by the services of their national administrative bodies as well as those of the Community, should draw up an overall programme divided into three parts: Community projects, single-nation projects and oint ones involving two or more states.

Community research projects

The Community would be an appropriate framework for providing a

European public research service (programme library, automated documentation), for constructing major instruments of research such as a particle accelerator or a material testing reactor, and especially for highly expensive prototypes – aircraft, reactors, computers, space vehicles and submarines. Defence materials present a special problem which we shall consider later. When joint activity has been decided on in a given sector, the member states should abstain for the duration of the enterprise from any national effort in the sector in question, to avoid the rivalry discussed above. This may seem too much to expect, but is in fact quite conceivable in sectors of advanced technology: in the association agreements between Euratom and various member states, the latter undertook to devote the whole of their activity to the purposes of the association, and a similar commitment figures in the Anglo-German-Dutch agreement on the gas centrifuge process.

Concerted programmes

For a second class of projects the Committee would aim at organizing concerted programmes which would remain national, but with a rational division of labour, with a view to organizing and guaranteeing each country's access to the knowledge resulting from the others' activity. This involves not only agreement to concert but also specific arrangements for the exchange of information, documents and staff, regular joint meetings and a suitable patents policy.

This method is at present in fashion as a result of the difficulties encountered with large programmes financed on a multinational basis. Experience will show whether the hopes placed in it are justified. The formula will only work if it proves possible, in practice as well as in theory, to assure Community businessmen in a given field that they will have access to commercially useful discoveries made by one of their number. It would doubtless be more effective if the Community is able to offer collective subsidies and thus play a catalysing role.

Once overall plans had been discussed and European joint efforts decided on, either as Community projects or concerted ones, purely national projects could fill what remained of the picture: at present, as we have seen, it is the other way about. The object is in no way to deprive those responsible for national programmes of their proper sphere of action, but to make them work to a reasonable scheme. It is the reverse of logical to decide first of all at the national level how much a country is prepared to spend on space activities, and then confer at the European level to see what joint enterprises can be undertaken.

It would, however, be a mistake to confine European action to those projects which are too expensive or difficult for a single country to carry out on its own. There are, after all, many spheres in which a European country might achieve useful results if it concentrated exclusively on them. Thus, for example, Portugal has earned world-wide recognition in the field of public works. The form of co-operation here envisaged would enable European countries to avoid this type of choice, provided they organize themselves to do jointly not only what they can no longer do singly, but also what they could do better or more cheaply as a joint effort.

For all these purposes, the first thing the European states need is a Programming Committee to provide the machinery for exercising rational options. The Committee's reports should be forwarded to the Council of Ministers by the Commission, which should give its opinion on the various national programmes, and refrain from endorsing those which for any reason it does not consider internationally valid. It should also recommend to the Council what Community projects should be undertaken and what funds should be provided from the Community's resources.

Community resources

The object, in short, is to apply to the new field of research and technology the Community's general principle that no plan is adopted which is not first recommended by the Commission. But, as has been seen with Euratom, this principle is weakened or evaded if the funds for the plan's execution come from national sources. For the principle to be thoroughly effective it must also be laid down that Community programmes must in future be financed not by governments but from Community funds. The funds in question would be those envisaged in the recent treaty on Community resources, supplemented as need arose. The Community might also be empowered to borrow money, as was done for the ECSC.

The Council, composed of the competent ministers, would then decide upon a programme for a fixed period, say five years, subject however to annual modification in the light of the latest developments, on the 'rolling budget' principle. The budget would be voted annually by the Council within this framework. Within the overall joint budget for each sector, existing or new specialized bodies would manage the funds in question. Under their supervision, and avoiding as far as possible the creation of fresh bureaucratic structures, the expenditure of the funds would be entrusted to the industry, to a particular firm or to *ad hoc* consortia.

In the case of atomic energy, which for historical reasons is regarded as more especially a Community responsibility, it would be appropriate to relieve the Executive of some part of its direct responsibility for the implementation of the Community research programme.

In fields such as high energy physics or space, which have never been covered by Community institutions, the latter should confine itself to determining the amount of resources to be made available within the general programme. The options would of course not be arrived at *in vacuo* but on the basis of proposals from the specialized bodies. In this way it would be possible to unite the various specialized institutions into a coherent whole, while respecting their autonomy and taking due account of the position within them of such countries as Austria and Switzerland, which do not intend to join the Communities.

In addition – and this is confirmed by the conversations now in progress – every new project should, unless there is special reason to the contrary, be open without reserve to the participation of any European country, and in some cases non-European ones as well. But this flexible policy with regard to individual projects would involve a general dilution and weakening of effort unless the members of the enlarged Community reach agreement through a single Programming Committee on the whole range of their national programmes of scientific research and advanced technology. To lay down this condition is not a form of 'Community imperialism': it is simply acknowledgement of the need for a method of choosing between the demands of different sectors at a level suited to the scale of the problems involved, i.e. the European level, through the single political institution possessing overall competence, namely the Community.

Parliamentary control

There is at the present time a vague but growing impression that the harm done by modern technology is at least equal to the benefits we can expect from it; and the conclusion is drawn that among the co-ordinating institutions needed are committees in which every new proposal would be criticized and its utility questioned. It seems to us that the structure we have outlined is sufficient to enable this indispensable function to be performed without introducing a sort of 'devil's advocate.'

The general utility of each project would have to be demonstrated to the Programming Committee, and this would be the time to examine any disutility it might have. Thereafter it would be for the Commission, a political organ responsible to the European Parliament, to approve or criticize the Committee's proposals. The Commission itself is a collegial and multi-disciplinary body and would not give its endorsement to proposals put forward by the Commissioner for research and technology without examining all their implications, especially in the economic and social fields.

But the main responsibility for systematically challenging proposals for expenditure rests with the European Parliament. For this purpose the appropriate Parliamentary committee should, like American Congressional Committees, possess a specialized secretariat and be empowered to consult experts as it sees fit. In addition the documents of the Programming Committee, with the technical annexes on which they are based, should be made public and available to the Parliamentary committee.

An open procedure of this kind, with publicity at all stages, is essential if members of the European Parliament are expected to do more than issue blank cheques. It may be a nuisance for officials and experts to have to give parliamentarians the information they want; but if the House of Commons and the French parliament, to name only those, had been given the necessary figures to make up their minds intelligently between different types of nuclear reactor, and if their specialized committees had had a chance to consult independent experts, the huge sums spent on natural-uranium reactors on both sides of the Channel might perhaps have been saved.

Objectors may say: Yes, certainly it is one aspect of the crisis of parliamentary democracy that it cannot exercise effective control over technological progress. But what reason is there to think that parliamentarians who can scarcely exercise this power on their home ground will be any more successful in doing so in the European setting?

There is no self-evident answer to this, but it is clear that one reason why national parliamentary control over research and technological expenditure in European Countries has lost all its meaning is precisely the fact that it *is* national, whereas the problems themselves are wider in scope. How can a parliament exercise control when it is asked to vote, not on a project but on its country's financial contribution to one? If parliamentary discussion and control were transferred to the European plane, at least the framework of the debate would be the same as that within which the project was drawn up and would, if approved, be carried out. One might hope, though it could not be guaranteed, that parliamentary control would once more become efficient and play its own indispensable role, provided it is organized at the level at which the problems actually present themselves.

Whatever may be thought of the merits and demerits of supersonic aircraft, the investigation by American Senate Committees of the SST project is a model of up-to-date democratic procedure which Europe might well take to heart.

Better decision-making

While the procedure must allow for all points of view to be heard and debated at every stage of the consideration of projects, there must also be some way of making the whole process sufficiently rapid. We may say bluntly that if the Community were to take as long to decide on the construction of a computer as it did to negotiate an agreement with Yugoslavia, the computer would be out of date before it came into existence and the Community might as well save its money. With the growing speed of technology, there is no comparison between time-limits that may be acceptable in the commercial field and those that are imperative in advanced technology if projects are not to go out of date before they are adopted.

In any case, the Community needs faster methods of decision-taking if it is ever to be capable of reacting as quickly as a national government should do in the event of a monetary or other crisis.

Once the programmes are decided on and the credits voted, the materials that have formed the object of joint study should in principle be bought by the public authorities of the member countries, who are very often the customers for the products of advanced technology. At the very least, governments should concert the placing of orders, which means that they should cease restricting purchases to their own national firms and should open their respective markets to competition from firms belonging to other Community countries.

Position of American firms

This raises the question of American firms and their European subsidiaries: is it either possible or desirable to keep them out of European public sector markets? It is accepted that the American technological advance is due to the scale of public funds involved and the size of the American internal market. This being so, European firms have an equal interest in penetrating the American market and in possessing a European market of comparable size: in securing a relaxation of the Buy American Act and in creating preferential conditions in Europe.

One might be tempted to distinguish between a European government buying, on the one hand, materials produced by an American firm producing in the United States and, on the other, those produced by the same firm's European subsidiary.

A double form of reciprocity might be envisaged, whereby European governments might agree to buy materials produced in the United States in return for the American government buying those produced in Europe, while European subsidiaries of American firms were allowed to sell to European governments in return for American subsidiaries of European firms being allowed to sell to the American government. But this would only be a paper form of reciprocity, given the disparity between the vast number of American firms in Europe and the very few European subsidiaries in the US.

The objective must be to bring about genuine reciprocity, so that firms of each continent and their subsidiaries have real access to the governmental market across the Atlantic. Here again, the institutions that Europe needs should play their part in the Atlantic dialogue. A European Committee for the Public Buying Sector, with the task of ensuring that the state market of each Community country is progressively opened to firms of other Community countries, would certainly be under pressure to agree that these markets should also be opened to American firms or their European subsidiaries. Europe's interest lies not in refusing such access but in trading it against a real, not merely theoretical right of access by European firms to the American public market.

Only if Europe equips itself with the necessary institutions will theoretical reciprocity become real. For this purpose the enlarged Community should organize efficient arrangements for information, liaison and negotiation with the Americans. Europe will need a spokesman for the different technical negotiations, for instance in regard to space, where hard negotiation will be necessary for the unrestricted use of American launchers for European applications satellites. Reciprocally, when Europe's contribution to the post-Apollo programme is on the tapis, it will be in NASA's interest to deal with a negotiating body capable of defending Europe's interests but also of guaranteeing that her undertakings will be met.[1]

Meanwhile the American government cannot be blamed for negotiating with Europe as it finds it, that is to say mainly with individual states; but people in Europe are not sufficiently aware of the long-term disadvantages of bilateral agreements with the Americans on co-operation and the exchange of information.

Such agreements give the American government access to the results of the various European programmes, which is not paralleled as between the Europeans themselves. Moreover exchanges of information, even if perfectly well balanced, automatically favour the party with the stronger industrial structure and the bigger programme, while the weaker party is often in no position to make use of the information it receives. Failing a network of agreements linking Europe as a whole with the United States, it is understandable that the European states attach importance to their bilateral ties with American institutions. But, as similar causes produce similar effects, they must not be surprised if their technological relations with the United States come more and more to resemble economic relations between the latter and the individual Latin American republics.

A European armaments agency

It is time to consider the defence sector. Historically, American supremacy in aviation, space, telecommunications, computers and nuclear energy is clearly linked to America's world-wide strategic responsibilities and to the way she has met them: a rich country and not densely populated, she has chosen the route of massive investment for scientific and industrial warfare.

No one has any thought of endowing Europe with a comparable military potential, i.e. one capable of matching the Soviet forces on its

[1]The European space conference held at Brussels in July 1970 has made a step in this direction by entrusting M. Théo Lefèvre with the task of negotiating with Washington. This is a sign of clear progress in the institutional field but, while necessary, it is not sufficient in itself. Not only must there be a European spokesman, but he must be able to negotiate on behalf of an institution capable of entering into commitments, as in the case of M. Jean Rey negotiating the Kennedy Round on behalf of the EEC.

own. Nor, on the other hand, does anyone think that Europe can rely wholly on the United States for its protection.

We are not concerned here with the general question of Europe's contribution to its own defence. But, from the viewpoint of this study, it is important to emphasize a major contradiction. On the one hand the members of the Community, and of tomorrow's enlarged Community, are endeavouring to create a Common Market with the fullest possible division of labour on a continental scale; while on the other they are pouring money into research and the construction of sophisticated military equipment in national programmes which cover the whole field of advanced technology. In these fields, which have most to gain from the division of labour on a European scale, it is in fact least in evidence. What is proposed is to put an end to this contradiction by extending to the field of armaments the process of economic integration which already applies to consumption industries within the Common Market. Europe's advanced industries must be provided with a market which they need as an outlet and which should henceforth be shared in common, namely the equipment of the European defence forces.

To this end a European Armaments Agency, should be established whose functions would be to define the needs of European countries for new armaments and to organize and finance the necessary research, development and industrial production for the equipment of European defence.[1]

It should be emphasized here that the present situation is an abnormal one. While European countries may rely on the Americans to provide the nuclear deterrent which stabilizes the situation in Europe, there is no reason why they should also have to rely on the American arms industry to provide conventional weapons which are not, as a rule, superior to European ones in quality.

The 'offset agreements' system, whereby the West Germans have had to buy huge quantities of American weapons to balance the hard-currency costs of maintaining American armed forces in Germany, has not only had the result of equipping German aviation with the notorious F104. It has also deprived the European arms industries of a natural outlet and led them to sell, regardless of price, to various third countries, a policy which the American government has often been the first to deplore.

It would of course be absurd to suggest that the American forces in Germany should be cut down in order to reduce the bill and restore a natural market to European arms manufacturers. But it must be clearly stated that there is a contradiction between the offset agreements policy and the development of advanced European industry.

This has come about because the problem of equipping the German army has been detached from its natural context, which is German and

---

[1]This would of course be quite distinct from the WEU armaments agency, which is merely a control body.

European, and related instead to a transatlantic system of military thinking and power relationships. What is advocated is that the problem should be restored to its context as an essential element in the process of European integration, which the American government supports. From this point of view plans by the British and Germans, and perhaps the Italians, for the joint construction of the MRCA are a step in the right direction, as is the recent Franco-German decision to manufacture a tactical support and trainer aircraft; but moves like these should be integrated in a European institutional framework.

The proposal therefore is to set up a European Armaments Agency within the enlarged Community, thus giving the latter a military dimension that it will need if it is ever to become a complete political entity. The Agency would take its place alongside the Programming Committee which we have already discussed. Even though there is no fundamental difference between the problems of building a fast reactor prototype and those of a new fighter aircraft, it is no doubt better to have a separate organization covering the research, development and production of new weapons. There would thus be two parallel systems: on the one hand an R & D Programming Committee making recommendations to a Council of Ministers for Technology, and on the other an Armaments Agency drawing up programmes for R & D, but also for the manufacture of weapons, to be approved and financed by a Council of Defence Ministers.

It may be objected that defence problems form a single whole: the formulation of defence policy, the part played by nuclear weapons with all the specific problems of their manufacture and use, the characteristics of new weapons systems, their construction, training troops to use them in peace-time, their deployment in case of a crisis and their use in warfare – all this constitutes a complex of political options and technical decisions which influence one another and from which it may seem artificial to single out one element. The objection may be summed up by saying that one cannot imagine a European Armaments Agency without a European General Staff, and that since European governments are not prepared to set up a joint General Staff they should therefore do nothing.

This is reminiscent of the strong arguments that were brought forward in 1950 to the effect that one could not have a Common Market for coal and steel without a Common Market for all other products. Those who argued thus were not wrong, but a start had to be made somewhere, and accordingly Europe first had the ECSC and then the EEC. What is proposed here is to apply the same method to defence problems, beginning with arms manufacture. As General Beaufre has said: 'When you are building a house you start with the foundations. The basis of a European defence organization is essentially logistic and industrial'.[1]

[1]In *Le Figaro*, 30 July 1970.

Possible strategies of development

All this does not mean that Europe must engage in a massive defence effort in order to equip itself technologically. On the contrary, she should on no account seek to imitate the American pattern of development. The United States achieved her present status in the field of advanced technology by tackling her problems with her own institutions and resources, neither of which can be matched in Europe. The day is far off when Europe will have institutions of similar power and wealth to the Department of Defense, NASA or the AEC, and in any case its problems are not the same as those of the United States: this is partly because the US has solved some of the problems for Europe such as the nuclear balance with the Soviet Union.

There are two other courses which Europe might take, and which complement each other. As regards 'conventional' advanced technology – if one may so call it – where, as we know, the Americans are paramount, the Europeans can try to ensure that their industries get the maximum spin-off from the American defence programme. The second and more important objective is for Europe to try to solve its own problems and develop new advanced technologies for the purpose.

Let us consider these two courses more closely. The first involves a particular state of mind: rather than saying '*L'Europa farà da sè*' – an attitude which led to such abortive technical ventures as the TSR 2[1] or the gas-graphite reactor system – Europeans should recognize American superiority where it exists and make the most of it. This, of course, is not a strategy for all sectors. In aviation, for example, it may be hoped that Europe will have enough political determination to refashion its industry on a European basis to give it the market it needs, organize European air space and in general re-establish itself in a strong position.

It is, on the other hand, quite possible that Europe will not try to fight single-handed against IBM's supremacy in the computer field and that European electronic firms will ally themselves with some other American concern. This would be similar to the usual strategy of the Japanese, who in such cases aim at joining not the biggest American firm in a given sector but one of lesser size, so that they will not be dominated.

This leads to our second point: Europe's best chance of achieving technical leadership in any sphere is to invent new technologies to solve its own problems.

If the American aeronautical industry today leads the world in long-range aircraft, it is because the American air force was obliged to develop long-range bombers during and after the war. Subsequently the size of the United States made it possible to use economically on such routes as New York – Los Angeles the types of aircraft which were also suitable for transatlantic routes.

[1]The British bomber prototype with special electronic equipment to enable it to fly at low altitude. It was abandoned as too expensive.

If the Japanese have brought about a revolution in shipbuilding it is because, having to import materials for their industry and to export its products on a large scale, they had to make ships as cheaply as possible. Incidentally, it is quite possible that the building of large tankers, ore ships and container ships, while it is not thought of as a particularly advanced form of technology, has done more to revolutionize the economic map of the world than, for instance, supersonic transport is likely to do.

In general Europe would do well to study carefully the strategies of economic development adopted in Japan, which are often much more suitable than American ones to European or Third World conditions.[1] The Japanese are in fact already co-operating with the Europeans in several Third World countries: e.g. with CIBA in South America and with a French firm extracting uranium in the Niger. The arrival of Japanese firms in Europe is imminent: they already have plans to build automobile factories in Spain.

Europe, for its own part, is in a good position to develop research aimed at improving or preserving the amenities of life: town planning, environment, tele-communications, pollution abatement, surface transport. In this last field (turbine trains, aerotrains, hovercraft) Europe clearly has a niche to occupy provided it develops industrial and commercial structures which are capable of exploiting the inventiveness of its engineers.

Likewise, in oceanic exploration and in research of particular value to developing countries, Europe is in a position to develop new techniques which may conquer world markets. We mentioned, for instance, the fact that Euratom spent $150 m on developing the Orgel reactor but that, while the enterprise was successful technically, it led to no result in the industrial field. Yet this type of reactor would have been particularly well suited for the construction of large desalination plants to make drinking water from the sea. If Europe had possessed proper institutions instead of a single body strictly confined to a purely nuclear role, it would have been possible to study the construction of a pilot desalination plant, to the potential advantage of the many coastal areas of the world where fresh water is lacking.

Bertrand de Jouvenel, in a penetrating analysis of the conception of research and development,[2] has recalled the well-known fact that most public expenditure in the United States goes on defence, space and nuclear programmes, while very little in comparison is spent on social problems or those of the under-developed countries. He quotes the remark of an American expert that 'The techniques of the temperate zone can only be applied to the tropics by means of applied research . . . Such research has received no support from the US or from anyone else'.

[1]See René Foch in *Le Monde*, 23 January 1969.
[2]Entitled *Arcadie, essais sur le mieux vivre*, Paris 1968.

This, as de Jouvenel observes, may be true of America but is not true of Europe. Britain, France, Belgium and the Netherlands, as a result of their colonial tradition, have retained links with their former overseas possessions and an expertise in development problems, for instance in tropical agronomy. Thanks to these, Europe is in a privileged position as regards the great present-day problem of aid to the Third World. Europe's positions of strength should be sought not in 'conventional' advanced technology but in new technologies which it is its task to discover and develop.

Conclusions

The time has come to bring our ideas into focus. Today, technological Europe is a cemetery of lost illusions, commemorating the failure of a series of chimerical national ambitions and ill-conceived plans for international co-operation. The reasons are clear enough: sectorial institutions paralysed by the obsession of a 'fair return', precarious budgets undergoing constant review, methods of management which have more in common with the Congress of Vienna than the Harvard Business School – all these factors have combined to prevent Europe setting up the modern industries it needs.

We shall not see a technological Europe until several conditions have been fulfilled. Firstly, a programme must be drawn up covering the whole range of proposed action in the field of advanced technology, at both the European and the national level. Secondly, the funds for these activities should be provided by the Community from its own resources and not be subject to annual pressure from governments. Thirdly, an enlarged Community must have the benefit of Britain's resources and industrial achievement. Fourthly, Europe as a whole must define its position *vis-à-vis* America, not only in the particular fields we have discussed but over the whole range of policy, economic and financial as well as military and political.

Having already devised institutions to manage its declining industries, finance its agriculture and organize aid to its former overseas territories, Europe must now set up the necessary machinery to create and finance the industries of tomorrow: a Programming Committee to enable the Council of Ministers to make rational choices at the European level, which is where the problems present themselves; a system of technical diplomacy so that Europe can speak with a single voice to Washington, and also to Tokyo and Moscow; a Public Markets Committee to ensure an outlet for the products of the new industry, not only on European markets but, on a basis of true reciprocity, on American public markets also; and finally a European Armaments Agency, since the various advanced industries tend more and more to merge into a single industry with the armaments market as one of its essential outlets.

Thus there is a long list of conditions to be fulfilled if Europe is to occupy a proper position in the vital field of advanced technology, in which it is at present steadily losing ground. Some people, while sympathizing with this analysis, consider it politically impossible to fulfil all these conditions in the immediate future, and hold that we must proceed by stages. They may well be right, but we must realize that in the field of advanced technology, unlike many Common Market activities, to do the best one can is not necessarily to make progress. One has to set one's sights on doing what is required and if – for lack of political resolution, finance or the right kind of institutions – one fails to attain a certain threshold, it is better to give up costly and barren efforts. They are indeed worse than barren, since if a country mobilizes thousands of highly qualified researchers for years on a programme that comes to nothing, it is harmed by being deprived of the fruitful work they might have carried on in other spheres.

Does it follow that Europe should do nothing until it has fulfilled all the conditions we have listed ? By no means. But until Europe develops the means of framing and conducting a truly European policy it must be content with the policy that its present means allow, doing its best to use existing forces to carry out its ideas.

From this point of view an interim strategy would consist in recognizing the dominant position of American firms in the sectors referred to in this study, while using the size of the market represented by European orders to persuade the big American concerns to operate in Europe in the way most favourable to European interests. These interests should be formulated on a European basis, since the existence of the Common Market means that if one Community country refuses to permit an American investment, the firm concerned can always go to another.

It should be recognized that the division of labour practised by these firms on a world scale is a positive element. Investments should be systematically preferred to outright exports from the United States, but they should no longer be the cause of a race for subsidies between European states. Investments in the form of industrial plant should be accompanied – IBM has set the example for this, and Westinghouse were prepared to follow suit – by the establishment of research laboratories in Europe, employing scientists who would otherwise be tempted to emigrate to the US. There seems no reason why European governments should not entrust research contracts to such laboratories, if a suitable patents policy can be worked out. The object, in other words, would be to hasten the development of large American firms with world-wide activities into genuinely multinational firms, to see to it that they have as strong an interest in Europe as in the United States and that they pay as much attention to the point of view of European governments as to that of their own. The strength of American firms would in fact be placed at Europe's disposal, but the rules of the game would be different: instead of the big American firms making European governments compete to secure their investments, it should be the European governments that make American firms compete with one another.

A strategy of this kind, which should not be dismissed as defeatist, presupposes a minimum of political cohesion among the European states. It would enable Europe to remain in the technological race pending the creation of suitable institutions, but it must be recognized that in these fields the time factor plays a part which is not met with in the other sectors of European integration. Time is of the essence, and Europe's technological lag is increasing daily.

Far from prejudicing Europe's future liberty of action, the object of this policy would be to safeguard it by creating nuclei of skill and potential in Europe against the time when the Europeans decide what they want to do. These nuclei will play the decisive role, and they will be constituted by private industry.

The purpose of this essay, as indicated at the begining, is to 'outline the institutions [Europe] must have in order to hold its own in the fields of industry to which the future belongs'. But within the framework of these institutions it will be for private industry to play the chief part. Technology is a matter for the private sector, as is shown – to choose one example among hundreds – by the Soviet failure with computers as compared with IBM's success.

This essay would give a completely wrong impression if it were read as suggesting that Europe's technological lag could ever be made good by means of institutions, even on a European scale. Actual enterprises must fill the gap, but they can only do so within the necessary institutional framework. This must be a European one, but the market must be world-wide. Europe's advanced industries must be planned on a world scale.

One may conceive of a mining enterprise or agriculture being protected at least on a temporary basis, but there is no sense in starting up new industries unless their products are going to be competitive very soon. In planning its advanced industries Europe should from the first set its sights on the world market, and especially the United States. It would be a mistake to think of starting with a protected home base for an industry which is eventually to become competitive on world markets. A first phase of this sort would no doubt be precluded by the extra-European interests of European firms; but if it did succeed, it would be the surest recipe for failure in the second phase.

Europe must provide itself from the very outset with the most modern forms of technology, relying on the most advanced firms whatever the nationality of their shareholders, aiming to produce the most up-to-date materials and sell them on the most competitive markets. Europe's problem is no longer – and this conclusion perhaps goes beyond the particular case of the advanced industries – to organize its internal economy while opening it in some measure to exchanges with the outside world. What Europe has to do is to create in its own territory a favourable environment for the great multinational companies on which tomorrow's economic growth will essentially depend.

Already the presidents of some multilateral companies treat on equal terms with the heads of European states, who receive them with as much respect as if they were fellow statesmen. Already we see the beginnings of the 'fabulous confrontation' spoken of by Robert Lattès: 'On the one hand nation states, on the other economic states in course of formation'.[1] But in fact no single European government can treat effectively with the great multinational firms, precisely because they are multinational. This can only be achieved by a Power capable of taking decisions, and ensuring respect for these, within a sufficiently large economic framework.

The enlarged Common Market will provide the frame; but it still remains to organize the Power.

[1] In 'Mille milliards de dollars'.

The Great Power Triangle:
Washington - Moscow - Peking

Michel Tatu

Foreword

For 16 years, from 1947 to 1963, the course of world politics was primarily determined by the rivalry of two 'superpowers', USA and USSR, and of the alliances formed under their respective leadership. The emergence of a non-aligned Third World from the process of decolonization failed to change this basic picture, for the ex-colonial new states, immersed in their own problems of development, were unable to form a cohesive third force that could have held the balance between the hostile blocs, and became partly objects, and partly exploiters of their rivalry. Nor did the internal tensions and crises within each bloc make a decisive difference to this 'bi-polar constellation'. For the fact that the Soviet bloc consisted of Communist party regimes, imposed in most cases by the leading power in its own image, put enormous difficulties in the way of any such 'satellite' leaving the bloc without a change in its regime, or changing its regime without provoking Soviet intervention; and as the cohesion of this 'ideological bloc' was forcibly restored after each crisis, its opponents were inevitably driven to restore the cohesion of their alliance as well. The system succeeded in maintaining a kind of balance and avoiding nuclear war – but it was a system devoid of any flexibility.

In 1963, however, the tensions which had long developed between the Soviet Union and Communist China led to an open break between the two main powers of the Communist 'camp', and China became a fully independent factor in world affairs – though not yet a world power on a par with the two other giants. From that moment, and increasingly as China developed a nuclear capability, the world scene was transformed: the bipolar constellation was in principle replaced by a triangular one, however uneven the sides of the triangle might remain for some time to come. From that moment, the alignment of the powers in any international crisis was no longer predetermined by their ideology, or rather their type of regime, since it could no longer be taken for granted that all Communist states would be on the same side on any given question. Instead, a new type of analysis was required to understand, and if possible forecast, the reactions of the three main actors to particular issues in the new constellation – an analysis of the factors which might cause each of them to give priority to the conflict with one 'main enemy' while seeking 'collusion' against him with the other.

In the present study, Michel Tatu has undertaken to demonstrate the principles of this new type of analysis. He does so in the light not only of the experience of the first seven years of the 'triangular'

101

constellation, but of our general knowledge of the factors which operate in classical power politics, and of his own special familiarity with the workings of Communist regimes, with both the clarity and subtlety that his readers in many countries have come to expect from him. He also displays the caution in his conclusions which is the mark of the scholar. Thus, while stressing the greater flexibility of a triangular international system compared with a bipolar one, he reminds us that this flexibility remains limited for only so long as Chinese strength continues inferior to that of the two 'senior' powers; and that only a Soviet-American conflict could lead to nuclear world war – because this fact forces both Moscow and Washington to focus their main attention on *their* rivalry and their common interest in survival.

In the short scope of this essay, Michel Tatu has naturally not been able to deal fully with all the various aspects of the new triangular age, such as the causes and consequences of the successive involvement of first the United States and then the Soviet Union in situations of 'overcommitment', and the more recent crises in the Atlantic and Warsaw Pact alliances and the different methods of overcoming them. If I have any criticism of his masterly analysis, it is that he seems at some points to overestimate the determining role of such geopolitical factors as the Sino-Soviet frontier conflict (which I am more inclined to regard as a dependent variable of Chinese domestic politics), and to underestimate the role of avoidable, and hence unforeseeable, error, as in the impact of a mistaken view of China's short-term aggressiveness on the American involvement in Vietnam. Seeing China's view of Russia as the 'main enemy' as more subject to change, and taking the realistic wisdom of American diplomacy less for granted than he appears to do in some passages, I am also less certain that the United States must be more or less automatically favoured by the mechanics of the triangular constellation.

But these are objections of detail upon which each reader will be able to form his own opinion in the light of Michel Tatu's sure methodical guidance. They do not impair the value of the basic insights and of the analytical technique he has demonstrated, nor do they affect his sober – and sobering – main conclusion: that a triangular world, because it contains more dimensions of rivalry but also more flexibility than the bipolar ideological confrontation which preceded it, offers fewer prospects for stable solutions but also more chances for restoring a new balance in shifting situations, thus avoiding the ultimate risk of nuclear war. It is hardly a comfortable conclusion – but at least it is not a hopeless one.

RICHARD LOWENTHAL

BERLIN, *December 1970*

The Great Power Triangle

A bstract concepts, and especially geometrical ones, should be treated with caution as a key to international affairs. Thus the notion of a 'bipolar' world which became a *cliché* after the last war never coincided exactly with the facts: the upsurge of Afro-Asian liberation, the unruliness of the super-powers' client states, and in general what has been called the diffusion of power, soon showed that the situation was more complex than any such tidy formula. In the same way, we should not take too seriously the concept of a 'triangle' which has made its way into diplomatic analyses since China became a thermonuclear power. The fact is still too recent, and the disparity in strength between the three powers involved is still much too great, for it to be possible to speak of a major reorientation of international relations. Nevertheless, the new formula has the advantage of ridding us once and for all of 'bipolarity', and it does correspond to something in the real world which will become more important as time goes on. Moreover, it suggests new prospects for the diplomatic activity of both the super-powers as well as of Peking, and it reflects an additional complexity in the international scene which already exists and which is worth examining in more detail.

The interesting fact about the 'triangle' is that each of its members is antagonistic to the two others, although, precisely because it is a triangle, their antagonisms may be modified in different sets of circumstances. Moreover, the antagonism between Washington and Moscow is not of the same kind as that between Moscow and Peking. Before considering the implications of the three-cornered struggle we should first review the bilateral relationships which form, so to speak, the sides of the triangle.

Washington versus Moscow

The Soviet-American rivalry which has dominated international affairs for the last quarter of a century is unlike the great national antagonisms of the past. By contrast with the old rivalry between England and France, France and Germany, Austria-Hungary and

Russia, and all the empires whose ambitions have made European history, the Soviet Union and the United States have no conflicting interests in the geographical sphere. Apart from the distant waters of the Behring Strait they have no common frontier, and therefore no territorial disputes. Before the advent of Russian communism the two countries had never been in conflict. (This is partly due, of course, to the shortness of America's history and the fact that, until about 1900, she weighed scarcely at all in the international scales).

Soviet-American antagonism was in a sense accidental, and there were two main reasons for it. In the first place, the Soviet Union and the United States were the two greatest powers in the world, in fact the only two great powers, at the moment of Hitler's defeat. Secondly, the communist ideology was still militant in Moscow, and it was therefore natural for the Soviet leaders to designate as the supreme enemy the chief capitalist power, whose methods and achievements were the most evident symbol of the social regime which must be overthrown. As for American involvement, it was due to realization of Moscow's overt and doctrinaire hostility, the need to contain communist expansion – who could have done so but the United States? – and finally the discovery that, with the development of modern armaments, the Soviet Union was the only power in the world capable of destroying the US. From these data certain basic features emerge:

ABSENCE OF DIRECT CONFLICT

Even at the height of the cold war, the American-Soviet conflict scarcely involved any national element in the proper sense of the term, other than the pride which comes from strength, and still less any racial or psychological ingredient due to past history. Stalin only opposed the Americans because he found them disposed to resist Soviet expansion in central Europe in 1945, Greece in 1947 and Korea in 1950. He would have behaved in the same way towards any other power that had blocked his path in similar circumstances. The United States for their part, despite certain phenomena of the 1950s, were opposed to the Soviet Union much less on account of its social system than because they found themselves forced to resist Soviet encroachments in areas which they had, sometimes reluctantly, undertaken to defend. The conflict was never a direct one – Russian and American soldiers have never fought each other on any battlefield – but was always on the periphery, away from national territory, at the points of contact between the respective spheres of interest that the protagonists came by degrees to acknowledge, tacitly no doubt but in a more and more binding fashion. If the encroachments and the expansionist policy had ceased at any time, the conflict would have lost much of its sharpness.

MUTUAL RESPECT FOR SPHERES OF INFLUENCE

This is more or less what did happen in the early sixties, when each of the super-powers gave up attempting to interfere in the other's sphere of direct influence – Khrushchev let West Berlin alone, while the West accepted the Wall; in Cuba the military *status quo* was restored, and in general the situation was consolidated as regards the 'hottest' sectors, i.e. those closest to the big powers' frontiers. At this time, too, owing to the Soviet nuclear effort and despite the clear American advantage in quantitative terms, the deterrent factor was at its strongest. Faced with the risk that the slightest clash between their armed forces might develop into a world holocaust, the United States and the Soviet Union came more and more to codify their relationships, delimit their respective spheres of interest and security thresholds, and consolidate their privileged position *vis à vis* other powers (the nuclear test ban and non-proliferation treaties). They even attempted, by means of the SALT (=Strategic Arms Limitation Talks) negotiations, to codify and stabilize the nuclear balance.

Does this add up to a *détente* between the two giants? The emergence of new weapons (Anti-Ballistic Missiles =ABM, and Multiple Independently Targetable Re-entry Vehicles =MIRV) threatens to upset, in the long term, the rules of the deterrence game as played hitherto; while the allocation of spheres of influence leaves enormous 'grey areas' around the world where rivalries and clashes may break out. But there are more specific reasons why the antagonism is likely to continue.

A USEFUL ADVERSARY FOR MOSCOW

A certain degree of Soviet-American tension, or at least opposition, is necessary to the survival of the Soviet regime in its present form. Of course Soviet diplomacy is no longer inspired by revolutionary ideology, if it ever was, and the repertoire of leftist slogans has lost its persuasive force inside the country. But these slogans and ideology continue to furnish the Soviet leaders with their sole credentials. In order to justify censorship, the persecution of non-conformist elements and the restriction of travel and other foreign contacts, the authorities are bound to advertise their hostility to the democratic system, to keep up a siege mentality and to foster belief in the permanent aggressiveness of the 'imperialist' enemy, that is to say the United States *par excellence*. This does not rule out political agreements and quite far-reaching economic co-operation with the capitalistic West, but the latter is cast firmly in the role of an artificial enemy, a pole of repulsion and a danger to Soviet society. A real *détente* which would mean the mingling of ideas and true contact between human beings is incompatible with the present reign of the *apparatchiki*.

DIFFERENT MOTIVATIONS IN FOREIGN POLICY

The two super-powers are also very differently motivated in the field of external affairs. The Americans aim at maintaining a certain world balance, a degree of order and stability conducive to movements of capital and trade exchanges. Their world-view, stripped of Wilsonian moralism, has become pragmatic as well as universal, while the Soviet leaders adhere to the more Manichean conception of 'us' versus the rest. This attitude, rooted in love for 'holy Russia', the revolutionary radicalism of the early 1900s, and the unabashed egotism of totalitarian states, means that national interests in the narrowest sense are given absolute priority. International equilibrium is a good thing wherever Russian ambitions are more or less sated, as they are for the moment in Europe, but it is and will remain subject to challenge whenever it appears too favourable to the imperialist adversary. From this point of view the Soviet Union displays symptoms of the 'eternal runner-up', the power that has only recently risen to the first rank and still has to achieve its place in the sun. Thus, while considerations of security and protection of the Soviet empire are important, they do not explain everything: if the Russians have gradually infiltrated into the Middle East and are sending their warships all over the globe, it is not just for security's sake but because there was a space which could be occupied at low risk, high though the material cost may be. This kind of opportunist expansion has been especially prominent in the last few years.

DIFFERENT METHODS

The two countries' methods also differ widely. The Americans rely on economic expansion, penetration by means of capital and technology, while the Russians rely on physical presence – above all military – and political subversion. On the Russian side this amounts to a costly type of perfectionism. For the Americans security is essentially the absence of a threat, and diplomacy an elaborate process of mutual adjustment: for the Russians it means maintaining or creating throughout their sphere of influence regimes which are carbon copies of their own, while they themselves display their military power, receive daily protestations of allegiance and eternal friendship voiced by press organs designed in the image of *Pravda*, etc., etc.

Even in areas which do not belong directly to the Soviet sphere of domination but only to its area of expansion, such as the Middle East, Moscow seldom seeks to triumph by means of economic, cultural or ideological superiority, but rather by the deployment of soldiers, technicians, agents, bases and other permanent installations. The Americans, on the other hand, tend to play down these expensive features in their overseas presence. This contrast is partly due to the

106

difference in their respective starting points: the Soviet leaders are just learning how to be a super-power, while the Americans are already well past that stage.

DIFFERENT VULNERABILITY

As a result, the vulnerability of the two powers differs a great deal both in degree and in nature. The American President is subject to pressure from public opinion, from the press and Congress, all of which tend to limit his freedom of action and, as a rule, to inhibit foreign commitments. This means that he can very seldom act in secret. Most of his decisions, especially if they involve voting new credits – as all forms of armament do – are not only known about, but discussed and criticized long before they take effect. His Soviet adversaries thus know all that is going on at Washington and can, by playing their cards shrewdly, increase the President's difficulties. At Moscow all deliberations are wrapped in secrecy, which gives the Soviet statesmen an automatic lead, while the lack of any organized and public opposition means that they have wide freedom of action.

However, there is another side to the picture. An open society of the American type is capable of weathering many storms. The constitutional mechanism accepted as valid by the overwhelming majority of the public, the system of elections and the alternation of parties serve to correct Presidential mistakes and facilitate the replacement of the team in power. The Soviet totalitarian system, by contrast, is like a too-perfect edifice in which every detail is essential to the stability of the whole. Any kind of jolt is dangerous to it; yet it is by abrupt means such as plots, conspiracies and palace revolutions that changes in the leadership are usually effected, since there are no generally accepted constitutional processes. The leaders' chronic uncertainty as regards popular feeling (cf. the warning against 'panic' launched by Stalin's successors when the dictator died), their anxiety to prevent damage to a fabric that they know to be artificial because it is based on force – in short, the traditional fears of autocrats whose rule lacks a legitimate foundation serve in part to explain Moscow's extreme prudence at times of international crisis; there is no predicting the effect of a prolonged conflict on the Soviet system and the empire as a whole.

The same vulnerability of the Soviet regime appears with regard to its system of alliances, with the difference that here Moscow prefers to anticipate danger by drastic action on a scale often disproportionate to the actual issue. Whereas the Americans did not have too much trouble in digesting France's withdrawal from NATO, Russian troops have been deployed or actually used four times since the end of the war to put a stop to misdeeds of far less gravity by

107

Western standards. True, American policy in Latin America – e.g. the intervention in Santo Domingo – has been known to resemble this type of Soviet perfectionism. But in general Moscow's presence in the Warsaw Pact countries is far more rigid and therefore expensive in material terms, more artificial and more vulnerable, based as it is on physical force and not on superior organization or a higher living standard.

Moscow versus Peking

The Soviet-Chinese conflict has all the marks that are not present in American-Soviet rivalry, and none of the latter's special features.

COMMON FRONTIER

The Americans and Russians have no common frontier. The Russians and Chinese share the longest frontier in the world, stretching over some 4,500 miles. Thus their antagonism is not accidental, as Soviet-American antagonism largely is, but represents a continuation of disputes caused in past centuries by Tsarist expansion in the Far East and central Asia. As we saw, Soviet-American hostility owes scarcely anything to nationalism and nothing at all to racialism: while the conflict between Moscow and Peking, though it began against the background of a shared ideology, was very soon exacerbated by both these principles.

The existence of a common frontier also means that confrontation is much more direct. While Moscow and Washington oppose each other through intermediaries on the periphery of their spheres of influence, in a sort of remote-control chess-match which does not involve the territorial security of either (except for the Cuba crisis of 1962), the Russians and Chinese confront each other without any intermediary and almost without allies, apart from Russia's Mongol protectorate and China's Albanian bridgehead. By contrast, their peripheral interests do not overlap to a great extent, except for South-East Asia and Vietnam. No doubt China's insistent propaganda in Africa, among the Palestine liberation movements, etc., is a nuisance to Moscow, but it is of no great consequence as long as it remains a matter of words and not deeds.

DISPARITY OF MILITARY STRENGTH

The disparity of strength between Russia and China is much greater than that between the United States and Russia. By and large, the Russians are today in the same position *vis-à-vis* China as the Americans were towards the Soviet Union in the late Forties and early Fifties, when they were free to use nuclear weapons virtually as they chose and the Soviet nuclear capacity was still rudimentary. But while Stalin was able to counterbalance this inferiority by huge conventional forces, today Moscow is far ahead of Peking in every type of armament without exception. The Kremlin was at pains to remind the Chinese of this during the frontier incidents in 1969, when allusions were made to the temptation of a preventive attack on Chinese nuclear installations. No doubt the size of China's territory and population and her aptitude for guerilla warfare are important deterrents, but the military inequality is none the less such as to make the situation infinitely less stable than that now obtaining between the Soviet Union and the United States.

WIDER ISSUES AT STAKE

The fact that the two powers share a common ideology and social system has several consequences. In the first place, the hermetic character of Chinese political life and decision-making places the Russians at the same disadvantage *vis-à-vis* Peking as the Americans are with respect to Moscow. Moreover the Chinese are equally in the dark about Soviet intentions, and this twofold ignorance is a factor of instability. More important still, the regimes opposed to each other are both monolithic, equally uncompromising in the defence of their interests and equally certain that truth is on their side. In addition to the schism between two rival churches professing a common doctrine, anathematizing each other with fraternal hatred, the situation is one of conflict between two rival cliques, both obsessed with the consciousness of authority and power.

Consequently the issue at stake is much wider than between Moscow and Washington. The Kremlin leaders are bent on containing and if possible reducing the American zone of influence in the world to their own advantage, but they are not interested in seizing power at Washington, at all events in the foreseeable future: whereas in the Moscow-Peking conflict the Kremlin is out to destroy Maoist power in China and the Peking leaders seek to overthrow the 'renegade socio-imperialistic clique' at Moscow. Even if each is obliged by circumstances to behave more circumspectly than its words suggest, neither party will consider itself secure until the other's 'treason' has been liquidated and the present animosity replaced by communist friendship of the official and 'eternal' kind – which, to each opponent, signifies the possession by itself of sufficient police, military and other resources to make sure that the situation cannot be upset again. A conflict between two 'tough' states must in the nature of things be doubly tough. Even a superficial lull, as when threats are replaced by negotiations, is largely due to the desire to weaken the rival power and sow dissension among its leadership, as well as easing the adverse effects of excessive tension on one's own position.

MUTUAL VULNERABILITY

Another feature is that the vulnerability which we noticed in the Soviet system as compared with the American is, in the case of Russia and China, common to both camps. What would be the reaction, in the event of a conflict, of the nationalities living on either side of the Kazakhstan-Sinkiang frontier? And would not the dissident forces at Moscow and the anti-Maoists at Peking seize the opportunity for a comeback? Here again the factors of uncertainty are cumulative, since each adversary may be tempted, rightly or wrongly, to minimize the risks in its own camp and overrate the advantage accruing to itself from conditions on the other side. It may be true that the worst does not always happen, but it is also true that miscalculation is not the least likely of possibilities, especially with totalitarian states entangled in their own propaganda. Thus the vulnerability of the two systems, together with the disproportion in military strength, is an element of instability in Russo-Chinese as contrasted with Russo-American relations.

RECONCILIATION UNLIKELY

The identity of the two political systems may have destabilizing effects for an opposite type of reason. Given the state of affairs in which the most important decisions depend on the secret deliberations of a very small group of leaders and sometimes even on the whims of a single man, no development can be ruled out *a priori*– not even the cessation of hostilities, which may be decided upon and put into effect as suddenly as they began. Of course a genuine reconciliation is not only improbable but unthinkable, given Moscow's present conception of its role: the Soviet Union has vassals, not friends, and there is no way in which China, a great power with a centuries-old enmity towards Russia, could sincerely accept the Soviet terms for rejoining the camp. But the two adversaries may perfectly well decide for opportunistic reasons, as they have often done before, to call off their slanging-match, which is highly artificial and dependent on orders from above, and re-establish a facade of unity. This would mean no more than frigid coexistence, but would have practical advantages for both sides: the Chinese would secure a modicum of economic and technical aid, and the Russians would get rid, for the time being, of a standing nuisance on their frontiers. Such a development might well occur, e.g., after Mao Tse-tung's death.

It is not certain, however, that such an outcome would be wholly to the benefit of the Soviet Union. A Moscow-Peking *rapprochement* would make China more respectable in the eyes of the satellite Communist Parties, and thus reintroduce her into a diplomatic game by which the Kremlin has nothing to gain. Indeed the most harmful period, from the Soviet point of view, of the conflict with Peking was between 1958 and about 1965, when China was still a member of the camp and took part, directly or indirectly, in its inner counsels. It was by taking advantage of the schism and playing the role of a mediator between the two giants that Rumania achieved the degree of autonomy she enjoys today. By virtually excluding China from the bloc – with the aid of the cultural revolution, by which Peking cut itself off from the world for several years – the Kremlin knocked this weapon out of the hands of would-be independents and 'honest brokers', and at the same time gained increased freedom of action in other fields. Peking being officially classed as an enemy, the Russians could ignore its clamour against their negotiating with the West – whereas Khrushchev in 1958 and 1959 had had to make excuses every time he held out a hand towards Washington – and were less embarrassed by Chinese attempts to outbid them in the third world. At the present time Peking's more moderate line in foreign affairs after the cultural revolution, plus its *rapprochement* with Bucharest and Belgrade, are a foretaste of what the new Chinese 'nuisance' might be for the Soviet Union. An *aggiornamento* in the doctrinal field, making China more respectable in general and perhaps helping to reduce tension with the Soviet leaders, would mean that Peking could once more make its presence felt in eastern Europe in order to encourage all anti-Soviet elements there, of whatever complexion.

Washington versus Peking

We shall describe this antagonism more briefly, since it represents the least important side of the triangle and involves many features that we have already discussed apropos of American-Soviet rivalry.

As with the latter, we are concerned here with an accidental conflict and not a deep-seated one – in fact, until recently the two countries were united by long traditions of friendship. On the other hand, there is a nationalistic element that does not exist between the United States and the Soviet Union: not only have American and Chinese soldiers faced each other in Korea, but American protection of the Formosa regime is the chief obstacle to Chinas' unification under Mao. Apart from this major source of contention, which seemes likely to ensure Sino-American hostility for a long time to come, the dispute boils down to very little; there is no peripheral clash of interests, since China has not expanded beyond her frontiers as the Soviet Union has done, and cannot hope to do so.

This is true, despite appearances, even in Vietnam. To begin with, Chinese aid to North Vietnam is of secondary importance compared to Soviet supplies of raw materials. President Johnson's abstention from bombing Haiphong between 1965 and 1968 was due more to fear of a confrontation with Soviet warships than the risk of destroying Chinese craft. Secondly, while it is true that Soviet and Chinese influences compete at Hanoi, it is a mistake to regard the Indochina conflict, as some have done in America, as a contest between great powers, waged by proxy in the Korean fashion. To a large extent the war is an expression of Vietnamese nationalism, more particularly of Tonkinese expansionism boosted by the victory over the French army in 1954 and sustained by particularly tough communist leaders. The two great communist powers, which had not started the war, were content to let it develop: the Russians on grounds of solidarity which they could hardly disclaim, the Chinese with more enthusiasm since their doctrine of the 'people's war' was identical with that of their Vietnamese neighbours. But that is the limit of Chinese intervention, and we may safely assume that Peking would reconcile itself to the non-achievement – which of course would be represented as temporary – of Hanoi's war aims, viz. the conquest of South Vietnam and the establishment of friendly regimes in Laos and Cambodia. In all probability, only an invasion of the North by American land forces and the overthrow of the Hanoi regime would have provoked Peking into positive action. Since this did not happen and the conflict is now confined within narrow bounds, Sino-American antagonism in this area appears very limited.

SPECIAL KIND OF ANTAGONISM

In any case, the antagonism is of a very special kind, given the overwhelming difference of military potential. The Americans have a first-strike capacity where China is concerned, i.e. they could destroy China's basic economic and military infrastructure without risk of reprisals on their own territory. Peking is at pains to counteract this inferiority by moral dissuasion; in particular, like Stalin in the late 1940s, by undertaking never to be the first to use its infant atomic power and trying to induce the other side to make a similar promise. In fact everyone knows quite well – and the Chinese themselves admit this – that the Americans have no intention of attacking China, and that the only serious danger to the Chinese is from their northern neighbour. This makes it all the easier for Peking to preserve its doctrinal purity by inveighing against 'American imperialism', a course of action which need not cause perturbation in Washington. From this point of view, and leaving aside Formosa, Sino-American antagonism is even more artificial than that between the United States and the Soviet Union.

The disproportion of strength and the unimportance of peripheral clashes also mean that the two adversaries, having few scores to regulate, have little to talk about. While the Russians and Americans are constantly in touch through all sorts of channels in regard to their bilateral interests (the SALT negotiations) and major world problems, and while the Russians and Chinese have found it necessary to keep tension within bounds by establishing a contact at Peking which has functioned regularly for over a year, the Americans and Chinese have only fitful conversations at Warsaw, interrupted by months and even years of silence, without this mattering seriously to either of them. In all respects, therefore, the Washington-Peking side of the triangle is the most unreal, giving the structure as a whole an unbalanced and artificial character.

Effects of the triangular situation

While the figure we have drawn is theoretically simple enough, its implications are more complex than they would be in Euclidean geometry. The triangle does not exist merely in the abstract, but consists essentially in the manner in which it is viewed from each apex. Moreover its development as time goes on has a logic of its own. At the outset it appeared as pure gain for the United States, who saw their chief enemy, an apparently monolithic communist camp a thousand million strong, split suddenly into two. Even today the triangle appears to be, if not purely and simply a 'good thing', at all events a phenomenon which is worth attention and can be turned to account in the quest for a world-wide balance which, as we have seen, is basic to American foreign policy. For the Russians, on the other hand, the effect of China's secession has been to add a new enemy, tougher and above all closer at hand, to the one they had already. The Soviet leaders, who are much less concerned with the world balance of power than with their own security and national interests, thus tend to see the triangle as involving them in a struggle on two fronts instead of one. It is they, in fact, who lose most by the situation. The Chinese, it is true, are in the same predicament, but it is one they have chosen and triumphantly proclaimed, and it has increased their liberty of action. Thus, while both communist powers see international relations as an egotistical game of 'us' versus the rest, their approach in practice is radically different.

Despite all this, the triangular set-up has its own objective implications, and each party endeavours, in different degrees and not always consciously, to turn them to its own advantage. To explain this in detail we may start from the basic observation that there is no such thing in practice as a struggle on two fronts, conducted with equal means and equal intensity against two adversaries who are also hostile to each other. In the nature of things, at some point or other each power must choose a principal opponent. This choice may not be openly recognized, it is often the result of external circumstances and may alter as time goes on; but it underlies the action of the State concerned, whose relations with 'adversary number two' become more fluid in character. Without going so far as to say 'The enemies of our enemies are our friends' – the interests involved, and the nature of international relations, are too rigid to permit such a *volte-face* – the original antagonism is diluted by a measure of collaboration or collusion. This in turn alarms 'adversary number one', who either reacts by denouncing – sometimes in excessive terms – the phenomenon of collusion, in order to discredit the other two, or else appeals direct to number two, who is thus in the gratifying position of an arbiter.

The term 'collusion' is of course an over-simplification, suggesting an explicit intention that may not be present. For instance a Soviet-American *rapprochement* might take place by the force of circumstances and have little to do with China. It might be more accurate to speak of 'parallel interests' or of 'weakened rivalry'. But the third person in the game, whether it be China or another power, sees the *rapprochement* between the other two as collusion, and we shall therefore continue to use this term.*

The theory of the game may be summed up in the following principles:

1. The existence of an 'adversary number one' leads to 'objective collusion' with number two.

2. Each of the three players aims to reduce collusion between the others to a minimum.

3. At the same time, it is in the interest of each to bluff or blackmail his chief adversary by threatening collusion with the other.

4. The surest way for any of the three to provoke the other two into collusion is to display undue aggressiveness.

We may now examine, in the light of these principles, the elements of collusion which, by the rules of a three-cornered struggle, modify the antagonisms that we have already described.

Collusion between Moscow and Washington

This is the most important of the three possible forms of collusion, owing to the degree of contact and mutual interests between the two greatest powers in the world. But again, this collusion takes on a different aspect according as it is seen from Peking, Washington or Moscow.

*Translator's note: the French term *collusion* perhaps carries less suggestion of trickery than its English equivalent.

CHINA'S VIEW OF THE 'COLLUSION'

Seen from Peking, Soviet-American collusion has been a major propaganda theme since the first days of the Sino-Soviet schism. From the Moscow Test Ban Treaty of 1963 to the 'Rogers plan' of 1970 for the Middle East, there has been no lack of subject matter for Chinese denunciation of the two powers' evil and usually 'anti-Chinese' machinations. It would even seem as if, contrary to the principle that each adversary aims to prevent collusion between the other two, the Chinese rejoiced at this phenomenon and did all they could to foster it by denouncing it in cases where it did not really exist. It should not, however, be forgotten that the Chinese, especially at the outset of their quarrel with Moscow, needed to discredit the Soviet Union *vis-à-vis* the rest of the communist world by denouncing the Kremlin's treacherous and pro-imperialistic game. In so doing they killed two birds with one stone, since their action also deterred the Russians from moving too far towards Washington, if it did not actually provoke a Soviet-American conflict. The shelling of the islands in the Formosa Strait in 1958 was directed not only against the American enemy but against Peking's ally the Soviet Union, which was put in danger of being involved in a military conflict with the United States. In the last few years the Chinese have introduced a subtler note into their denunciation of American-Soviet collusion, by describing the relations between the two super-powers as a mixture of collusion and rivalry, a definition which is not far from the truth.

MOSCOW'S VIEW OF THE 'COLLUSION'

Seen from Moscow, American-Soviet collusion can only be envisaged in a restricted sense, given the rigid ideas of the Kremlin leaders; As we saw, the triangle means to them having two enemies instead of one, and there is no question of their ceasing to pursue Soviet interests in the West because of anything the Chinese are doing. This state of affairs could only change if China presented an imminent and inescapable threat, so that Moscow had to 'give up everything' to make sure of being secure in the east. As this is not so, a secondary effect of the triangular situation has come into play, with the Russians using the Chinese threat not in order to buy a rapprochement with the West at the cost of concessions, but to convince the West that they deserve concessions by virtue of their special position. Arguments of the type 'We are defending the whole civilized world by standing firm on our eastern frontier; you ought therefore to show understanding towards us, especially in Europe' were often heard from semi-official Soviet sources in 1969, when tension on the Ussuri was increasing. In March of that year there was a curious instance of the triangular game when Moscow accused

Peking of staging the Damansky Island incident in order to help Bonn succeed in its objective of holding the election to the Federal presidency at Berlin. China in fact had no interest whatsoever in that far-away issue, and we may wonder if Moscow was not using the frontier incident as an excuse to explain to Ulbricht its inaction over Berlin.

In any case, except perhaps for the period of the first American bombing of North Vietnam, we may say that Moscow habitually considered China its principal enemy, implicitly and at times even explicitly, from 1963, when open and direct polemics began between the two countries, until the autumn of 1969. Since then, while there has been no 'thaw' properly speaking, the Kremlin seems to have tried, with a good deal of success, to 'freeze' its quarrel with Peking (especially by the Kosygin - ChouEn-lai conversation in September 1969 and the resumption of frontier talks, followed by the exchange of ambassadors and the despatch of a commercial mission) in order to redeploy its energies westward, especially towards the Middle East and Europe. This evolution suggests two remarks.

Even during the years when Moscow regarded China as her chief enemy, collusion with Washington did not go to the length of a *rapprochement*. The Kremlin's military superiority over China was such that it had no need to make concessions in the west to allay its anxiety in the east. It may even be said that during this period, from 1963 to 1969, Moscow was fairly inactive as regards East-West relations. Signs of this were the Russians' obstructive attitude towards the efforts of Herr Brandt, who became foreign minister in December 1966, to unfreeze the European situation; their reluctance to enter into the SALT talks, their passivity in the Middle East, etc. The Soviet leaders certainly did not want fresh tension, but it was as if they felt too weak to negotiate.

On the other hand, the lull in Soviet-Chinese tension at the end of 1969 coincided with renewed Soviet activity in the west. In the space of four months Moscow entered into the SALT talks, responded to the advances of Herr Brandt, who had meanwhile become Chancellor, and in January 1970 decided on a military commitment to the United Arab Republic which is almost without precedent in the history of the Soviet regime. This simple juxtaposition of facts throws a great deal of doubt on the theory which is still widespread that Moscow's 'overtures' to the West reflect a desire to 'safeguard its rear' on account of the threat from China. It would be more to the point to suggest that the Russian leaders decided at the end of 1969 to 'safeguard their rear' in the east by reducing tension with China so as to pursue a more active policy in the west. Be that as it may, we cannot regard all Moscow's recent diplomatic initiatives in the west – from SALT to the plan for a European security conference, and including the Bonn-Moscow treaty and the revival of co-operation with France – as due simply and solely to the desire for a *détente*, that is to say collusion with the western powers. Whenever the Soviet leaders resolve to engage in a dialogue it is part of a dynamic plan, serving the same objectives as the other weapons in their diplomatic and military armoury.

WASHINGTON'S VIEW OF THE 'COLLUSION'

Washington's point of view as regards American-Soviet collusion is different again from that of the other two powers. Officially the United States refuses to designate an 'adversary number one', and she is more successful than the others in avoiding the necessity to do so. But, antagonism or no, a great many problems have to be discussed with the Soviet Union, and this leads the Americans, willy-nilly, to embark on a course of collusion. They might even be tempted, in the event of a Soviet-Chinese conflict, to 'sell' a Soviet-American alliance to Moscow in return for solid concessions; but China would have to be much stronger than she is today for such a bargain to hold water. For the time being Washington's concern for world equilibrium is too great for her to desire to see a clash between the other two giants, and the best course she can pursue is to declare herself neutral, as Mr Rogers did in 1969.

Irrespective of either side's intentions, however, Soviet-American collusion, or at any rate parallelism, has become a reality wherever the two powers' essential interests demand it. The best example is in Asia, where they have a common interest in keeping China at arm's length. This was seen over the Formosa Strait issue in 1958, when Khrushchev and Eisenhower each did their best to impose moderation on Mao Tse-tung. When the Sino-Indian conflict in the Himalayas broke out a year later, the Russians and Americans found themselves on one side of the barricade with China on the other, to the greater detriment of 'socialist solidarity'. In the same way the Russians and Americans have found a tacit but common interest, pursued by very different means – the Russians by attempts at 'salvage', the Americans by aiding rival political groups – in thwarting Sukarno's activities in Indonesia, those of the various pro-Chinese Communist Parties in Asia, and in general all movements openly working in Peking's interest. It has even been contended that Moscow did not want North Vietnam to win the war in Indochina because this would play into Peking's hands by justifying the latter's theories of revolution. This is a doubtful argument since, as we have pointed out, the war is an essentially Vietnamese enterprise, and also because Moscow has given so much military aid that it would be no less entitled than Peking to claim credit for a Northern victory.

In any case the effect of the 'triangle', in some Asian countries at least, has been to bring about a genuinely peaceful coexistence between the two super-powers: this is so in India and probably soon will be in Indonesia, where Soviet and American aid complement each other harmoniously, each government preferring the other's presence to that of Peking. Similarly it was because of China that Moscow intervened so promptly, by the Tashkent arbitration, in the dispute between India and Pakistan, while the United States openly welcomed this successful stroke of Soviet policy. Thus the triangle here plays a stabilizing role, Soviet interests coinciding with the maintenance of equilibrium. This state of affairs could only be strengthened if China were to adopt an aggressive posture, as in 1958, 1959 and 1962.

THE SALT NEGOTIATIONS

The other instance of collusion is the SALT talks, although the anti-Chinese implications of these are much less obvious. The specific motives which led the two great powers to embark on these talks – the need to limit the arms race and achieve some control of the strategic balance – exist independently of China, and the talks would have happened even if the United States and the Soviet Union were the only nuclear powers in the world. It is not clear what effect the negotiations at Vienna and Helsinki can have on the Chinese nuclear programme, but clearly the talks must take account of China's growing potential; and this factor tends to make American-Soviet agreement harder, not easier, to reach. The Soviet Union, which is the immediate target of China's nuclear arsenal, can reasonably maintain that it needs additional strategic potential to meet this threat, i.e. that it must have more than parity with the United States. It is true that Russia's defence against the Chinese threat consists chiefly in its intermediate and medium-range missiles which, according to the Soviet government, are not on the SALT agenda. But the Americans for their part can claim that China's intercontinental missiles will soon threaten American territory and that they must guard against this situation by achieving more than parity with the Soviet Union as regards ICBM's and long-range ballistic missiles, which are the main subject of the SALT talks.

The other question is that of ABM's. The Chinese threat has often been cited, though not always consistently, by Mr McNamara and President Nixon to justify the Sentinel and Safeguard programmes, and indeed the protection these offer is at present most credible in relation to Chinese missiles, which are relatively few and unsophisticated. As the Russians can invoke exactly the same argument, this might easily lead to another round of the arms race. For this reason some people in the United States have suggested that the right course is to give up ABM's and come to terms with the future by admitting China now to the nuclear deterrent club. This is an interesting idea, especially as its long-term result should be to include Peking in the SALT talks, which of course would not make these any easier. But it would involve crediting China with a deterrent force which she does not possess at present, and presupposes a degree of idealism which is not universal in Washington and certainly not in Moscow.

In other words, the triangle in this case produces contradictory effects: the emergence of a third party impels the two super-powers to seek agreement with each other, but also to step up their respective armaments. Pursuing the argument to its full extent, any agreement involving parity between Washington and Moscow, even at a very high ceiling, would be impossible to achieve, because the Chinese potential would increase in relative importance year by year as it came closer to the ceiling. The Russians and Americans must choose: either they want to maintain their quasi-monopoly at all costs and keep the Chinese at a distance, and for this purpose they must keep up the arms race; or else they can come to an understanding which will limit their defence costs and risk *vis-à-vis* each other, shutting their eyes to the Chinese factor; but then they must be prepared to see China play an increasing part in the strategic equation and one day upset their calculations. The more the SALT negotiators ignore China, the more heavily will its shadow fall across their deliberations.

To sum up, Chinese influence on American-Soviet relations has hitherto been limited as regards time (the intermittent periods of Chinese aggressiveness) and space (India and South-East Asia), or has been confined to certain aspects of international affairs (SALT). The bluff whereby one super-power threatens Peking that it will ally itself with the other has been used by Moscow more than Washington, since the Russians are more at odds with China than America is. But it has never gone very far, partly because the Americans have generally refused to play and partly because the Russians have always been in a position of strength *vis-à-vis* China and have not felt the need to offer concessions to the West. In the future, however, this gambit might take on greater importance if China's potential becomes more alarming to Moscow, even without any special aggressiveness on her part. Since the Russians will be the soliciting party, the Americans will be able to choose whether to accept or refuse closer collaboration with the Soviet Union according to which communist power they regard as their 'number one enemy'. They may accept, but unless they feel as much threatened by China as Russia does, they will exact concessions in return; so that once again the three-cornered situation appears more to America's advantage than Russia's.

Collusion between Moscow and Peking

There has never been a great deal of this, the essential reason being, as we saw, that the antagonism between the two communist powers is too fundamental. Moreover the Russians have less room for manoeuvre *vis-à-vis* Peking. In their relations with the United States the Kremlin leaders can display some elasticity, since as a rule their antagonism only comes to the fore when it is a question of scoring points in some peripheral area like the Middle East, Africa or Berlin. In relations with China, on the other hand, the security of the Soviet Union is directly at stake. It follows that collusion would involve more costly concessions, of a kind that neither party would consider except in the presence of a grave external threat.

One period during which there might have been 'objective collusion' between the Russians and Chinese was after the United States embarked on the bombing of North Vietnam in 1965. At the outset at all events, both powers must have been alarmed by this aggressive measure against a communist state, and Moscow launched a major campaign for 'unity of action' in aid of Vietnam. In so doing, the Russians had a double purpose: firstly to deter the Americans by a show of unity – most of President Johnson's critics in fact predicted that this action would reinforce Sino-Soviet solidarity – and secondly to put pressure on Peking to return to the fold, or at least moderate its hostility to Soviet 'revisionism'. In this aim they were not unsuccessful, for some of the Chinese leaders – for instance Peng Chen, then mayor of Peking, and perhaps Liu Shao-chi and others who were stigmatized some months later – seemed inclined at this time to endorse the 'unity of action' campaign. One of the key issues in the Peking debate which culminated in the 'cultural revolution' was indeed whether American imperialism or Soviet revisionism was to be considered the chief enemy. Although the question was never openly answered, Mao plumped for the latter, and his view prevailed. Soviet-Chinese tension, in the political and propaganda spheres though not in the military, was never greater than in 1966–67, with the besieging of embassies and the huge anti-Soviet demonstrations in Peking, at the very height of the struggle in Vietnam. This did not prevent Moscow and Peking concluding an agreement for the transit of Soviet war material to Vietnam, but it required long negotiations and much insistence from Hanoi. The two powers were not reconciled, nor did they 'collude' against America in any real sense.

More recently, as we have seen, the Soviet Union seems to have ceased to consider Peking its 'number one adversary', and this should in theory mean collusion between the two. But while the Soviet leaders may take this view, as they have damped down their attacks on China and are seeking to normalize relations, there is no sign that the Chinese have ceased to regard the Russians as their chief enemy. While accepting, as is only prudent, the degree of normalization offered by Moscow, they are showing complete intransigence in the frontier negotiations and have launched a vast internal campaign of 'preparation for war', which can only mean a diplomacy in various Western countries since 1969, they are most probably for many a wish to find allies in the controntation with the Soviet Union. If Peking has any sort of collusion in mind, it is likely to be with the West and not the Kremlin, whatever the latter's wishes. And, while power may practise antagonism on its own, collusion is a game for two.

It remains a question whether this state of things may change with time, especially as Chinese power grows. So far, the few traces that can be discerned in Soviet foreign policy of a disposition to play the 'triangular' game have pointed to a one-sided conception of its rules. Moscow has practised a sort of sham collusion, in a minor key so to speak, with both the United States and China: it has made play with its eastward anxieties in the hope of inducing the Americans to be more accommodating in Europe, while at the same time appealing to the better nature of the Chinese to bring them back into the Soviet embrace. None of this is in conflict with the Kremlin's fundamental aims of encroaching on the American sphere of influence in the west and putting an end to the Maoist schism; nor will this situation alter as long as the Kremlin judges both its adversaries to be 'manageable', the Americans being unaggressive and the Chinese too weak to do harm. The first of these circumstances is unlikely to change much in the foreseeable future, but we may wonder what will happen to the Kremlin's strategy when China becomes more powerful. As we suggested, the most likely eventuality would seem to be a closer *rapprochement* with Washington and concessions to the latter, but what of the opposite course, viz. genuine collusion with Peking?

Certainly this cannot be excluded, since, as we saw, the unpredictable nature of the regimes and of their decision-making processes leaves the field of speculation wide open. The twists and turns of the cultural revolution indicate that Mao's choice of the Soviet Union as 'enemy number one' may be reversed by his successors. The one thing we can be sure of is that unless the Russians were to do another 'Prague coup' in Peking, which is most unlikely, any *rapprochement* will be more tactical than real on China's part, and will require substantial Soviet concessions. Moscow would have to agree to settle the frontier dispute, resume economic aid and agree to consult the Chinese over world policy and make room for them in the communist movement – in short, the Soviet leaders would have to jettison practically all their traditional ideas and modes of behaviour in the matter of alliances. We need not fear this happening overnight. Until it does, the Chinese have every interest in maintaining their present line of cautious toughness, while building up their strength as fast as possible.

Collusion between Washington and Peking

From the very beinning of the Sino-Soviet schism, Moscow accused Mao first of 'objectively playing the game' of the American imperialists and then of becoming their active ally. While Soviet propaganda on the subject of collusion was rather less systematic than that of Peking, it was at times very sharp and quite unembarrassed by any regard for truth. When American forces put in at Hong Kong, this was denounced by the Soviet press as proof of Chinese aid to the interventionists in Vietnam; China was attacked for trading with the capitalist countries, and so forth. More recently, at the beginning of 1970, the Soviet weekly *Za Rubezhom*, commenting on the renewal of American-Chinese talks at Warsaw, spoke of 'perfidious attempts by American military circles to disturb relations between the Soviet Union and the Chinese People's Republic', while the Novosti agency went so far as to 'reveal' a 'secret meeting' between Mr William Rogers, the American Secretary of State, and communist Chinese emissaries at Hong Kong. The object of this crude propaganda was apparently threefold: to discredit Peking within the communist movement, to force it to take a tougher line with the Americans and even provoke them, and finally to serve notice on Washington that any flirtation with China would prejudice the American-Soviet dialogue. By and large, however, Soviet charges of collusion are directed against China as the prime mover rather than the United States, or else against 'accomplices' of the second rank such as Japan and West Germany (of course before the Moscow-Bonn treaty).

We may understand the Soviet Union being alarmed by anything that might look like an alliance of the other two powers against it. If at any time both Peking and Washington regard Moscow as their principal enemy – and, as we have seen, Peking has done so for some years past – they have an evident interest in a mutual *rapprochement*. Moreover there is a clear application here of the principle that a display of aggressiveness by one of the three powers tends to bring about collusion between the other two. Among all the reasons which led the Chinese to resume the Warsaw talks with the Americans, first at the beginning of 1969 and then, more successfully, in January 1970, a high place must be given to the invasion of Czechoslovakia (which suggested a precedent for China) and the Soviet military pressure throughout 1969 on the Ussuri and in Kazakhstan. The substance of the Warsaw talks is tenuous enough, but the fact that the double encounter took place in 1970 was a clear instance of Peking using 'collusion blackmail' against Moscow – the more so as the talks were held for the first time in the respective embassies and not within earshot of Polish, and therefore Soviet, listeners. We may expect that any future Soviet activity which both Peking and

Washington regard as dangerous will give rise to new developments of this kind.

LIMITS TO A SINO-AMERICAN 'COLLUSION'

At the same time we should recognize the limits of this collusion. As far as the Chinese leaders are concerned, their virulent anti-imperialism – sustained all the more vigorously as it goes down well in the Third World, and Peking does not feel directly threatened by the United States – prevents them taking any but very small steps towards Washington. Moreover the Chinese, not without reason, detect Washington's hand in Japan's presumed ambition to rearm and play the part of a 'gendarme of Asia'; consequently an accommodation with the United States would be regarded as equivalent to normalizing relations with Tokyo, which would mean a difficult adjustment of roles between the two great Asiatic powers. Finally, and overriding everything else, there is the problem of Formosa: it is hard to see how Mao or his successors could accept a *rapprochement* with Washington without some concession on this essential point.

On the American side, the basic question is whether the Soviet Union or China is 'enemy number one', or whether any power should be given this rating. Clearly it is not China, except perhaps in parts of Asia where, as we have seen, the situation has led to advantageous 'collusion' between Washington and Moscow. On the plane of world relations the Soviet Union is certainly the chief adversary, but also the chief negotiating partner, the power with which a number of vital issues have to be constantly examined and adjusted if a disastrous confrontation is to be avoided. Thus, while Washington has a strong interest in using Peking to restrict Soviet power, there is much force in the argument so often used by Moscow that an American-Chinese rapprochement would impair Soviet-American relations and interfere with the organization of coexistence. This fact, no less than the deadlock over Formosa, explains why American governments over the past years have accomplished little more on the Chinese front than purely formal gestures such as exchanges of teachers and journalists, which have failed to lead to anything more substantial.

TOWARDS A REAL TRIANGLE?

This brings us back to the point we made at the outset of this study, that the disequilibrium of the three parties is too great for a genuinely 'triangular' situation. As long as the key to thermonuclear war, and therefore the fate of world peace, is in the custody of the two super-powers alone, possessing a first-strike capacity against every other nation, Washington and Moscow have no alternative but to carry on a private dialogue to the exclusion of China and other secondary powers.

However, Peking's growing strength opens up new prospects in the fairly long term. Initially it will no doubt cause a reflex of solidarity between Washington and Moscow, reinforcing their mutual understanding; the more so as it will be very surprising if Peking does not take advantage of its new strength to make fresh moves on the Asiatic chessboard, and this aggressiveness, diplomatic and political if not military, would intensify collusion between its rivals. But at the same time Washington will no longer be able to neglect the third party to the game, and will have to start negotiating current issues with her. There will have to be a Washington-Peking dialogue, even at the risk of weakening the 'hot line' to Moscow and offending the Soviet Union. When this dialogue takes place the triangular set-up will have become fully operative, and the United States will probably be in the most advantageous position of the three powers. Being less fettered by doctrinal prejudice than the others, having no need for permanent adversaries and seeking none, the Americans should be in a better position to react to the hostility of each of the other two and bring about the world equilibrium which is their main objective.

Things have not yet reached this point, but the last observation at least suggests that while the triangular situation upsets familiar notions of bipolarity and involves many uncertainties, it is not necessarily unfavourable to peace. Even at the present time, the position is on balance fairly reassuring. One sometimes hears it suggested that each of the three powers may be tempted to push the others into war so as to reign over the resulting devastation; this may serve as a propaganda argument, but it has no basis in fact. In the late fifties, it is true, Mao Tse-tung gave the impression that he was not averse to such a solution, but it would take more than this at the present day to induce the two super-powers to betray their thermonuclear responsibilities.

On the other hand, while no one in Washington seems seriously to desire that Sino-Soviet antagonism should degenerate into an armed conflict, the existence of the triangle is one of the factors restraining Moscow from settling accounts with Peking by force, since Washington could not fail to benefit by the weakening of the Soviet Union in a long conflict. Finally, one may reasonably feel that an American-Chinese war would not suit the Kremlin, since it could hardly stand by while its former Chinese ally was being crushed; and *a fortiori* that one of the many reasons which prevent an American-Soviet war breaking out is the fact that only China could gain by it, as de Gaulle pointed out to Khrushchev as far back as 1960.

While the existence of the triangle is thus a factor tending to prevent war, it does at present lead to the adoption of forceful attitudes by each of the three powers, and does nothing to encourage a *détente*. It is partly in order to outface China that the Soviet Union has developed its military potential in the last few years, deploying its fleet in distant waters and particularly the Indian Ocean, to the alarm of the Western powers also. Again, the danger of Chinese expansion has contributed no little to the American involvement in South-East Asia and the Soviet presence there. We have seen that China's progress in the field of strategic armaments is likely to make the Russians and Americans step up their own nuclear programme. Finally, the virulence of Peking's anti-imperialist propaganda and the Chinese presence in the Third World would, if continued and intensified, oblige Moscow to exert greater efforts in that area. None of these consequences can be avoided. But the situation in a bipolar world, where both local engagements and direct confrontations could and did take place, was hardly more satisfactory.

A Future for European Agriculture

A report by a panel of experts

D BERGMANN   M ROSSI-DORIA

N KALDOR   J A SCHNITTKER

H B KROHN   C THOMSEN

J S MARSH   H WILBRANDT

PIERRE URI *Rapporteur*

Introduction

O N the initiative of the Atlantic Institute, and under a grant from the Fritz Thyssen Foundation, a group of economists and agricultural experts from various countries, whose names are appended below, held a succession of meetings in Paris on the subject of European agricultural policy in its internal and external repercussions.

Professor Hans Wilbrandt acted as Chairman and M Pierre Uri acted as Rapporteur and was also responsible for the original draft of this Report. The group was assisted in its research by M Mario Levi and Herr Gerd Jarchow. Mr. Albert Simantov, Director of Agriculture, OECD, and Mr. Robert Brand, Economic Minister, US Embassy in Paris, attended some of the meetings as observers.

The present Report was thoroughly discussed by the group and represents the highest common measure of agreement among its members. But as is inevitable with a collective work of this kind, no individual member should be regarded as being fully committed to this Report in every detail or to the emphasis given to various aspects.

The members of this group wish to emphasize however that they are in full agreement with the following major findings of the Report:

(1) There is an urgent need for a radical redirection of agricultural policy within the Community, both for Europe herself and for Europe's relationship with other countries.

(2) While the members of the group are in full agreement with the principles for the reform of agriculture proposed in the Mansholt Plan, they consider that, as an essential complement to the proposals made in that Plan, the emphasis of policy should be shifted towards income support and away from price support.

(3) They consider that the concrete proposals made in the present Report provide a constructive and significant new approach to a solution of these problems. While they recognize that many important issues remain to be discussed and resolved in detail, they believe that the proposals put forward in this Report afford a valuable framework for further consideration and study of the various issues.

There are, of course, a large number of points which particular members of the group would have expressed differently if the Report had represented their individual views and was not an expression of the joint view of the group as a whole. There are a limited number of issues on which individual members wish to express specific reservations. These are given at the end of the Report.

M DENIS BERGMANN
Directeur de Recherches, Institut National de la Recherche Agronomique, Economie et Sociologie Rurales, Paris.
Prof NICHOLAS KALDOR
King's College, Cambridge.
Dr HANS-BRODER KROHN
Directeur Général, Commission des Communautés Européennes, Brussels.
Mr JOHN S MARSH
Department of Agricultural Economics, University of Reading, England.
Prof MANLIO ROSSI-DORIA
Senatore della Repubblica Italiana.
Mr JOHN A SCHNITTKER
Vice President, Robert Nathan Associates, Washington DC.
Dr CARL THOMSEN
The Royal Veterinary and Agricultural College, Department of Agricultural Policy, Copenhagen.
Prof PIERRE URI
Counsellor for Studies, Atlantic Institute, Paris, and University Paris IX.
Prof Dr HANS WILBRANDT
Direktor des Instituts für Ausländische Landwirtschaft an der Georg-August-Universität, Göttingen.

130

Summary

part from the completion of a Customs Union, the Common Agricultural Policy has been the major task to which the European Community has applied itself.

Its actions in this field can only be judged fairly if one bears in mind the extreme difficulties which had to be overcome. It was a formidable task to establish the free circulation of goods between markets divided by large price disparities, and to agree upon a common system of market intervention in lieu of a wide variety of policies, often of the most uneconomic kind.

However, it must now be recognized that this agricultural policy has not attained its objectives. It involves financial burdens which increase at an almost intolerable rate. In spite of this farmers within the Community justifiably complain about the low level of their incomes. This contradiction arises because the Community has concentrated its agricultural expenditure on a few products which must either be stored or exported at a loss. By the level of its protection and the prices at which it liquidates its surpluses, the Community contributes to a disruption of international markets. Moreover this distorted pattern of prices is likely to cause serious balance of payments difficulties to those countries which want to join the Community.

If the sacrifices incurred for the sake of agriculture bring no better results, it is clear that the methods must be changed.

The Mansholt Plan represents a bold initiative. It is based on the acceptance of a fundamental principle: agricultural income can only be maintained if the reduction in the agricultural population is accelerated, and if farms rapidly reach an economically viable size.

But this policy of structural reform is not enough. Unless it is complemented by a change in price relationships, including a reduction in the prices of surplus products, there is no assurance that surpluses will not increase further under the spur of improved productivity which structural changes will accelerate. The present prices may also keep on the land many farmers who should leave the industry.

On two central points, the task confronting the working group was to reconcile the seemingly irreconcilable.

The re-establishment of equilibrium requires the reduction of certain prices – and yet the understanding and consent of the Community farmers.

Hence such price reductions must be compensated by income subsidies – yet of a kind which does not retard but accelerates the restructuring of agriculture and the redirection of production.

On the first point it should be emphasized that certain prices, which represent an income to some producers, are a cost to others, as is the case with cereals. The subsidies paid in compensation for price reductions will give an immediate advantage to the majority of agricultural producers, who do not however account for the major part of production. Compensation will be calculated by reference to *average* yields. The poorest farmers, whose yields are below average, will therefore receive more in compensation than they lose through lower prices. This system will thus serve not only to maintain agricultural income but also to improve its distribution. It thus responds to the oft-repeated demand for a replacement of price support by income support.

In order to secure the necessary change in the structure of agriculture, it is envisaged that income support should be confined to the present generation of farmers. Compensation cannot be transmitted from one generation to the next, except in certain cases for a limited duration. It would be discontinued if the same small farm were operated by another owner; on the other hand, it would continue to be paid, up to a certain maximum of years, if the farm were amalgamated with others into a viable economic unit. The subsidy compensating the price-reduction on a particular product would be maintained even if the farmer switched to other products; thus the maximum incentive would be provided for the reorientation of production.

In this way the surpluses should be rapidly eliminated. The disappearance of the financial burden which they entail would free funds necessary for income support. The entitlement to a subsidy retained by a farm absorbed into a more viable unit would increase its value: as a result the selling price would of itself include an indemnity for leaving the farm. This would reduce the public outlay contemplated by the Mansholt Plan for that purpose.

All the elements of the scheme are clearly interrelated.

Such are the essential features of the policy recommended for the Community in order to serve its own interests and to provide a way out of the present *impasse*. It would also entitle the Community to propose to the large agricultural exporters of the world the rejection of dumping practices which disorganize the world markets.

A second prerequisite for the restoration of an international market is the establishment of international stabilization schemes. Until now such measures have been a national or a Community responsibility. It is vain to expect freedom in agricultural trade unless effective stabilization schemes are established on an international scale. This requires the creation of international buffer stocks which are operated so as to offset variations of current production relative to current consumption, by releasing stocks in times of pressure and absorbing them in times of glut.

There can be no question of adopting this new policy in any definitive manner before Britain joins the Community. But by clarifying its nature and objectives we can obviate a discussion at cross purposes which is likely to block the negotiations. The Community asks Britain to accept the Common Agricultural Policy. Britain's answer is that she would like to, but cannot if the burden is too great. Each of the parties knows, as is shown by the Mansholt Plan, that the policy must in any case be changed. It should therefore suffice to agree on the principle that income support and structural reorganization should gradually replace price support. It should suffice to agree that the concrete methods in which this principle would be embodied should be devised by the enlarged Community, that is to say with the participation of Britain.

The Present and Prospective Situation

Twelve years after the Treaty of Rome came into effect, and eight years after the first decisions which concerned cereals and their by-products were made, and the first financial statutes established, the Common Agricultural Policy is in an untenable situation. The Community's expenditures have increased at a substantial rate. At first this reflected the gradual widening of its powers and the growing number of products covered by the Common Agricultural Policy, but more recently it has been due to surpluses, mainly of cereals, sugar beet and milk.

The Community has filled its granaries and cold storage rooms at a high price. Of course it is always possible to liquidate surpluses by selling them at cut prices or giving them away but, economically, surpluses exist when a part of the harvest must be sold at a loss, either because goods are stored with no certain prospect that they will ever be sold at a price sufficient to cover total costs, or because the product is exported to external markets for a fraction of its internal price and costs of production.

The Cost to the Community

This is exactly the present position. In the 1969-70 season butter surpluses will have cost $518 million against $384 million the previous year, and support for milk products as a whole will have risen to $550 million in 1970 from $329 million in 1969. The cost may be lowered in 1971, but it seems certain to rise again as surpluses return. Altogether payments from the Community fund have risen from $29 million in 1962-63 to $2,783 million for 1969-70, six-sevenths of which consisted of price support.

Nevertheless expenditures by member countries have increased at an incredible speed. In some countries this has resulted in increases of 30 per cent per year over a run of years. The farmers are forced to recognise that changes must be made. Such cost increases, compared with gains in Gross National Product of members, which remain around 5 per cent per year, bring nearer the time when public expenditure for agriculture will outstrip total resources. Today a total of seven thousand million dollars per year is absorbed in financial aid and subsidies, counting both Community and national expenditures.

Even this sum does not cover all the charges borne by the Community. One must also count the excess cost to consumers of agricultural products, including imports, whose prices are raised by means of import levies. The total value of Community agricultural production in 1967 reached 25 thousand million dollars at internal prices. This was worth only 19 thousand million dollars, when valued at prices similar to those paid to British or Danish farmers. At world prices, based on American export or British import prices, the total value of Community production in 1967-68 was 17 thousand million dollars.

Given the present disorganized state of world agricultural markets, world prices are themselves arbitrary. The Community itself, by its subsidies for exports, contributes to their low level. The fact remains that to 7 thousand million dollars of public expenditure must be added 6 to 8 thousand million dollars additional burden which the consumers of the Community bear in the form of inflated prices. The tax levies which raise the import prices help to finance public expenditure which, however, amounts to some 2 thousand million dollars, and this latter sum should not be included both in higher prices and in public support expenditure. With that correction the burden appears to be in the range of 11 to 13 thousand million dollars per year. This is equivalent to half the value of agricultural production, calculated at internal prices. On a gross overall product of 400 thousand million dollars this is a burden equivalent to nearly 3 per cent of Gross National Product. This is far from negligible. National resources are already largely committed to personal consumption, investment and public services. Expenditure on these items cannot be easily reduced. Three per cent of the Gross National Product is for the various countries between three quarters and one hundred per cent of what they now spend on education: in this field the needs are enormous and unsatisfied. Access to education is a fundamental aim in reducing inequalities; moreover it has been demonstrated that the level of education in a country is one of the decisive factors in rate of growth. Again in most countries resources on this scale could increase the rate of new house construction by 50 per cent, or make possible fundamental improvements in transport or communication systems. By using so large a proportion of resources to prop up declining enterprises, whether in agriculture or in industry, the Community foregoes the opportunity to undertake such necessary improvements.

The total French government expenditure for agriculture alone represents $2,000 per farm per year.[1] At the Community level the total cost in terms of public expenditure and of excess prices paid by the consumer is still $2,000 per farm.[2]

If, in spite of sacrifices such as these, farmers can still claim that they do not obtain, and by a long way, an income equivalent to that of other sectors, something must be wrong with the way money is spent. New methods must be devised.

The Development of the Common Agricultural Policy

How has this situation come about? The Treaty of Rome explicitly included agricultural products in the Common Market so that they might benefit from a common agricultural policy. The report made in 1958 about the economic situation in the countries of the Community, shortly before the establishment of the Common Market brought one conclusion into clear relief. With regard to industrial production, while overall production levels were very different, structure of production, i.e. the share of each of the main types of industrial activity in the total, was surprisingly alike in the different member countries. By contrast, in agriculture there were no such similarities. The proportion of the agricultural population to the whole of the working population; the proportion and type of land available for cultivation; the extent of mechanization and the

---

(1) 3 thousand million dollars for 1,600,000 farms.
(2) There are 6 million farms in the Community, to be related to the overall cost indicated in the text.

use of fertilisers; the yield per unit of production; the proportion of agricultural production to overall food supplies; the prices guaranteed in each country to domestic producers and the ways in which production was shared between different enterprises, varied widely between countries. Again, while vigorous protection and state intervention to maintain farm incomes prevailed everywhere, the instruments themselves varied according to the role accorded to trade and farmers organisations, or publicly controlled central bodies.

It could even be said that there is no measure, however uneconomic, which cannot be found in one or other country. Absolute price guarantees, denaturing of products or their transformation into alcohol, quantums or production quotas, the destruction of wine or of fruit trees, outright import prohibitions – all prevail only too frequently. Whatever the difficulties that have evolved in the Common Market, it is only fair to keep in mind the basis from which it started: disparate national circumstances and chaotic policies.

It is from this angle that the measures taken by the Community must be judged. In order to succeed within a given period, and to allow goods to circulate freely throughout the Community, protective systems of long standing had to be dismantled. To accomplish this, and to establish common prices, meant either introducing considerable price increases in some countries, which ran counter to economic equilibrium, or imposing important cuts in prices which would have evoked strong protests by farmers. One can hardly be surprised that the result does not correspond to the needs of the present situation, especially since the technical transformation of agriculture has accelerated rapidly during the period in which these decisions were being implemented. Today we have at least a point of departure, experience from which we can learn, and the embryo of a policy which can be transformed. As Napoleon said: "One has to have a plan, if for no other reason than to be able to change it".

The objective of the Common Agricultural Policy was to arrive at the free circulation of farm products between member countries, to maintain Community preferences and to provide joint financial responsibility for the common policy. The method chosen was essentially to establish import levies which would be progressively lowered until they were eliminated between member states, but which would be maintained on imports from non-members. The revenue from these levies would meet an increasing share of the Community's expenses and be supplemented by contributions from member states. Thus the financial arrangement formed an integral part of the Common Agricultural Policy. Throughout the entire transition period, the most important discussions and the most threatening crises have centred around finance.

In its latest form, the financial regulation provides for a definitive solution to be approached by degrees. The Community will receive appropriate resources for the whole of its budget. These include from the start the whole of the agricultural levies, supplemented by a rising proportion of the customs duties. The contributions of the member countries will ultimately be replaced by a fiscal resource which, following the example of the value-added tax, will represent a uniform fraction of the gross product of the member countries.

One must not confuse the mechanism of the policy with its content. The introduction of levies, their disappearance inside the Community and their continuation outside it, is the equivalent for the agricultural sector of the elimination of customs duties and the institution of a common external tariff in the case of industrial products. A further feature takes account of the peculiar circumstances of agriculture. Instability of world agricultural markets required a variable element of protection to ensure internal producers the necessary degree of stability. This is the variable levy for agricultural products, a device which has gone far beyond stabilization. But the level of prices has not only been stabilized but has been entirely divorced from any reference to external influences.

It is not the principle of levies that is in question but the amount of the levy, which automatically increases with any growth in the difference between internal and external prices. Joint financial responsibility is not in question, but doubts must exist concerning the objects to which the funds raised are applied. Since, at the agreed price, surpluses multiplied, it was necessary to increase without any restriction expenditure incurred on purchases for storage, or on compensation for the loss on exports to external markets at world prices. Thereby a vicious circle is set up: variable levies enable the prices to be fixed at a level which causes surpluses, and these in turn are paid for by the levies.

For this development neither individuals nor institutions can be blamed. The incentives written into the system work in this direction. Levies which invariably bridge the gap between the lowest import price and the internal maintained price have given the illusion of a large degree of freedom from market discipline. They lead to a failure to appreciate the effect of prices on production, or the fact that external protection in itself does not suffice to ensure a market for production generated by the protected internal price.

The levy system cannot be applied without prices being fixed internally by common accord. This price reference is necessary so that the amount of the import levy can be established on the basis of the difference prevailing each week between the level of import prices and the internal price level. There is, of course, a constant jockeying for position aimed at keeping domestic prices high. If one Minister wishes to ensure high returns for his costly agriculture, the others will be in no position to resist. How can they explain to their own farmers that a lower price might make it possible for them in time to outbid those competitors who are in a less favourable position, and thus to earn a higher income? Such an argument is less immediately clear and less persuasive than an immediate increase in prices. In practice, this has been the way in which Ministerial decisions have been taken.

This tendency is all the more dangerous since decisions about prices and market organization continue to require unanimous agreement, contrary to the principles embodied in the Treaty of Rome for the third stage of the transition period. Such a regressive trend in the development of European institutions should not be allowed to continue.

Finally, there is a basic contradiction of immense significance inherent in the fact that while the price support operations and export aids are the joint responsibility of the Community, any measures or policies for controlling the volume of production are left to the individual responsibility of each member country. These procedures seem to be designed to bring about both excessively high prices and surpluses. Price decisions are taken as a result of political bargaining with the pressures varying from one product to another. This can only result in a set of product prices which are out of balance in relation to each other, and which bear no relation to the market situation.

The scale of intervention varies according to the products involved. This is not only a consequence of the practical difficulties originating in differences among markets, but also of economic logic. The less elastic the demand for a particular commodity the more the maintenance of a stable price is dependent on guaranteed purchases. If, on the other hand, consumption varies markedly with changes in prices, as is the case with fruit and eggs for instance, the market will respond more readily to any reduction in price, leaving a relatively satisfactory return to the producer. An apparent inequity comes about because of this. The products which receive the strongest support happen to be those of the North rather than the South, cereals rather than livestock and (except for milk) large farms rather than small ones.

Prices and Incomes

The existing mechanisms cannot bring about the maintenance of, let alone any increase in, farmers' incomes, especially of those farmers who are the most needy. It is not only difficult, it may even be contradictory, to identify increased incomes with increased prices. Incomes are not prices; they represent the difference between returns and costs. To the extent that some farmers use agricultural products as inputs, their costs are increased as the prices of these raw materials are fixed at a high level. Cereals or, to a small degree, molasses are inputs for pork, poultry and eggs. They can be used for stock breeding as is shown by British agriculture. No doubt the prices established for these latter products, and the levels of protection which they enjoy from external competition, take into account this rise in costs. However, an indirect effect remains. Insofar as we are dealing with products for which demand fluctuates with price, the size of the market may decline and overall returns may diminish. The importance of price relationships has also been neglected. Milk and meat are in competition with each other. Support of milk diverts production from meat, which takes longer to produce. Thus a product of which there is a surplus obstructs the expansion of a product in short supply. Again, between cereals and meat there is competition for the use of land. Land which could yield an income based on an increasing demand for beef, is being diverted towards production which is constantly in need of support.

This is not all. Prices influence the level of costs. This is most markedly true in the case of land. We have witnessed extremely rapid increases in the price of land used for wheat. In a way, if the farmer owns the land, he gains twice, both in income and in the value of his capital. Cost-calculations which include the value of capital immobilized in the land (which has been increased as a result of high product prices) involve a vicious circle. On the other hand, in the case of farmers who do not own their land, actual costs are higher due to the increase in their rent payments.

We can go even further. We can question the advisability of setting common prices, when the economic conditions of agriculture differ so considerably from region to region. Economists teach us that to obtain the best distribution of resources, we must measure the cost of inputs, particularly the cost of labour used in the production of any one commodity, not (or not necessarily) by its actual remuneration, but by the value which these same inputs could produce in the best available alternative use. This is the theory of 'opportunity costs'. Thus, in a highly industrialized region of Germany, farmers must earn high returns in order to be retained in face of the competition for labour and the rising salaries offered by industry. In Southern Italy, on the other hand, surplus labour in agriculture has no other alternative than unemployment; even barely productive work is an improvement on none, a low income preferable to no income at all. These differences do not only prevail between member countries of the Community but also between areas within each country; indeed internal regional differences can be greater than those between countries. A conclusion can be drawn from this: part of the remuneration which should go to the farmers in the poorest regions is not based on the economic value of their activity but on social necessity. Raising prices uniformly in order to ensure an adequate living standard for the poorest farmers provides large windfall gains for more prosperous farmers, which are not justified by social needs. This problem can only be resolved if it is faced squarely: *that is to say, by basing market prices on market conditions and by providing discriminatory financial aid assuring a minimum income for the poorest farmer.*

The method of supporting incomes through supporting high prices entails, on the other hand, the risk that farmers will receive no corresponding benefit.

137

No one knows, when surplus products are bought by the intervention authorities, what part of the price paid by them will actually reach the agricultural producer. To this uncertainty must be added the enormous costs of sheer waste. Apples and pears must be discarded, beets must be distilled in order to be sold to the alcohol industry at a rock-bottom price. In most cases, exports do not even go to meet the food needs of people in the Third World countries who are hungry. Rather, they may effectively subsidize the food industries of competing countries, by supplying them with cheap agricultural raw materials furnished by the Community which may be processed into products which could then well be sold in the EEC's own market.

Increasing surpluses condemn the Community to a perpetual vicious circle. If too much sugar is produced, surplus molasses used for feed will limit the outlets for cereal feeding stuffs and the distilling of surplus beets will be in competition with the distilling of surplus wine. The wine agreement forbids any subsidies for planting additional vineyards, but nothing has yet been done to restrict government or even Community aid to finance orchards and cowsheds: this is a situation in which fruit has to be left to rot, and the cost of storing and subsidizing butter for export amounts to two dollars per pound.

Common Market and World Market

A few years ago, it was still possible to assume that continuously increasing world demand would allow us to consider the accumulation of surplus production as purely temporary: the latter was to be reabsorbed by the needs of the Eastern European countries, and even more so by the developing countries. The reports from international organizations were alarming: the explosive rate of increase in world population, the lag in the Third World's agricultural production, seemed to make famine a real threat. Faced with such great needs, it was not absurd to count on a rise in world prices. Given this prospect, the high prices within the Community would not have required strong support measures for very long; an overall evolution would even things out. These were, in particular, the premises of the Baumgartner/Pisani Plan, which proposed to allocate surpluses to an aid-in-kind, similar to that made by the Americans under the terms of Public Law 480. From a universal point of view, disregarding the division of markets according to nations, there is something irrational in slowing down production and even, as in America, reducing the acreage under cultivation, while so many countries are suffering from chronic malnutrition or deficiencies due to lack of proteins, and while so many countries take such trouble to grow crops in arid climates or on rocky soil.

The export of agricultural surpluses as aid was not necessarily the best way of helping development. It could slow down the greatly needed increase of production in the poor countries. At the same time it enabled rich countries to avoid the necessary reorientation of their production.

In any case world food prospects are changing. The developing countries are in the process of achieving a rapid increase in production, thanks to the introduction of relatively cheap techniques such as the improved selection of seeds. Market forecasts are taking on an entirely different aspect. The FAO as well as the OECD foresee increasing surpluses of cereals on a world wide scale, if North American production continues to grow at a fast rate. Whatever may be the failures encountered by the socialist countries, no doubt due to the fact that a collectivized agriculture does not offer the necessary incentives for the expansion of production, the shortages of the past cannot be extrapolated. Rising agricultural investment in tools and implements, the growing supply of fertilizers as well as the technical progress in new varieties of seed must all lead to an alleviation of shortages. If we look particularly at Great Britain, which is the largest importer of agricultural products in the world today, we see that farm production is continuing to increase – in fact it has increased, in the period 1960-66, at a higher annual percentage rate than that of any other Western industrial country. Britain seems likely to remain an importer of dairy products, but if she enters the Common Market and applies the price level fixed by the Community, she would be capable of increasing her cereal production to the point of becoming a net exporter.

All this calls for a reappraisal in more realistic terms of the Community's place in the world. Too narrow a perspective may conceal the underlying facts of the situation, which should best be considered in a worldwide context. Moreover, the financial mechanisms established by the Community can lead to a distorted view. It would seem that milk involves the greatest net burden. This feature derives from the structure of European farming. For the vast number of tiny farms in the Community, milk represents a regular income, even if the surplus of butter accumulates at a vertiginous rate. In a worldwide context, by contrast, the production forecasts, particularly in North America, demonstrate that even if it has been temporarily reabsorbed, the most serious surplus seems likely to be that of cereals.

The imbalance of agricultural prices within the Community stems from the high price fixed for wheat, which shows the largest gap between domestic and foreign prices. This high price has discouraged the production of other cereals and led to wheat surpluses. Further, the use of wheat for feeding stuffs is discouraged by its high price within the Community. Increases in the yield of wheat should have led to a reduction in the area used for this crop, the more so since rising real incomes in Europe have diminished the use of wheat for human consumption and created a greater demand for livestock. As a result a changed relationship between the price of wheat and that of coarse grains has become imperative. From a purely accounting point of view this need is concealed by the mechanism of the Common Agricultural Policy. Since the Community is a substantial net importer of cereals, mainly coarse grains, the higher the level of internal prices the higher the import levies which accrue. In this way high prices appear to be a source of revenue for the Community.

In the international context, the Community's activities tend to disrupt the world market, and to distort the division of labour and the flow of goods between countries. As a result, the Community has on several occasions found itself in conflict with powerful trading partners. The United States constantly seeks to maintain a market in Europe for its cereals and to expand its output of cereals despite surpluses in Europe and shortages elsewhere, and despite its own policies designed to prevent the importation of European dairy products. The figures for Community agricultural imports suggest that the United States has not been the main victim. For a while, American exports to the EEC continued to increase at a moderate rate, although more recently they have tended to stagnate or decline. The main victims of the protectionist stance of the Common Agricultural Policy have been the developing countries which export sugar or rice; it was the Community's policy for these products which prevented them from finding a market in the Community.

The meaningfulness of world prices may be questioned in the light of the present distorted nature of the world market. One method of determining world prices is to examine the prices paid by the largest importing country, Great Britain. Such an examination shows that for cereals this price is about the same as the prices received by producers in the main exporting countries, the United States and Canada. Even under the favourable conditions of production in Canada, there is an element of subsidy in the prices. Moreover, the similarity of the world price to prices received by producers in exporting countries disappeared when the International Wheat Agreement was broken. As a result prices in world markets fell below those paid to producers in exporting countries.

America bears a major responsibility for the low significance of world agricultural prices. Post war policy in the United States set agricultural prices at a level which bore little relationship to international values. When surpluses occurred plans were introduced to reduce the amount of land devoted to the production of unsaleable commodities. Yet the surpluses continued to increase, and with growing surpluses there was increasing pressure to sell these at cut prices in the world market – despite the fact that the United States has also given food aid to the tune of some two thousand million dollars annually. It could be said that world prices in the 1950s were roughly in an inverse relationship to domestic American prices. The Community has entered into this game wholeheartedly. When the Wheat Agreement was broken in 1969 it decided to make all the sacrifices necessary to undercut the lowest cost producers in the export markets.

The agricultural policies of the industrialized countries are increasingly caught up in a vicious circle: they all contribute to the collapse of world prices, and at the same time they are all condemned to protect themselves from the effects of low world prices in an even more uncompromising manner. Butter is the most extreme example. Under a regime of free competition the world market price would be established at a level that would just cover the costs of production of the highest cost producer whose output was still needed to meet the demand. What happens is the very opposite. The costs of production of the producer most favoured by climate and technological advance, New Zealand, should provide the basis for world prices. However, the Community being unable to find other outlets for its butter, subsidizes its export to the point of selling *below* the New Zealand price and thereby continually forces the New Zealand price to decline. The price for one hundred kilos of butter in London once went as low as $47.25; today it is $68 whilst the internal price of the Community exceeds $187.

Agricultural Policy and the Common Market

The Community has at least succeeded in achieving its objective of an agricultural Common Market and thereby ensured internal stability in agricultural prices.

It might have been expected that the gradual establishment of an agricultural Common Market would result in a better distribution of resources within the Community. This would have involved the expansion of production in low-cost areas and its decline in high-cost areas. Indeed, for most products, the objective of the free circulation of goods across the Community's internal frontiers has been progressively established as planned, and this process was completed by 1967 and 1968. For some products such as wine, which were initially excluded, it is being accomplished now.

But the establishment of the free circulation of goods has not led to any redistribution of production; on the contrary, everything has been done to prevent this from happening. Since the fundamental mechanism relies on fixing prices, price-competition is in fact extremely limited despite freedom of circulation. For cereals it operates only within the margin between threshold-prices (which form the basis of protection from outside) and intervention-prices (which are generally 7 per cent or 8 per cent lower) at which purchases by publicly financed bodies come into effect to maintain guaranteed price levels.

Large variations in inter-country purchases have taken place only in times of monetary difficulties. Prices are fixed in terms of a common currency unit, but each country translates these into its own national currency. Since the margin of exchange fluctuation permitted by the International Monetary Fund continues to operate between the countries of the Community, tensions in the balance of international payments, which caused variations in the exchange rate within the permitted margins (the German mark in one direction, the French franc in the other, before the latter was devalued and the former revalued) caused price fluctuations between countries in commodities with a fixed price in terms of the common unit of account. Thus in 1969 it was suddenly advantageous for Germany to make massive grain purchases in France. These were, in fact, cancelled after stabilization at the new rate of exchange.

The new price relations resulting from the revised rates of exchange were immediately accepted for industrial goods. But for agricultural products Germany at first maintained her old domestic price; from January 1st 1970 she had to accept the lower price, corresponding to the new rate of exchange, but has been authorized to compensate her farmers for the price reduction by subsidies taking the form of bonuses per hectare. France has raised her domestic prices only gradually after devaluation, though these should have been raised immediately if parity with the price expressed in units of account was to be maintained. Because of controls at the frontier and subsidies, the unity of prices in the Community was thus broken and has since remained a fiction – the prices specified in units of account are no longer applicable to either of the two largest producers within the Community. In abnormal times, as well as in normal times, the replacement of uneconomic by economic production has been carefully avoided.

Two factors in particular tend to favour these trends. The joint agricultural policy is limited to fixing prices, to protection by import levies, and to the financing of surpluses. Nothing prevents governments from extending national subsidies which distort cost relationships and, in particular, from promoting investments which compensate for natural disadvantages. Two distortions are particularly worthy of note. Among the countries of the Community, France alone finances the social security of farmers almost entirely through the budget. The normal system of social security is one of contributions based on earnings. This means that each branch of activity is taxed in proportion to the labour it employs. This is the basis on which the relationship of prices and exchanges is built. When a sector of activity like agriculture bears only about one-fifth of the cost of social security assessed in this way, the cost of those employed may turn out to be artificially low, and the monetary cost of their employment to be below its real cost.

In contrast, Germany subsidizes capital expenditure on land improvement much more generously than other countries. The result is a distorted relationship between investment and production. Subsidized investment tends to compensate for deficiencies in land and climate. The expenditures involved explain why costs remain high despite a high output per hectare.

The financial mechanism is really designed to avoid any serious reorganization of production between the different regions within the Community. If the market functioned normally, the producer who enjoyed the most favourable conditions would expand his production at the expense of other producers. Less well-placed farmers would be forced either to curtail their production, or to find a market at the best available price outside the Community. This means that, if the market were really 'free', it would be not France but Germany which would prove to have excess production and which would have to seek export markets to dispose of her output. Financial solidarity in buying up surplus production masks this effect, but also leads to the worst misunderstandings. When a German Minister complains that Germany bears a heavy financial burden because there are too many farmers in France, he is right in a way. His argument would be even stronger if he underlined the fact that French production would not appear so profitable, and the reduction in the number of farmers would proceed faster, but for the fact that Government expenditure on agricultural support is so much higher in France than elsewhere. But there is also another side to the problem. In the absence of a common effort to divert surpluses towards external markets, French supplies might be so large as to upset German markets and the German peasantry. Thus, it is equally true to say that Germany is paying a heavy financial contribution to protect her own farmers. In a word, a common agricultural market has been established only by divorcing that market from all its economic functions.

Unity of prices, whether it is the result of decision by the authorities or the result of market forces, has another justification. A part of the logic of the Common Market is to avoid some of the distortions arising in a free trade area. The system of the European Free Trade Area is familiar. This was designed to dispense with a common external tariff, and it excludes agriculture. The result is that industries competing with each other may receive imported supplies at different prices. Thus price differences remain in the case of food, which constitutes a basic factor in the determination of the level of wages and consequently in the conditions of industrial competition. In some countries wage rates are officially related to the consumer price index, and in the principal countries of the Community the weight of food expenditure in the construction of such indices is between 40 per cent and 45 per cent. This weight is considerably higher than the proportion of food expenditure in total consumer expenditure, and reflects the added importance of food in the budgets of low income consumers.

A customs union and an economic union, covering agriculture as well as services, and relating not only to products, but also to the factors of production, was intended to guard against such distortions. In particular, the unity of agricultural prices aimed at making it possible for the industries which process the products of agriculture to compete on fair terms. On the other hand, when we come to deal with the question of industrial wage costs, the decisive factor is not the prices of agricultural goods at the production level, but the prices paid by consumers. Since distributive margins and tax systems differ greatly between countries within the Community, uniformity of producer prices by no means ensures uniformity in the cost of food to the urban consumer.

Distortions

For want of direct action on the reform of the structure of agriculture and on real incomes, the Common Agricultural Policy hardly appears to be a policy. Because intervention at the national level is not regulated, and because the uniformity of prices has been disrupted by monetary problems, it is not truly common. When one considers the central role played by discussions of levies, contributions, subsidies and restitution payments, it appears to be more financial than agricultural.

AMONG COUNTRIES

The mounting number of difficulties could bring about a change. Since present policy causes blatant distortions, the resulting tensions between divergent interests might provide the key to the solution. It is possible to rouse certain groups, to stir up factions of public opinion, and to mobilize parts of the agricultural community. In other words, there might be a political issue for those who wish to bring about necessary changes. Serious distortions exist between member countries. The principle of financial solidarity between member countries in matters relating to agricultural policy is justified by the logic of the Common Market. However, it would seem rational that the size of each country's contribution should be in proportion to the size of its national revenue, and within each country it might further be related to individual income. But this is not the case, and the basic character of the problem derives from the fact that agriculture employs too many people. This accounts for lower productivity than in other sectors, as well as for a lower level of income. The redeployment of the farming population, which is inevitable, needs to be greatly assisted. The cost of improving productivity, raising incomes and facilitating departures is heavier the larger the proportion of the total active working population that is engaged in agriculture in a given country. On all these scores, it would seem obvious that the relative contribution of Italy should be the lowest, and the financial aid it receives the highest. However, the principle of the financial regulations which allocates all import levies to the common budget, results in Italy's paying into the Agricultural Fund for Orientation and Guarantee more than she receives. It should be possible to introduce, without very radical changes, a more logical and equitable distribution of Community payments.

AMONG CONSUMERS

Between the citizens of each country, another distortion arises.

The mechanism set up by the Community involves an intolerable contradiction. Nothing makes this more obvious than a brief comparison with the British system. If we exclude certain exceptions to the rule, such as high customs protection given to horticulture, and occasional import levies on imported cereals, the principle applied in Great Britain is to import at world prices for the domestic market. At the same time, farmers' returns are supplemented by means of deficiency payments, which make up the difference between guaranteed prices and the average market price. This system ensures that subsidies act in a normal manner. While maintaining a certain incentive level for farmers, they make it possible for consumer prices to be kept relatively low. What the taxpayer contributes in subsidies is partially restored to the consumer. The Community's mechanism consists not only of raising the cost of imports to the level of internal prices, but also – since this protection is insufficient – of supplementing such protection by public intervention to maintain internal prices. Everything that cannot find a normal outlet on the internal market must be financed out of public funds. The public authorities take on the financial burden of storing and denaturing products, and of the enormous price reductions which are sometimes necessary to export surpluses. Public expenditure in this case does not serve to lower prices but to raise them. The taxpayer, having contributed to finance exports, pays once more as a consumer through high prices.

It is a well-known law that the cost of food absorbs a proportion of income that is all the larger the lower the level of income, and the larger the size of the family. Therefore, a policy of high prices for agriculture, and more particularly for the basic products of agriculture such as wheat, automatically redistributes income at the expense of those who are the poorest. This would be seen more clearly if we imagined for a moment that agricultural prices were lowered and the decline compensated by equivalent payments financed from the budget. Nobody would dream of covering these additional public expenditures by indirect taxes imposed exclusively on food, still less by direct taxes on the lowest income groups – there would be immediate cries of inequity. Such is, however, the exact manner in which a policy of high agricultural prices affects the distribution of real income.

143

The British system operates in the opposite manner: the consumers benefit from favourable prices, the producers' returns are raised by deficiency payments financed by a progressive income tax and highly differentiated indirect taxes, from which food products are exempt, and which are heavier on the more luxurious articles of consumption. Although we do not here recommend that the British system be applied within the Community, that aspect of it which relates to the distribution of the costs of policy between taxpayers and consumers gives food for thought.

AMONG PRODUCTS

The most obvious distortions exist among different agricultural products. The most progressive agricultures, such as those of Denmark, Holland and Great Britain, have been engaged in the processing of farm products into goods of higher value for which there is a growing demand. From this point of view, the agricultural policy of the Common Market is a regressive one. It favours cereals and sugar beet and thereby raises the costs of processed products such as poultry, eggs, pork and beef. The important exception to this, the duty-free imports of oil seeds and oil cakes, is also an obvious contradiction. It is true that cereals and molasses provide the carbohydrate, while oil cakes provide the fats and proteins needed to feed cattle. However, as in human diets, the precise ratio between these different types of food is not fixed. Under the pressure of high cereal prices oil cakes can be substituted for cereals in greater or lesser degree.

Another type of distortion between products occurs because cereals and wheat benefit from unlimited guarantees, while intervention in fruit and vegetable markets is much more arbitrary. Unquestionably these products are much more varied and subject to extreme seasonal fluctuations, which make it more difficult to have an organized market. We have already noted the relatively higher elasticity of demand for these products, so that in times of increased production, larger volumes of sales compensate to a certain extent for lower prices. In the case of fruit trees, however, difficulties may arise from the time-lag between the decision to produce and the first crops harvested. Production may be reacting to the shortages and consequent high prices of several years earlier. The result is that for apples and pears, no other solution has been found for surpluses than to destroy them. It is most regrettable that horticultural produce, for which demand is growing, seems to be at a disadvantage compared with cereals, at a time when wheat represents a constantly decreasing fraction of the human diet.

Finally we must consider the effects of policy on the use of land for the production of cereals, meat or milk. Despite growing shortages of meat and surpluses of milk the only contribution which has been made to a better use of resources is the introduction of premiums for the slaughter of dairy cows. In fact the operation of the policy means that despite rising consumer prices for meat products the producer of livestock lacks the necessary incentive to increase his output.

Inequality between products necessarily entails distortions between different types of farms. Cereal cultivation is for the most part concentrated on large farms. The difficult working conditions facing some farmers serve as an alibi for the high level of prices, but these prices benefit the more fortunate ones in proportion to their size, their use of more modern methods and their ability to achieve economies of scale. Inequality in returns between farmers has increased under the Common Agricultural Policy.

It is one thing to observe that small farms cannot be profitable, that they condemn a man who works alone to the loss of all freedom and of any possibility of rest or vacation; it is another thing to increase the difficulties of such a farmer in a misguided attempt to protect him. In fact, this is just what results from high prices for cereals and sugar beet. The situation of the small stockbreeder or milk-producer is made worse, first by the fact that his costs are raised, and second because the financial resources of the large farms which compete with him are unduly increased.

AMONG FARMERS

Nothing is more misleading than to believe that agriculture represents a homogeneous entity. It is largely in response to the claims of the small farms that the large ones have obtained the greatest advantages. These now turn out to be to the detriment of the very small farms they were intended to help. There are at least two kinds of agriculture. It cannot for a moment be denied that the more competitive farms must expand or that the more backward must be absorbed into new units. The main task is to facilitate this gradual transformation of the structure of agriculture. However, it is the worst-placed farmers who are today the more numerous. Their support can only be obtained if it is possible to improve their lot immediately. It is on this basis alone that a course could be adopted which, by transforming agriculture, would raise the standard of living of all farmers.

Fundamental Ideas for a Policy

An agricultural policy is indispensable. Market instability arises less from changes in demand than from unforeseeable variations in weather and production conditions which affect the volume of output from year to year. Technical progress, such as irrigation, drainage, improved seed varieties and better control of plant and animal diseases has reduced instability arising from natural causes. It is possible to envisage a stage at which the industrialization of farming will largely protect it from such ups and downs. Even if in the more highly developed countries farmers succeed in reducing the impact of changes in the weather, less developed competitors will still be affected by such unpredictable changes giving rise to an instability which is inevitably contagious.

Another factor of prime importance is that agricultural production requires time – several months for crops, several years for some livestock production. Thus, production which is encouraged by prices ruling at any one time may no longer correspond to market requirements when the products become available. This results in cycles which have been the subject of empirical as well as theoretical studies. To be sure, industry must cope with similar uncertainties, and the gestation period of investment in industry is generally even longer. However, industry is more capable of maintaining its own prices by regulating the supplies reaching the market than is agriculture. The agricultural situation is made more difficult because production in excess of market needs is likely to be accompanied by a sharp fall in prices, thus greatly reducing income.

The delay between the decision to produce and the subsequent availability of the goods produced and the response of both supply and demand to price changes varies greatly between products. For example, a drop in the price of cereals is unlikely to enlarge the market, while a fall in milk prices might, at least within certain limits, encourage small farmers to intensify their production or increase deliveries to dairies in order to maintain their level of returns. Products such as pork, poultry and eggs, take less time to adjust to price changes, whilst consumption reacts more strongly to price fluctuations. New fruit orchards take a long time to mature, but there is some consolation in the fact that consumption expands when prices fall.

The implication is that stabilization measures cannot be dispensed with. They are all the more necessary since regularity of income is the major incentive encouraging technical progress and greater productivity in agriculture. Moreover, the fluctuations to which primary agricultural production is subject are well known, as are the disastrous repercussions that sometimes occur in developing countries. There can be no question of abandoning agriculture to such fluctuations; on the contrary, everything possible should be done to extend a degree of stability to the rest of the world. Until worldwide stability can be attained, there remains an obligation to discover a means, on a national or community level, to limit instability.

As soon as production is separated from market conditions we face further difficulties.

The Level of Productivity

The fundamental problem lies elsewhere. Agriculture, in Europe at least, is essentially directed towards food-production. Its contribution to the textile industry is entirely marginal. It is well known that the demand for food increases relatively slowly with increases in real income. This causes the total incomes earned in agriculture to rise more slowly in comparison with the incomes earned in industry; to maintain the same rate of growth of incomes per head is only possible if there is an adequate rate of decline in the numbers engaged in agriculture.

Given the conditions within which the average farmer works inside the European Economic Community, his productivity may provide him with only a shockingly low income compared with average income levels ruling in member countries. What counts here is not the yield per acre: in certain regions and for certain crops these are the highest in the world; what determines income is the net production per working person, that is to say, the value added by the industry, divided by the number of people involved. A high output per acre may result from the use of inputs bought from other sectors, which do not form part of the value added by farming. These costs must be deducted from total receipts before calculations can be made of the sum available to remunerate land, capital and labour.

Productivity comparisons are rather ambiguous. A general measure can only be obtained by considering the value of total production; this calculation immediately raises the objection that high prices for agricultural goods result in an artificially high estimate of productivity. Prices existing within the Community, shielded by protection and benefiting from public purchases of surplus produce, are much higher than those in neighbouring countries, such as Great Britain or Denmark. If we were to apply world market prices to Community production we should arrive at considerably lower figures for the value of production, and for productivity.

There are certain rough comparisons which are nevertheless helpful. The Community, which produces a surplus of some products, but imports others, is self-sufficient on the average. It employs 14 per cent of its working population in farming. Such an average conceals great differences between member countries. The proportion of work force engaged in agriculture is about 22 per cent in Italy, 14 per cent in France, 10 per cent in Germany, 8 per cent in Holland and 5 per cent in Belgium.

Here again, we could argue at length about figures. The number of wage-earners and of farm owners is clear. However, the comparison with other sectors raises the question of the number of hours per year actually worked. These may be considerably higher or lower in agriculture than in industry. To estimate the number of family helpers, women and children, presents almost insuperable difficulties. Depending on the country, statistical conventions sometimes count each one as a full time worker, or may apply a reduction coefficient which takes into account the fact that in most cases family helpers provide only part-time work. Thorough studies are being made in the Community to attempt to find homogeneous equivalents for a full time unit of measurement. The results of this more rigorous system of measurement would perhaps bring the population actually employed in agriculture nearer to 12 per cent than 14 per cent. This correction is essential for comparing incomes in the agricultural sector with those in other sectors, but it does not alter the hard facts.

It suffices to look at those countries where agricultural techniques are most advanced. In the United States today, only 5 per cent of the working population is engaged in agriculture; of this it is estimated that one quarter contributes three quarters of the products sold. With so low a percentage of the labour force in agriculture, the United States is still the largest exporter in the world. In New Zealand only 7 per cent of the population is engaged in farming, but three quarters of its production is exported. Great Britain produces some 60 per cent of its food requirements although only 3 per cent of its working population is employed in farming.

The conclusions seem inescapable: under circumstances which are normal in other advanced countries, the Community would be able to satisfy its own needs with only one third as many farmers as now.

These rough figures are in agreement with overall findings regarding the value added per capita. In the three main countries of the Community, per capita value added in agriculture is approximately half that in industry and services. The comparison would appear even more unfavourable if the method of calculation had used prices lower than those maintained in the Common Market.

The past weighs heavily in this matter. In the 19th century, when agricultural products began to flow in from the new countries, Germany, France and Italy chose to protect their own agriculture. Great Britain allowed low cost imports to enter freely and accepted the inevitable contraction of her agriculture. Holland became a specialist in buying cereals as a raw material for the manufacture of food for animal products of much higher value.

The recent past has also had its influence. War and post-war shortages led to incentives to increase agricultural production at virtually any price. West Germany, cut off from the agricultural areas of East Germany, increased her subsidies for investment in land. Italy, suffering from massive unemployment, had no desire to reduce the number of her farmers. This would have simply added to unemployment. In its Fourth Plan, France, relying on the prospect of the Common Market, made the mistake of setting as its objective an increase in agricultural production without proper regard to the costs involved.

The Limits to Labour Mobility

This situation is changing. The rate of growth of agricultural productivity is greater than that of industry almost everywhere: if this continues long enough, the difference in productivity levels would disappear. But this spectacular progress, at the rate of 6 per cent to 7 per cent per year, creates as many difficulties as it resolves, for it mixes inextricably two essentially different elements: one is a technical revolution, the other a reduction in employment. The volume of agricultural sales increases much more slowly than that of industry.

Workers leave the industry because of the relatively unfavourable situation in which they find themselves. Such migration is evidence both of the increased efficiency of labour, given the systematic use of new techniques, and of the high degree of hidden unemployment which exists in farming. In effect, the marginal contribution made by labour to output has only been apparent, since in fact far fewer people could produce the same volume of goods. The Mansholt Report estimates that 80 per cent of the farms within the Community are unable to provide full time employment even for one person. At this stage the human problem comes to the fore. The reality confronting agricultural and employment policy is the limit set to the possible number of departures from the industry. The task of policy is to accelerate the rate of outflow, while facilitating re-employment and softening its painful aspects.

If the composition of the active agricultural population is considered in greater detail, several elements can be seen to operate which are likely to cause the outward movement to take place by fits and starts. The category of employment which has diminished most rapidly is that of the agricultural wage-earners. These no longer represent more than a small fraction of agricultural labour. Family helpers, too, are turning towards other activities. The hard core is represented by the farmers themselves. It is impossible to be insensitive to their attachment to the land, to their wish to preserve their independence, or their desire to avoid falling into the status of wage-earner. Thus, for the time being, the Community is likely to see a slow-down in the rate of reduction of the agricultural population, despite the fact that this is the main method by which the value of production per capita in agriculture may be raised to the level of other sectors. There is, however, another factor of major importance. The average age of farm owners is very high – 57 years. In due course there should be a sudden acceleration in the reduction of the farming population, provided that the matter were well handled. The Community's sense of solidarity ought to operate generously for those currently working the land, but it is necessary to avoid extending to later generations the benefits which are justified for the present one. To do so would needlessly perpetuate an untenable state of affairs.

The difficulty is even greater than averages reveal. The agricultural problem is intermingled with the regional problem. Today, within each country, there are enormous disparities from one area to another in the proportion of the working population engaged in agriculture. France still has some regions in which it rises above 30 per cent, Italy some above 50 per cent. Contrary to what is needed to attain a satisfactory equilibrium, it is in the regions where the proportion of the population in agriculture is greatest that the rate of reduction is the slowest. This is almost to be expected. Agricultural workers in the proximity of industrial urban centres have been lured away already. In some cases their exodus has been so rapid that some farmers are short of workers. As a result the age pyramid becomes unfavourable: productivity falls, owing to the small proportion of the agricultural labour force which is at the height of its powers. The farther agricultural workers are from the centre of industrial growth, the larger the proportion of the population working in agriculture, the lower is their productivity and the slower their rate of re-employment in other sectors. Worse still, in many such areas traditional industries, organized on too narrow a basis, are soon jeopardized by competition from other areas, so that difficulties accumulate. Often unemployment in industry bars the only remaining exit from hidden unemployment in agriculture.

These changes cannot be ignored at the present stage of industrial development. As fresh air, pure water and open country become more and more scarce it becomes increasingly urgent to prevent the formation of deserted regions, existing side by side with over-populated urban centres. Thus there is a new aspect to agricultural policy. It merges with regional policy and provides an opportunity to create a new service industry devoted to the conservation of natural reserves, made more necessary by the frightening progress of pollution, and more profitable because of the growth of tourism from the cities associated with greater leisure and higher incomes.

Market size and Farm size

For these immense tasks, the widening of markets alone is not enough. Where industry is concerned, the free circulation of products and the creation of large scale common markets in themselves bring about a redistribution of production and specialization by factories which permit the exploitation of economies of scale to an increasing extent. Each component can be produced on a mass-production basis in specialized production units integrated into a continuously expanding overall programme. In broad outline, this is the secret of industrial expansion and of the strength of multi-national enterprises which can fully utilize this method of increasing productivity. In agriculture, things work very differently. Market size does not seem to affect production costs greatly. No matter how large a farm may be, it never represents more than a tiny fraction of the total supplies on the market. Thus, the existence and size of the European market alone is not sufficient to transform the profitability of agriculture.

In agriculture economies of scale operate on a completely different level. Below a certain size (which varies with the nature of cultivation) farms are unable to provide full time employment. The Mansholt Report sets standards. With modern techniques, cereals cannot be economically cultivated in Europe on a farm of less than 80 to 120 hectares; the production of milk requires 40 to 60 cows; the production of meat 150 to 200 head of cattle, that of pork 400 to 600 head, and of chickens, 100,000. These figures relate to the present state of techniques which are themselves rapidly changing.

With modern industrialized methods of pig or poultry husbandry, the area of land involved is of little importance. In its final version, the Mansholt Plan meets this difficulty by establishing a measure which is more widely applicable. This is the value of production sold from the *farm*, less the purchased agricultural inputs used in the process of production. The amount so calculated is referred to by the rather mysterious term 'rectified gross product'. It is on farms which fall below a minimum value of 'rectified gross product' that the whole problem comes to light, especially where a farmer works alone. Not only is his income bound to be low, but particularly when he is engaged in livestock production, he is condemned to near-slavery which makes it impossible for him to take a day off or to go on holiday.

Economies of scale can be analyzed in greater detail. In terms of the number of people employed, the level beyond which productivity no longer increases and costs in terms of hours of work do not decrease is soon reached. This condition is probably satisfied on farms employing no more than 4 or 5 people. For some types of enterprise it may be as low as 2 persons. This situation is in strong contrast to that obtaining in manufacturing industry where economies of scale are not exhausted even when the individual business employs many thousands of workers. However, in agriculture, economies of scale are very important when the size of the farm in terms of area covered is suboptimal, which invariably involves a misallocation of labour in relation to land. Gains can also be obtained by increasing the scale of operation in the purchase of inputs and the marketing of output. Moreover in agricultural processing activities economies of scale are continually increased by technical progress in the same way as in other types of industrial activity. Hence unless agricultural production is redistributed into optimal-sized units the gap between the structure which is technically possible and that which actually exists will continue to widen.

As things stand, agricultural employment involves considerable hidden unemployment so that output per worker is only a fraction of what it could be; this factor is mainly responsible for the very large differences in productivity between more and less efficient farms. We are dealing here with a vast, but relatively new, problem. So long as agriculture depended essentially on manual labour, with the aid of such primitive tools as the plough and the scythe, the size of the farm was of no great consequence, any more than the size of the market. Today, it is possible to operate profitably on farms with a small number of hectares only in the case of market gardens which supply nearby urban centres: this requires an intensive labour input as well as considerable capital investment. But apart from this case, the technical revolution created by machines that are capable of sowing, spraying or harvesting vast areas of land has caused the size of production units to become a decisive element in costs. The situation is worse for those farms which comprise a number of widely separated parcels of land. Under these conditions, modern methods cannot be fully exploited and the problem is compounded by time lost in going from one piece of land to another. The only possible remedy is the consolidation of land holdings. Schemes to secure this have often been introduced; their execution requires Penelope's never-ending patience; they are retarded by peasant resistance, as well as by the chronic shortage of land surveyors, and their effects are constantly undermined by new partitioning resulting from inheritance.

So far as agriculture is concerned the competitive process which causes efficient units to replace inefficient ones faces a peculiar obstacle. In the case of manufacturing industry it is always possible for an expanding firm to enlarge its capacity by building new factories – it does not have to acquire the use of existing buildings from other firms in order to enlarge its production. In agriculture on the other hand – excepting the case of pork, poultry and egg production which no longer require a sizeable land area for large-scale production – the enlargement of a farm necessary for high-productivity output depends on the additional land being made available. It is only as some farms disappear that the remaining farms can expand the area which they cultivate. Although the agricultural population is falling at a rate of 3 per cent a year only 1–2 per cent of farm holdings are abandoned each year. Moreover there is no means of ensuring that the land of the abandoned farm is integrated with existing farms in such a way as to improve the ratio between the area of land cultivated and the work force employed – which is the decisive factor in the modernization of extensive agriculture.

This is the basic difference between agriculture in North America or the Soviet Union and that of Western Europe. However rapid progress there may be, as a result of technical improvements and outward migration, the level of output per worker is only a fraction of what it would be if the individual farm unit had sufficient land at its disposal. In Europe, even in the largest and most modern agricultural enterprises there is generally more equipment and labour than can be fully utilized. If the same labour and capital input could be spread over larger areas, and effectively used for many more hours per year, cost of production would be greatly reduced. But in the agricultural sector (in contrast to industry) the growth of the successful farm is inescapably linked to the disappearance of others. It is only through a large-scale reduction in the number of farms that economies of scale in farming can be properly realised. Thus, the most consistent, the most humane policy, designed to make land available and provide the farmers with more productive employment, will at the same time raise the standard of living for the poorer farmers and make for accelerated progress in agriculture as a whole.

Nothing would be more dangerous than to underestimate the difficulties. There are no miraculous solutions. The differences in climate and the quality of land are enormous, and so are those in the training and skills of the population. Such differences exist within regions and not only between them. The required investments are not only in material assets but also in human resources. Furthermore, since vast numbers of farms are involved, most of which are of a very small size, it is doubtful whether these small units can adapt to the market, or their separate response to even the best thought-out policies correspond to the needs of a satisfactory overall balance.

Obstacles to the International Division of Labour

Apart from the question of the internal restructuring of agriculture, there is also another policy issue which is even more difficult to implement and which presents another contradiction. Different parts of the world possess widely differing advantages for the production of particular products, depending on differences in climate, the quality of the soil and the cost of labour. All countries would gain from a division of labour which enabled them to concentrate production on their most highly productive agricultural operations. This would result both in higher income for agriculture and lower costs for the entire economy, particularly for industry. No fundamental justification can be found for agricultural protectionism.

The whole development of economic thought in Great Britain during the first half of the 19th century was based on a gigantic campaign for the repeal of the Corn Laws. From 1815, following the temporary cessation of imports during the Napoleonic Wars, import quotas were fixed on wheat in such a way as to stabilize internal prices. Below a certain level of price, imports were prohibited; above a certain level they were freed altogether. With the repeal of the Corn Laws, England drew rapidly ahead of all other countries in the development of her industry; this involved accepting free competition in agricultural products and, as its sequel, the rapid reduction in the size of the farming population.

But several considerations militate against the acceptance of this economic logic in Europe. The first is time – that is to say the necessarily long period needed to reduce the size of the agricultural population. The second is the experience of two wars and the interruption of maritime transport which they brought about. Thus, during the Second World War, Great Britain intensified the exploitation of her soil and also the efficiency of her farmers. What is this argument worth today? The Swiss use it to justify their farm policies and their ridiculous price levels. Nevertheless, it is hard to conceive in present circumstances that the maintenance of an excess population in agriculture could, in case of conflict, constitute a military advantage. First of all, there is no given relationship between the volume of production and the size of the working population engaged in it – quite the contrary. Second, one must bear in mind that in case of conflict there are only two possibilities: either essential transport will be maintained or the conflict will be so global and will reach such a high degree of escalation that producers on the inside as well as suppliers on the outside will be unable to continue their production or to deliver it. Such remote hypotheses can offer no justification for a constant weakening of the economy.

A third problem, the burden placed on the balance of payments by agricultural imports, has led Germany during her period of reconstruction, as well as Great Britain in more recent years, to encourage agricultural production, thereby slowing down the rate at which labour leaves the land. This is a risky business – what is gained on one side of the account may be lost on the other. If the rise in food costs, which constitute the very base of the cost of living, reduces – through its consequential effect on money wages – the competitive capacity of industry, losses in exports may exceed the savings made on imports.

There is, finally, one other major consideration. No one denies the necessity to limit fluctuations in the market so as to obtain economic conditions of production and to secure tolerable living conditions in agriculture. But stabilization schemes remain a national or, in the case of Europe, a Community affair. The very incomplete and precarious international agreements which have been made – for example for wheat, and in the case of tropical products, for coffee – have been of limited effectiveness, and have periodically broken down. However, freedom of trade on a durable basis, which would be to everyone's advantage, cannot be conceived unless it is accompanied by price-stabilization schemes on an international scale.

Such are the contradictions waiting to be resolved. The European Community might have provided the opportunity to initiate more rational policies than individual countries have been able to accomplish in the past. Up to now this opportunity has been missed. But another opportunity remains. This is to bring to bear on world affairs the considerable weight of the group of countries already constituted (and which will soon be even greater if it is enlarged by the entry of other countries) in order to persuade their principal trading partners to accept a policy of market stabilization which would permit freer trade in agricultural goods.

A Fundamental Choice

The Community must itself have a policy in the proper sense of the word. It can only have one when a fundamental choice has been made. The Community must determine whether it seeks an agriculture so efficient that it can export on a large scale, and meet competition in outside markets, without financial aid or subsidies. In this case an effort at rapid rationalization is necessary. This requires an unswerving reduction in over-employment, a concentration of production into large units which can use the most modern techniques, and the attainment of the highest possible productivity for agricultural labour.

Until now the Community has taken the opposite road. Its system of variable tax levies, the strong protection it applies to its agricultural market, and the unlimited subsidies that it authorizes in order to maintain the internal price of commodities with export surpluses, has allowed its price level to be entirely out of line with that of its competitors. It is as though the Community's major criterion were the need to be self-sufficient and to treat both imports and exports as anomalies.

In one of his phrases, as vigorous as it was irrational, General de Gaulle declared that the mark of a Community was that it produced its own food. Why food rather than energy or industrial goods? An over-protected agriculture does not succeed in ensuring a living wage to the majority of its farmers and, because of the expenditures it entails, constantly reduces the competitive capacity of the rest of the economic community.

A third road remains open. The Community need not decide in advance to be a net importer or exporter. This should depend for each product on the prices at which it is able to sell profitably by comparison with its principal competitors. This method would allow the farmers' income to be maintained through their own efforts, it would operate for the better use of their resources, and for raising their standard of living, and finally would confront international trade in agricultural products with its opportunities and *raison d'être*. It is a change which cannot be effected in a day. The transformation of structures, the delays and limitations imposed by concern for the fate of individuals, set a minimum to the time required. But the more time that is required for a plan, the more urgent it is to embark upon it.

Such are the essential lines of action without which there can be no effective agricultural policy. Past experience, however, teaches us that agricultural policy is often considered in too isolated a context. To work satisfactorily it must be integrated in an overall economic policy with which it must form a coherent whole. Above all, action to raise the living standards of farmers, by enabling them to find new jobs, depends upon industrial and regional policies, which lie outside the limits of agricultural policy as such.

An Industrial Policy

Here, too, the difficulties are enormous. The Commission of the EEC has tackled both of its tasks. The delay which occurred in formulating an industrial policy seems all the more astonishing since agriculture, which has been the object of so much attention by the different institutions, represents only 7 per cent of total production as against 50 per cent for industry. In industry also, there are acute structural problems in the Community, and the most spectacular aspect of industrial change is the growth of the large concern and the movement towards concentration which in the last few years has led to the amalgamation of some firms which had already been among the largest.

But this phenomenon is perhaps misleading. As the big enterprises expand, their turnover is sometimes inflated mainly by an increase in their purchases from external suppliers. In other words, the concentration is less evident when we look at their added value, or the labour employed, than if we measure it by the volume of sales. The most precise structural data available derive from an industrial census carried out in all the countries of the Community, based on data relating to around 1962. So far as we can judge, there is an undeniable trend in Germany towards the concentration of the labour force in the most important enterprises. In Holland, where industry is essentially a creation of the last 25 years, we find not only some of the largest enterprises in the Community, but also medium-sized firms which are considerably larger than those elsewhere. In France, Italy, and Belgium on the other hand, it would appear that the structure of industry – that is to say, its distribution over enterprises of different sizes – remains substantially unchanged, except for the steady contraction of units of less than ten persons – i.e., those enterprises which do not, properly speaking, belong to manufacturing industry.

Fortunately, size is not everything. The essence of economies of scale is specialization. That is what makes it possible for large enterprises, and particularly those working at a multi-national level, to produce, or to acquire, each part of each article from establishments which manufacture them at the lowest cost. We can see the outlines of a structure in which small enterprises could, as in the United States, prove themselves to be perfectly competitive thanks to a form of specialization which integrates them into wider industrial processes. They may even be so efficient that they do not become dependent on a large enterprise, but can negotiate on an equal footing with several large firms competing with one another.

The fundamental problem of industrial policy is not only to enable Europe to have a secure place in the most advanced technological sectors. This particular task requires a co-ordinated effort going beyond national frontiers, organizing a division of labour between the countries and abolishing the various forms of protection which stem from the current exercise of government controls by the separate states. Nor is it a highly complex problem of how to expand enterprises which are already enormous, without guaranteeing them a monopolistic position that would stifle their energy. The basic and most difficult problem is to transform the general structure of the innumerable enterprises which today manufacture on a small scale goods that can only be efficiently manufactured on a large scale. These firms must become far more specialized, and it is this alone which would enable them to provide steadier employment and a higher standard of living for their workers, through the enlargement of their markets and the reduction in their costs.

A Regional Policy

This remodelling of industry can contribute to the renovation of agriculture the more it is linked to an effective regional policy. Efforts to slow down the concentration of industry and services in a small number of increasingly congested areas, and the encouragement of industrial development in the so-called agricultural areas, is a fundamental part of any efficient plan for agriculture.

All countries attempt, by tax reductions or by public subsidies, to encourage decentralization. These efforts encounter numerous obstacles. No country succeeds in making the enterprises in the large industrial and urban centres bear the true costs of their development, costs which increase extremely rapidly for land, for the organization of transportation systems, or simply for the supply of water. No local fiscal system charges all these social costs either to industry or to the inhabitants. The result is that, by and large, these concentrations are subsidized by the rest of the country, through the public purse; in effect by a sort of back-handed redistribution, by not taxing them enough in relation to other enterprises. In this way, part of the direct aid allocated to decentralization serves only to moderate the discrimination against them, which provides an artificial stimulus to concentration.

In certain countries, moreover, the efforts to develop infrastructures, especially for transportation and communication, without which outlying regions cannot develop, are wholly inadequate. It is also doubtful whether the instruments used to distribute financial aid to the regions are appropriate for their purposes. They generally take the form of assistance for investment. This encourages industries utilizing heavy equipment rather than employing labour in large numbers. In order to re-employ redundant farmers, as well as workers employed in archaic industrial enterprises or in costly forms of distribution, it is necessary to give incentives to industries or services to employ as many men as the conditions of profitable business can justify. In this respect, it must be recognized that the methods now in force in Britain are more direct, and are better adapted to the situation. Their practical effect is to tax employment in services and in congested areas, and to use the financial resources so gained to subsidize industrial employment in decentralized areas.

In any case the decentralization of education, and the multiplication of institutions designed for retraining, form a fundamental part of any policy of growth and modernization, and of any regional policy. Farmers are legitimately sensitive to the obstacles they encounter in obtaining for their children an education comparable to that available in the towns. If it is admitted that subsidies to farming must be limited in time, and be given only to the present incumbents and not be transmitted to their successors, it becomes all the more imperative that their sons be given the means to follow a different career and be trained for different professions.

The prospects opening up for modern society make it clear, moreover, that the reduction of the agricultural population is not to be confused with rural depopulation. The need for clean air, for relaxation after having worked in the city, makes green spaces additionally valuable, and lends greater importance to those services which cater for a new type of tourism – that of weekends. This creates a variety of secondary activities which can complement the work of farmers, one of whose functions is their role as guardians of open spaces. An important conclusion emerges. The creation of new industrial growth-points in various regions, the better distribution of industrial location to provide the job opportunities and their combination with the new occupations in the countryside, and last but not least, the development of an infrastructure without which there can be no development, cannot be accomplished except by regional planning. These interdependent objectives must be considered as a whole.

Proposals for an Agricultural Policy

The very announcement of a change is already a change which produces salutary effects.

No time should be lost in modifying present policies. Current investment will continue to influence the level of production for a long time. Mistaken investment decisions involve two types of cost: the immediate cost of the new equipment and the longer run cost of coping with surplus output. Everyone is aware that considerable sacrifices must be made to reform agriculture. A long history of relatively low productivity means that a rapid reduction in the number of people employed in the industry must be achieved or incomes will compare increasingly less favourably with those in other sectors. There is, however, a fundamental difference between expenditure which will reduce the long-term cost of adjustment and that which, by adding to output, will simply involve an ever growing level of expenditure in future.

The Mansholt Plan

The EEC Commission has clearly recognised this and since 1968, guided by its Vice-President in charge of agriculture, Sicco Mansholt, has courageously proposed a total recasting of agricultural policy. It recognizes that a policy which has protected markets, supported prices at a high level, and financed from common funds the storage and export of surpluses, has not provided any basic solution. It therefore suggests a direct and vigorous attack on the problem of changing agricultural structures. Based on the memorandum known as the Mansholt Plan, the first plans for regulations have just been drawn up and will be submitted to the Community's Council of Ministers. They constitute a *detailed implementation* of the proposals contained in the Plan.

In essence, they contain interrelated measures designed to accelerate and facilitate a reduction in the agricultural population and to attain a better utilization of land by regrouping farms and by attaching parcels of land, available from more rapid outward migration, to larger units. Four provisions complete this scheme. One reduces the area of farmland by using part of it for reafforestation or the creation of national parks and recreation areas. Another leads to the grouping together of farmers, so that they can bypass market intermediaries and come into direct dealings with processing industries.

The third provision emphasizes the role of training and knowledge in order to secure better understanding among farmers of opportunities and obstacles. Finally, the Commission has drawn attention to the consequences of the difficulties encountered in Community procedure: the lengthy discussions in the Council, the manifold crises, the bad compromises, and the administration's

156

constant responsibility for making detailed decisions; and urged that the farmers' organizations should take over the essential function of market management.

In all these aspects, the Mansholt Plan is revolutionary in character and offers decisive progress in comparison with the past. Up to now, despite the declarations of intent, the major part of the expenditures has been used for price support. What remained of Community funds for market orientation has been used to subsidize investments in storage or the modernization of fixed equipment. It has often happened, as with expenditures by individual governments, that this financial assistance has ignored market conditions and contributed to increasing surpluses of cereals, milk or fruit.

The structural policy proposed now is quite a different matter. Through the association of small farms, or the strengthening of more advanced ones, it aims to establish production units of sufficient scale to permit the lowering of costs, the liberation of farmers from the slavery resulting from working alone, and adaptation to market changes.

This restructuring would be accompanied by financial aid to units forming groups or seeking to expand. Within a very few years, things might develop to the point where only those farms which were capable of using appropriate methods and which attained a certain minimum size – either on account of their own expansion or of their association with other units – would be allowed to benefit from Community or State support.

Additional measures are designed to assist a more rapid reduction in the number of farm owners. Some of these are intended for all farmers, regardless of age. Farmers would be offered large sums to put their land at the disposal of larger units, while retaining ownership of the land if they so chose. These premiums would be granted as a contribution to restructuring. Other measures are aimed at older farm owners and offer them a substantial retirement pension which could be taken from the age of 55. Unlike the measures adopted in some countries (in France for example) such assistance would only be given on condition that land which the pensioners agreed to leave would not be cultivated again in the same uneconomic conditions, but would become part of a larger unit.

At the other end of the scale, it is proposed to help younger farmers to find new employment by means of education and retraining. The Plan pays insufficient attention to the fact that the chances of successful reorientation attracting farmers to better jobs in industry or in services will be the greater the more there is a sustained rate of economic growth throughout the Community. The memorandum refers to efforts which must be made towards a regional policy. Agriculture is all the more deprived, and the reduction in its working population is all the slower, in areas where industry is but little developed or where it is inefficient, or where existing industry tends to disappear owing to outside competition.

We cannot help but admire the vigour with which the Plan stresses some of the more serious difficulties, and the vigour with which it sets about transforming the structure of farming. We must also admire the courage and perseverance with which its originator confronted the agricultural world, tried to overcome its first hostile reactions and to avert misunderstandings; and tried to make as many farmers as possible understand where their true interests lie. The real choice for most farmers is between continuing an increasingly mediocre and oppressive existence, or accepting a new status enabling them to make better use of the land, to retire with a substantial income, or to prepare themselves for employment in other activities. The situation is aggravated by the fact that certain political parties seek to exploit it demagogically, by attempting to persuade the peasant masses that they could survive with their outmoded farms if only they were spared competition from more modern enterprises. This amounts to deliberately misleading them about the possible income to be derived from such a retreat into backwardness, and also about the limits to the amount of assistance which the rest of the community will be ready to accept, if agricultural aid continues to grow at an insupportable rate.

Additional Measures

We would like to be able to say that the Mansholt Plan is an effective answer to the problems of European Agriculture. But further analysis reveals certain contradictions which will stand in its way unless it is complemented by other provisions. There is no honestly conceived agricultural policy for the European Community which does not spring from the Mansholt Plan and does not retain its essential provisions. Even so, we cannot overlook the additional measures which will be called for. It is in this spirit that the proposals which follow are made: they bear in mind the necessity of presenting a policy as a whole in which seemingly unpalatable measures are inserted into their proper context, and are accompanied by counterparts which make them not only acceptable but attractive.

In this perspective, it will be easier for agricultural policy to be integrated into an overall policy. First we must take into account the difficulties that the Mansholt Plan, which lacks some important elements, would leave unsolved. In essence, it relies on the development of an improved structural organization of agriculture in order to raise the standard of living of those who work the land. It anticipates that larger farms, or farms working in partnerships (exercising an embryonic form of economic planning) will adjust their production more adequately to the market. It also provides that farmers should be able to negotiate contracts directly with the processing industries, thus bypassing intermediaries who currently stand between production and processing, and often absorb any increase in the price of food to consumers without passing it back to the benefit of agriculture.

Will these methods suffice, however, to raise agricultural income to the level of that of other categories of the country, and above all, to adjust production to needs? It may be asked whether the minimum farm dimensions which this Plan considered as economically viable (and which can only be established gradually) are so only in relation to the present level of prices. If large farms alone were sufficient to bring about a balance, there would be no American agricultural problem; and perhaps even English farms, which are on an average three times as large as those of the Community, would not need Treasury subsidies amounting to almost the whole of their net income. In other words, do not the prospects offered by the Plan confuse two issues which relate to two different time periods – future structures and present prices?

The financial difficulty cannot be escaped. The hope is expressed in the Mansholt Plan that a resolute effort to transform agricultural structures would make it possible to reduce progressively, and finally to eliminate, expenditures for price-support which are now spiralling at a dizzying speed. American experience, and the persistence of surpluses in Canada and Australia, suggest that such expectations are too optimistic.

To begin with, we must not forget the difficulty which stands in the way of an immediate increase in total Community expenditures on agriculture. Of the total expenditure on agriculture (whether by the national markets or through the Community) France absorbs the preponderant part, which is perhaps not so surprising since half the arable land is situated in France alone. The cumulative total of expenditures on price subsidies, which cannot be immediately reduced, and the supplementary expenditures for structures already go, in her case, beyond all possible limits.

One contradiction dominates this analysis. Any restructuring of agriculture will accelerate the growth of productivity and increase the proportion of total output on the market. Unless there is a fundamental redirection of productive resources it is hard to see how an acceleration of surpluses can be avoided. The proposal progressively to withdraw from cultivation 5 million hectares out of a total of 71 million hectares does not represent a sufficient counterpart any more than the direct contracts between associated producers and industrial processors. Price stabilization measures, far from being made redundant by the reorganization of the industry, may have to be maintained, or even increased.

Control of Production by Quantitative Restrictions

The producers' organizations are well aware that the present situation cannot be maintained indefinitely. Already, for sugar beet and refined sugar, a complicated system has been agreed in which the price guarantee covers certain qualities only, after which, and up to a second limit, the sugar producers pay a tax created to finance the reabsorption of surplus production: and beyond that, returns correspond only to sales prices in outside markets. But the guaranteed quota exceeds internal consumption. This means that the domestic market is protected regardless of the interests of countries which produce sugar cane. Such protection makes it impossible to reach a satisfactory equilibrium in the sugar market and is an extraordinarily awkward device for arriving at an average price which, in fact, is lower that that apparently guaranteed.

Contemporary discussion of the control of production centres on the reduction of surpluses. Many advocate the re-establishment of a quota system. A reduced production as a result of quotas would alleviate the financial burden. But there is need for clarification.

Are we speaking of *fixed quotas*, that is to say, a limitation of the quantity of wheat for example, which each country or each farmer is permitted to produce or to sell? The political difficulties of distributing quotas among countries are formidable. Decisions allocating quotas to each farm require a standard of reference. As a result, the structure of production may be frozen, halting progress and discriminating in favour of those who have already reached a high level of production and against those who might be capable of expansion at lower cost.

Or are we thinking of a more flexible solution, which would allow quotas allotted according to past performance to be *negotiable*? In other words, farmers who believed that they could expand profitably would buy the right to produce more from those who were prepared to cease production. The result would be payments to some farmers not to produce; other farmers would face an increase in costs insofar as they would have to buy the rights to additional production.

In any case, whether quotas be fixed or negotiable, the process of cutting surpluses of one product is likely to cause overproduction of others. Unless land is laid to waste forcibly, those farmers whose production is limited or those who have sold their rights, will put their land to a different use. Gradually the application of a quota system to a limited range of products would be extended, with all its disastrous consequences, to agriculture as a whole.

Some organizations suggest re-establishing, on a Community scale, the quantum system which was applied for a long time in France. The producers obtained the full price only within a certain tonnage limit. Beyond this limit, production was subject to a reabsorption tax. This meant that producers contributed to financing expenditures necessitated by over-production, whether for subsidizing exports or for denaturing products. Such a system, and the redistribution that it demands, would not be possible on the Community scale without severe political difficulties. It is hard to see, moreover, why a reduction in the average price should be sought in this indirect and distorted form. It leaves the root of the problem unaffected. It is important, however, to fix the price paid for cereals by farmers who transform them into animal products, so that a more favourable relation is established between meat prices and cereal prices. If the producers' organizations are resigned to see their average income lowered, nothing is better than a general and uniform reduction in price.

The difficulty must be tackled head-on. There can be no hope for an accelerated reduction in the agricultural population, upon which hopes for a higher farm income must depend, if prices are calculated so as to allow marginal enterprises to survive. Another formula which would demand no such formal decision could be entertained. This would be to leave the nominal prices for agricultural products unchanged but rely on increases in other prices to reduce their real value.

However, to make permanent inflation a basis for a policy is unacceptable. Furthermore, this system of decision by default would affect all agricultural prices in the same proportion, changing neither their relationship to prices in other countries, not their relationship to one another.

Price Relationships—An Overall Plan

What matters is not the historical relationship of present day prices to past ones, but rather their relationship to current market conditions, both as regards outlets and competition from other producers. By this yardstick the relationship of prices within the Community is utterly distorted. It would be a bad service to agriculture to encourage the belief that it can go on producing what is not wanted, and even worse, to raise prices in the face of falling demand. This process is bound to come to an abrupt end: agriculture's interests are better served by gradual adjustment.

The necessary redirection of production is inseparable from far-reaching changes in relative prices. This presents the most difficult decision. Agriculture has for long been accustomed to seek increased income mainly through increased prices. But the average level of prices is misleading. High prices for some farmers involve high costs to others: to those who rely on agricultural inputs. There is no way out unless prices can be lowered on surplus commodities, some of the most important of which serve as raw material for the production of others, and unless such changes bring about a reduction in production costs and create a more favourable price relationship for products in short supply. In effect, such a modification in price relationships, far from diminishing the overall income of agriculture, may adequately improve income for a large section of the industry.

A radical change in the agricultural policy is thus essential. This is beginning to be recognised by all those, including certain producers' organizations, who have perceived that price support must be replaced by income support. This recognition arises from a growing awareness that price support does not distribute income benefits equitably. Within agriculture it is in fact likely to increase the disparity of income between those who are poorest and those whose incomes are relatively high. It is one thing to refer to the principle of direct income support. it is another to set out a concrete formula for its application. The main objective of this study is to present precise solutions on this issue. Such solutions are essential if the changes in agricultural policy, agreed to be necessary, are to become technically feasible, politically acceptable, and socially justifiable.

It is out of the question to propose such price adjustments without compensatory measures in the form of direct aids, which will mitigate their effect on income, and without effort to establish more normal and stable prices in international markets. An overall plan must ensure that production would tend to adjust itself to outlets, that price changes would not reduce agricultural income but enable it to maintain its level, and finally, that the inequality of income which is now growing, would be reduced both between agriculture and the other sectors and among the farmers themselves. This is the basis of the proposals which are put forward here. These proposals form an entity. They confront the question of price levels for different products by linking a new system of subsidies for farmers with concrete measures designed to reorganize the international market.

It is clear that these measures will have to be spread out over a period of time and accompanied by other reforms in the field of agricultural and regional policy. In due course these would lead to a coherent whole, placing structural policy in harmony with that of prices. This in turn would be linked to a commercial policy for agriculture more akin to that applied by the Community in other sectors.

Such is the overall plan, the elements of which we shall now consider one by one.

PRICE REVISION

We have seen that all measures which have been considered for the control of production amount to a lowering of prices. In devising an overall policy we need to have the courage to plunge into the simplest method, which envisages a stage by stage reduction of prices of surplus products.

It is proposed to begin with those products whose prices within the Community are most in excess, and least defensible, in comparison with those of other large producers. This immediately designates two products for which Community decisions have created prices that are much higher than those which previously ruled in the member countries selling at the lowest prices: namely, cereals (particularly wheat), and sugar beet. Price cuts for these products are the key to an agricultural equilibrium, since they constitute the raw material for the production of pork, eggs and poultry, meat and, to some extent, milk; and also because they are in competition for the use of cultivable land.

No doubt, following the decisions made when the agricultural Common Market came into being, farm prices have remained relatively stable although the general level of prices has risen. It should be noted, first, that it is consumer prices which have risen, particularly as a result of a rise in the cost of services, and in consequence, of distributive margins. Industrial prices have remained generally stable. Second, prices do not in any way express changes in income. For example, the refrigerator industry has not ceased to increase its production despite the fact that prices have fallen by 80 per cent during the last few years as compared with the average prices of other industries. This has been possible because new methods have brought about a sharp rise in productivity. In this situation profits could only be maintained or increased as sales increased with lower prices. In the same way, it is in cereals and sugar beet that the growth in agricultural productivity has made the most spectacular progress. Moreover demand for these products will be increased if measures taken to protect various markets are better co-ordinated. So long as cereals and sugar are protected, it is inconsistent to import oil cake free of duty, since it competes with these products as cattle-feed.

A gradual decline in prices of certain surplus products is a necessary condition if a satisfactory pattern of meat prices is to be reached. Meat is the product for which demand increases most rapidly in response to rising real

161

income and of which there is a shortage, not only within the Community, but on a worldwide scale.

There are no products, not even the dairy products so troublesome to the Community, which do not respond to changes in price. It will not be possible to put an end to intolerable surpluses and gigantic losses through storage and exports except through a reduction in prices, and this in turn requires that the price cuts reduce farmers' costs as well as prices and that compensatory aid related to their ability to withstand lower prices, is available to the cultivators.

COMPENSATION PAYMENTS

The second and most fundamental element of the overall plan is a method designed to maintain the income of farmers as prices are lowered. This section contains the outline of a possible scheme.

The principle must be to substitute, gradually, income support for price support. The latter leads to surpluses and the intensification of inequalities; the former would be able to respond more directly to the needs of social equity. The problem which confronts our society concerns farmers rather than farming. Solutions to this problem must satisfy three requirements: those of favouring development in a more economic direction, of satisfying the desire for social equity, and of being relatively easy to calculate and simple to administer.

It goes without saying that if each producer were completely compensated for a fall in price, subsidies would be only a more complicated substitute for excessive prices. The incentive to produce would be the same and the desired effect, a certain redistribution of income, would be nil. This is the principal reason why we do not propose adoption of the British system of 'deficiency payments' or some equivalent. Since these payments from the budget are the equivalent, for each farmer, to the difference between the price guaranteed per unit and the average price realized in a market which is open to imports, they constitute, as do the Community's methods, price support but *not* income subsidy. The incentive to production is not appreciably different from that of high market prices. This kind of 'customs-duty-in-reverse' constitutes a form of protection, and thereby limits the market for outside producers. Since both the deficiency payments and the duties which apply to certain products are not uniform, there remains, just as with the Community system, distortion in the use of resources which represents a loss to the economy.

The essential difference between the Community and Britain does not lie in the mechanism by which prices are guaranteed: it lies in the lower level of prices guaranteed to British farmers, as against those in the Community, and in the methods followed in adjusting those prices. If the British methods were applied to the Community, and if they compensated in full for higher prices, they would give the same incentive to over-production. This would run counter to any attempt to reach an equilibrium between supply and demand. A comparable method has been tried out in the Community, for olive oil and durum wheat. This was intended to avoid raising the market price of a product for which one country, Italy, supplied only a small part of the total market requirement, the rest being imported. The worst possible confusion resulted.

The method proposed here would combine four essential rules. The first of these would compensate for lower prices on the basis of the average yield in the Community. The second would fix payments depending upon the area under cultivation *in the years preceding* the decision to lower prices. The third would involve minimum and maximum time periods and would limit the subsidy to the life of the farm operator, so that it could not be passed on to his successors. The fourth would make it vary inversely with the size of farms.

Each of these points needs clarification and detailed comment.

162

Average Yields

The idea of using 'average yields' as a basis can be illustrated by an arithmetical example. Supposing the price of one quintal of wheat is lowered by one franc, the average Community yield being 32 quintals per hectare, the basis for compensation would be 32 francs per hectare of wheat. Again, if milk were to drop 1 centime per litre, and the average yield was 2,500 litres per cow per year, compensation would be based on the figure of 25 francs per year per cow. In other words, price reductions would be compensated by a standard unit of quantity, whether quintals of wheat, hectolitres of milk or tons of sugar beet, independently of the quantities actually produced by a particular farmer. The administrative advantages of this rule are obvious. It would not be necessary to know the current production per farm. The simplest information, namely the areas under particular crops or the number of livestock would suffice for calculating the compensation payment due. This formula has also a precedent. When Germany revalued the deutschmark, agricultural prices expressed in European units of account became lower than before. She was authorized, for a temporary period, to compensate producers for their reduced returns in marks. To do so the system of a uniform subsidy per hectare was applied. The formula proposed here is a generalization of this solution, making it applicable to various products, in terms of livestock, as well as to crops in terms of the area of land involved.

The Standard

The standard which would form the basis of compensation for the reduction of price would be calculated for each producer on the average number of 'units' he had assigned to the products in question, in the three years preceding the decision to lower the price. Subsequent increases in the area of land under cultivation for any particular crop, or of the number of livestock applied to, say, milk production, would not entail a right to further compensation. To do so would run counter to the basic purpose of using the price mechanism to adjust supply to demand. In the same way, the subsidy should not be reduced in the event of a *reduction* in the 'units' assigned to these products, since this would run counter to the intention of causing a readjustment of production by means of price adjustments.

In this way, it would be possible to shield the farmers from the income-effect of price changes, without thereby giving incentives to maintain uneconomic production.

In the case of *successive* price reductions, the same principle should be applied – the additional compensation should be calculated on the number of 'units' employed prior to the *last* reduction of price. This number however must not be higher and should normally be lower than the previous one, otherwise the purpose of the scheme might be defeated. Of course the compensation would continue on the same basis as before.

Delays

The third rule, which ensures that compensation is paid only during the lifetime of the recipient, further reinforces the divorce of income support from the production process. Compensation should be paid only to producers who are still in business. It could not be passed on to an heir or to a new buyer of the farm (except in circumstances explained below). Such conditions are fully in accord with the objectives of the Mansholt Plan. Such provisions, though apparently severe, are clearly in the long-term interest of the farming community, since without them the necessary structural changes would not take place. This means that compensation payment should not be paid beyond the time when the present head of the farm becomes entitled to a substantial retirement pension, i.e. after the age of 55; however, there would need to be a special provision in favour of those who are close to this age limit, and this could take the form of a minimum period of, say, five years, for the payment of compensation either to the farmer himself or to his wife and children, in any particular case. Compensation payments cannot be continued indefinitely. It seems sensible to suggest a maximum period of compensation of 15 years. This would mean that farmers over 40 would receive compensation up to the point of retirement. Younger farmers should be able to find other employment or, provided structural reform were pursued with sufficient vigour, be able to derive a satisfactory income from farming without the need for compensatory payments.

A further point that requires to be settled follows from the basic objective of the Mansholt Plan for the consolidation of farm land by the amalgamation of groups of farms or the enlargement of existing units. To strengthen the incentives to the formation of groups or the enlargement of holdings, it will be necessary, therefore, to provide that the separate entitlements to compensation of the individual farms which are thus amalgamated or absorbed into larger units, should continue in force for 15 years from the date of the first payment. The incentives to concentration would thereby be strongly encouraged.

Moreover, the farmers who surrender their land in connection with any such concentration scheme should receive the discounted value of such subsidies as part of the price received for their land; in this way the market itself will indemnify farm owners who leave their farms, and the public expenditure necessary for implementing this part of the Mansholt Plan will thus be reduced.

In this way, the farmer would receive, as part of the sales price, the capitalized value of the subsidies to which he was personally entitled. He might even receive a much higher sum. A situation could arise in which the farmer would, in fact, have received payments only over five years; his selling price, however, would include the value of his subsidy rights for the whole fifteen year period.

Another less advantageous option would be open to those farmers who chose to leave their farms. They could collect immediately the capitalized value of the compensatory payment to which they were entitled. Should the subsidy thus be paid out in a lump sum, it could not be transmitted again if the farm were to form part of a group or be absorbed into a larger farming unit.

Degression

Excepting the above provisions to concentration schemes, the compensation payments should contain a degressive element; the compensation paid per 'unit' should be smaller, the larger the number of 'units' per farmer. Thus, compensation per hectare would decrease as the number of hectares of wheat or sugar beet per farm increased, or the number of milch cows per farmer. This scheme of reducing compensation per hectare with the size of the farm should obviously only begin to operate beyond a certain size.

Large farms with substantial herds of livestock do not require the same price per unit as small marginal farms in order to earn adequate profits. Furthermore, large units can more easily adapt the pattern of their production. Finally, economic efficiency is not determined by high yield measured in physical terms but by profitability related to the true value of the produce to the market. Where farming is based on prices fixed at an artificially high level, farms should be strongly encouraged to adapt their production to outlets based on unsupported prices.

Several schemes can be envisaged to determine the limit beyond which degression would begin. If it begins early enough, total subsidies will be less costly. As a result, larger funds could be allocated to restructuring agriculture or supporting the lowest incomes. However there is a danger that the profitability and the capacity for expansion of those farms with the greatest promise for the future might be seriously impaired. The simplest solution would be to apply degressive rates of compensation to all farms which by Community standards are larger than the average. One difficulty is that an average of *all* farms conceals the very considerable variation in farm size from region to region. It would no doubt be preferable for degression to begin at the level considered in the Mansholt Plan to be the minimum for efficient farming: say, 100 hectares of wheat, 60 milch cows. Whatever the system of degression chosen, the rate at which compensation was reduced would need to be slow. For example it would fall only by 2 per cent of the basic rate of compensation for each additional hectare or head of stock. These scales of degression would determine a maximum beyond which no compensation would be payable.

Objections will, no doubt arise, because of the inequality of treatment of farms of the same size depending on whether they existed before the application of the Plan or whether they are formed by an amalgamation of already large farms, or by an amalgamation of a mosaic of small farms. In the latter case the small farms will have brought with them their individual rights to compensation payments and the degression will not apply to the farm as a whole. This is not a real injustice because it is obviously far more difficult to create a large farming enterprise from a mass of small farms. The encouragement should be proportional to the effort required.

Net Costs

We must try to estimate the costs of applying the system outlined here.

First, it must be clearly stated that it covers only the maintenance of incomes and is not intended to compensate for capital losses. Normally, compensatory payments relating to price reductions will moderate the fall in land values. It is in any case desirable to slow down or bring to a halt the rise in the price of land. However, should land prices fall, the system proposed here is limited to temporary income-compensation; it is not meant to compensate for capital losses. This is an application of a more general principle. When, on account of a change in economic circumstances, industrial assets are reduced in value no one suggests that the owners have a right to be indemnified for loss. More specifically, when the value of assets has been inflated by Government intervention – such as protective tariffs or price maintenance – this does not confer a right on the owners to demand compensation should the preferential treatment subsequently be abandoned.

In calculating the expenditure on compensation a distinction should be made between the overall cost to the economy and the fiscal cost to the public purse. It is obvious that the overall cost to the economy is bound to be less than the cost of the present system. The actual cost is composed of the sum of public expenditures for agriculture plus the excess prices paid by the consumers. Since the reduction in prices, thanks to the degressive character of the subsidies, would not be *fully* compensated, there would necessarily be a reduction in the overall cost to the Community.

In terms of budgetary cost, however, this is not necessarily true, because of the difference between production and sales. The compensation payments are calculated in terms of the average yield. They thus apply to the *whole* of agricultural production. On the other hand, the prices which are to be reduced are paid, not on the whole output but only on that part of it which is sold in the market. In the case of cereals only about two-thirds of total production reaches the market. To avoid an increase in public expenditure on account of this, the scale of compensatory payments would have to be adjusted by reference to the proportion of total production actually sold.

However, such an adjustment may be found not to be socially desirable when the causes for the differences between production and sales are taken into account. Some part of the difference is due to home consumption by farmers. This declines rapidly as a proportion of output the larger the income of the farmer, and the more diversified his diet. Hence if the basis of compensation is production rather than sales, this gives a differential benefit to the poorest farmers (for whom the proportion of unmarketed output is the highest) and thus ensures that the compensation is most ample where it is most deserved.

Another cause of the discrepancy (and this probably accounts for the major part) reflects the use of cereals as feeding stock for animal products (pork, poultry or eggs) and to milk used to feed calves. There is a close relation between the price of these inputs and those of the end-products. For example, the price of pork will decline if cereal prices fall. Under these conditions, again, the best solution is also the simplest – to gear the compensation payment to total production, which would serve to make up for the reductions in prices of those products which are used as agricultural inputs.

The maximum budgetary cost cannot of course exceed the reduction in the price per unit multiplied by present tonnages. The actual cost will be less than this partly on account of the degressive character of the compensation payments: this will depend on the scale of degression adopted for the different products, as well as the proportions of output produced by farm units of different sizes. The latter type of information (indispensable for any rational agricultural policy) is unfortunately not at present available. There would also be important savings in relation to present expenditure, particularly on export restitutions, partly on account of the lower domestic price and partly on account of the reduction in the size of surplus production on which such restitutions have to be paid. Such savings, taking into account the second factor as well as the first might be very considerable. Further, since it is envisaged that the discounted value of compensation rights would be included in the price paid to farmers who sell their land – which will enhance the value of the land to the buyer – this will make it possible to regard the higher price paid by the buyer as a substitute for the indemnity to be paid to those who leave farming – which constitutes the largest item of expense envisaged in the Mansholt Plan. The total public expenditure on agriculture may well, as a result of these savings, be less than it would be if prices are neither reduced nor compensation paid. But even if public expenditure were to increase on balance, and the increase financed by a rise in indirect taxes, the consequent increase in the cost of living would be more than offset by lower food prices, with a more than proportionate benefit to lower income groups

There is moreover something paradoxical in the fact that food products are subject to indirect taxes, albeit at rates which are generally lower than those for industrial products. This means that consumption of particular importance to the lower-income groups, especially to those with large families, is being taxed, and the regressive character of indirect taxes thereby accentuated. Such taxes reduce the outlets for farm products, despite the fact that taxes are partly destined to finance costly measures to relieve the market of surpluses. It would be better to reduce these indirect taxes which contribute to the creation of surpluses.

The Community system rests on the value-added tax, in which the tax paid on purchases is deducted from the tax imposed on sales. It should be modified by exempting industrial products necessary to agriculture: essentially, agricultural machinery and fertilizers. Lower prices would result, as well as an incentive to greater productivity. This would help to increase the net income of agriculture by economic methods.

166

The rationale

The system proposed here may be justified both from an economic and a social point of view. An immediate comparison with the quota system shows that these proposals avoid the waste and rigidity imposed by fixed quotas. They also avoid the high prices associated with negotiable quotas. The effect on income is more advantageous than that which would result from a quantum system where prices were guaranteed for all producers, up to a certain tonnage, and where additional quantities were taxed to finance their removal from the Market, or simply abandoned to market vicissitudes.

Where farming conditions are difficult, and productivity per hectare low, there would be an immediate addition to income, since the rate of subsidy is related to average yields in the Community. Those whose yields are below average will benefit immediately, but their advantage is limited to the lifetime of the existing farmer. The scheme would thus impose no obstacle to structural reform but could easily be combined with the provisions of the Mansholt Plan for the reorganization of agriculture. Dr. Mansholt's plan outlined the forms of aid which would enable the older as well as the younger farmers to leave agriculture. It lacked a formula which would meet the needs of middle-aged farmers who have neither the inclination nor the ability to find immediate employment in other sectors. The arrangements proposed here meet this need. The features of the scheme which fix compensation by reference to average yields and which make subsidies degressive according to size are also justified by economic logic: it is the larger enterprises which contribute most in terms of volume of output to the lack of balance in the market; they are also the farms which can most easily adjust. It is thus both more equitable and more efficient to give these larger units incentives to reduce their output of surplus products and to increase production where a shortage exists – for example, by shifting from wheat to coarse grains or from milk or sugar beet to beef production. By this device a gradual economic transformation may be reconciled with an immediate improvement in the position of the poorest farmers, and an encouragement to the more prosperous farmers to reorganize their production to meet market exigencies.

This proposal should encourage those farms which are most likely to become modernized, in particular the largest ones. The proposals of the Mansholt Plan which aim at assisting the reconstructed and modernized enterprises to get off the ground are retained. For larger farms, the most pressing needs are to increase the amount of land at their disposal and to facilitate their access to capital. An agricultural development fund could be established along lines similar to the social and economic development plan which was set up in France some time ago, and which has its equivalent in all the other member countries of the Community. The capital is lent for a given length of time, and as the loans are repaid they can be lent out again to others.

In any case, the objective is to increase the profit-earning capacity of the farms which will remain. The scheme could not succeed if they continued to produce for surplus markets. Thus, they require an incentive to change the use of their resources in accordance with market trends.

It may be contended that the reshaping of agricultural policy will not be sufficiently rapid to prevent the continued accumulation of surpluses. Such an argument underestimates the effect of measures announced in advance. Experience has shown that the Common Market made its impact even before it was fully operational. Industrial enterprises reviewed their ability to compete, reorganized and invested in the light of the coming abolition of protection. The announcement of plans for restoring a balance between farm prices would produce the same reaction in the development of agricultural production. Thus, quotas would not be required even for the immediate future.

It is quite possible that a new price policy would result in a less intensive level of farming than exists at present and would help to reduce surpluses. The current high price of land justifies expenditures designed to secure the highest possible yield per hectare, due to the price level of basic products. A reduction in these prices would contribute to lowering the price of land, and thus would make for a better balance between value of production and the value of the inputs used to obtain that output. In a different context, there is no doubt that the price of farm land is influenced by the increase in the price of land for building purposes. It would be out of place here to discuss methods which might slow down this increase in the value of building land which is so detrimental to town planning and housing, and thus worsens the quality of life for a large part of the population. However any measure which tends to reduce the price of land for building would, by the same token, contribute to a solution of the agricultural problem.

Reform of the World Market

No policy, however well thought-out, can be carried out if the international context is ignored. An economic power as vast as the Community cannot maintain an attitude of unconcern in everything beyond its own frontiers, or be blind to the repercussions of its acts on other producers throughout the world. The real interest of the Community compels it to pay attention to its competitive strength. It must be recognized that the level at which international negotiations on agricultural products have been undertaken in the past is on a par with the worst kind of bargaining. Each country does its best to maintain its exports so as to rid itself of its own surpluses, without a thought for the surplus problems created for other countries.

It has not been possible to come to any agreement about the conditions under which world prices should be determined. As long as each country remains free to subsidize its products at will, there is no guarantee that the development of trade will correspond to a reasonable international division of labour. An attempt was made by the Community at the time of the Kennedy Round. It proposed that the financial aid and protection which each country provided for its own agricultural products should be added together and expressed as a single sum. This total, called the 'amount of support', would have been considered equal to the difference between the level of returns guaranteed to internal producers and the international price level. Having thus calculated this sum it could later be reduced in the course of further negotiations.

The basic idea was attractive. It had the merit of treating as equal all kinds of intervention, whether tariff protection, variable levies, quantitative import restrictions or British-style subsidies for certain products. Even direct assistance to incomes or investment could be included by making it appear in the farmers' returns. Its application, however, contains a fault: an escape clause allowed for protection to be retained in the event of internal inflation or abnormal price reductions on world markets. A further difficulty was that the 'amount of support' varied greatly between countries. As a result it was found that the simple calculation of an 'amount of support' and its gradual reduction by easy stages would not remove differences in the degree of protection. So the consequence remained uncertain. Even if parallel reductions in the 'amounts of support' were negotiated, those participants who were initially most protected would be able to preserve this dubious advantage, making other countries' markets more open than their own.

In any case, the Community which conceived this idea should apply it to competition among its own members. The operation of the Common Agricultural Policy, and of government aid to farmers, has made it impossible to know which products should be developed on economic grounds in preference to others. No true comparison can be made as long as the French budget bears a major share of the cost of social security in agriculture, or the Federal Republic spends far more than her partners on land improvement. It is anomalous that the Community has failed to provide itself with the right to inspect all forms of state intervention. This is especially unfortunate at a time when France is gradually raising farm prices to the Community level from which she departed by devaluation. This process will result in extra profits for her farmers that will exceed the sum assigned to agricultural social security in the budget. This should afford an opportunity for eliminating, in a fair manner, a discrepancy between member states by applying social security charges to agriculture in the same manner as to the other sectors of the economy.

If assistance by national governments were co-ordinated in this way, the Community would make the Common Price Level more realistic and would establish, in agriculture, the beginnings of a common incomes policy. It would put itself in a position to tackle from a sounder base those international tasks for which its commercial power makes it particularly responsible.

If a new policy of agricultural trade is to have a fair chance of success, two conditions must be fulfilled. The first is to reconstitute a market in which international prices have meaning and in which they cease to be the result of competitive dumping, a process which, as we have seen, causes world prices to fall as a result of high internal prices. The other condition is that stabilization mechanisms, which are indispensable for agriculture, should not be separately established within the borders of each country, but should result from a joint effort.

ELIMINATION OF DUMPING

To deal with the problem of dumping the Community, which has abolished quantitative restrictions on agricultural imports, albeit in favour of a strongly protectionist levy system, must insist on the modification and eventual abolition of import quotas by its partners. Dumping can only exist if the exporters' home market is protected; without such protection products sold at low prices on outside markets would find their way back to the domestic one. In this way a progressive and concerted reduction of protection by all the large producers would make it possible for world prices to find again a level which reflected actual production costs.

If this attempt succeeded, the Community would have available a standard with which to compare its own conditions of production. International prices would not differ from the internal prices of the main producers. Within agriculture price would be determined in the light of international conditions, price policy thus forming one part of a coherent commercial policy.

The Community requires a valid reference for its price policy, even if agreement cannot be reached with other producers to establish more economically realistic world prices. Should this be the case, the EEC should announce that, in accordance with rights granted by international agreements, it will apply anti-dumping legislation to sales made on its market by external producers at prices lower than those ruling on their own domestic market. Unlike tariff legislation, anti-dumping legislation can be particularized according to the country, the supplier, and the time. In this way the Community would find the reference it is seeking, which is the price established in its domestic markets by the main producers. Moreover it would, as the world's leading commercial power and the biggest importer of agricultural products, have at its disposal a means of exerting exceptional pressure on other producers to adopt a more rational policy, since they would no longer be able to dispose of their surpluses to the detriment of their competitors.

There are three kinds of international agreements for the stabilization of prices and incomes. The first sets minimum and maximum prices for trade between members and is illustrated by the International Wheat Agreement of 1967. The signatory countries agreed on minimum prices but had no secure method of preventing price cutting. In the event prices that had been set too high in 1967 gave way under the pressure of surpluses and the ex-partners plunged into a race to undersell each other.

The second type of agreement allocates markets between participants. It is analagous, on the international level, to a domestic system of quota control of production. Prices are maintained by restricting access to the world market; but they are difficult to police since each participant tries to increase his share, and no one can prevent non-participants from starting or expanding production.

It is only the third type of agreement – the establishment of international buffer stocks – which relies on an economic mechanism that is inherently effective. This seeks to establish international stocks of goods in times of surplus in order to place them on the market when shortages occur. Some of the British marketing boards have attempted this function and so have France's agreements with the countries of the old French Union.

It is often argued that the financial cost is liable in a short time to become so great as to make such schemes unworkable. This ignores the fact that in *every* case where production exceeds consumption, a surplus is created and a cost incurred to finance it. If part of the surplus is financed by an international organization, the burden is no greater than that which would otherwise be borne by governments and private traders. If, as can reasonably be expected, prices were gradually lowered when stocks of a particular product exceeded certain limits, the total cost of carrying stocks might be less under an international scheme than the actual cost (to Governments and consumers) in its absence.

It is essential that the Community should use its power and influence to launch the idea of an indissoluble link in agricultural trade between market stability and freedom of exchange. This is the principal aim to be pursued for international trade in years to come. It permits the integration of agricultural policy into the overall economic policy of both individual countries and groups of countries.

COMMERCIAL POLICY AND PRICE POLICY

More normal and stable world prices would allow the Community to complete its policy for domestic agricultural prices and re-establish the coherence of its commercial policy between industry and agriculture.

All that would then be needed would be a decision on the proper level of Community preference for agriculture. The appropriate level of protection for agriculture in the longer term should be considered in the context of a world market no longer distorted by present agricultural policies, and of a Community within which structural reform had made substantial progress. One thinks here in terms of a period of ten to fifteen years ahead.

These two changes in the situation should enable the Community to set itself as a target a level of protection in agriculture which should not be out of all proportion to the one enjoyed by industry. The rates or duties could conceivably be two or three times as high. It would be indefensible to keep them twenty or thirty times higher: on some products protection rates reach some 100 or 200 per cent while they are gradually going down to around 76 per cent on manufactures.

In practice, however, plans which seek to liberalize the Community's policy cannot start from the hypothesis that international stability of agricultural prices would be fully established. For basis products variations in freight rates alone might have an important destabilizing effect. International freight is often subject to violent fluctuations. It is difficult to conceive that agriculture, which requires stability, should be fully exposed to the vagaries of competition with so different an activity as shipping.

To eliminate the effect of such short-term fluctuations protection, or more precisely, Community preference, would have to be based on the average level of external prices over a period of five years including both high and low points. In order that Community farmers should not be totally isolated from world market conditions, the basis for calculations would be adjusted regularly, establishing a rolling average. Inasmuch as there would be a structural tendency for the prices of some products to fall and of others to rise, such changes would need to be incorporated into the Community's price policy so that producers might plan accordingly. But as a result of these long-term tendencies, fluctuations cannot be altogether eliminated. Therefore to satisfy the aim of stability, it would normally be necessary to complement the fixed tax expressing Community Preference by a variable levy which would be increased when prices dropped rapidly, and diminished, or even changed into a subsidy for imports, whenever prices rose too fast.

It may be questioned whether compensation for fluctuations should be total: whether in fact stability should be perfect. It is important that farmers should not only take long-term trends into account in planning their production, but also that they should sell what has been produced at the most opportune moment. This aim would be satisfied by ensuring that the variable levies did not absorb the whole range of price fluctuations.

This is the system which should be negotiated progressively. Its implementation would ensure the coherence and efficacy of a new agricultural policy.

Contributions of Member States

Another condition is essential for the Community. It will be necessary to reconsider the formula which determines contributions made by each country to the Common Agricultural Policy as well as the payments each receives from the Community. Two considerations are involved. One is the need to make gross contributions to the European Fund proportionate to the capacity of each country, and net receipts from the Fund proportionate to the financial burden for its agriculture. We have a need for both equity and parity in competitive conditions within an overall common market. The other consideration relates to the direction in which these various possible systems guide the actions of Member States. A system which makes the receipts from the Community turn on a country's surpluses and the cost of removing them from the market, is fundamentally out of order – it gives the wrong incentives. It is necessary to provide incentives which operate in the opposite way by encouraging each country to reduce the size of its agricultural population by the most humane method possible, and to reorient its production in accordance with the trends of demand.

In practice, one cannot avoid separating two elements of public expenditure for agriculture. As long as it is necessary to subsidize exports, restitutions can only be made directly by the Community. Since, within the Community, products circulate freely, their origin (when they are exported to other countries) is unknown. The Community has a similar responsibility for storage which is not closely linked to the point at which the products originated. Expenditures to improve structures can on the other hand be identified with precise localities.

A simple idea would be for payments by the Community on account of agricultural policy to be centred on its fundamental problem, the excessive size of the agricultural labour force. Member countries should receive payments from the Community in proportion to the expenditure they are required to make in order to reduce the size of their active agricultural population. The costs of such a policy are likely to be higher the more numerous the agricultural population. The Community's contribution cannot amount to a blank cheque. Countries should be entitled to draw on Community resources only when they can prove that the expenditure they have incurred corresponds to the objectives of reformed farm structures and price levels.

Since the earliest days of a common agricultural policy it has been accepted that import levies would constitute the principal basis of contributions. This situation is changing. The most recent financial regulation has gone beyond agricultural matters and is designed to cover all common expenditures. The regulation requires that the customs revenue from the common external tariff should be paid into the Community budget. The logic of this arrangement – already envisaged when the Rome Treaty was negotiated – derives from the recognition that a product's point of entry into the Community tells us nothing about its actual destination: what enters by way of Rotterdam may, as a result of freedom of internal trade, end up in Germany or France. A different logic initially governed the allocation of import levies on agricultural goods to the Community budget. The argument was based on the ill-considered notion that the more a country imported, the more of its own production became surplus. The conclusion drawn was that imports should be made to pay for the subsidies on exports necessary if internal surpluses were to be disposed of abroad at world prices.

Nevertheless for the Common Market in agricultural goods, the argument which is valid for customs-duties is also, to a certain extent, valid for import levies. The point of entry into the Community does not necessarily indicate the final destination of imports. However, this question needs to be examined more closely. Obviously, whatever comes in via Rotterdam is as likely to go to Germany or France as to remain in the Netherlands. For Italy, on the other hand, one would hardly expect imports to arrive simply in transit to Germany or France. If Britain joined the Community, her imports would also stay within her borders, and not normally cross the water to enter other member countries. Thus in the case of Italy, and above all in that of Britain, these import levies, which raise the price of food to the domestic consumer, result in a substantial net cost to the balance of payments when the proceeds of the levies are transferred to the Community.

However, nothing would be more imprudent than to bring back into the arena of discussion the financial regulation which it has taken so long to negotiate, which assures the Community its own proper resources, and which serves to prevent potentially even more flagrant inequities. Whatever the reason, it was foreseen that as a result of falling imports the revenue from levies would decline. In the new system of finance they would contribute not more than 20 per cent of the Community's budget. As a result greater reliance has had to be placed on the allocation to the Community of a fraction of the value added through the total of economic activities of each country. The policies for agriculture which are proposed in this Report will make these regulations more acceptable and more effective in their application. As internal and world prices became more closely aligned, receipts from import levies would fall, and the burden on the balance of payments of importing countries would be alleviated. The elimination of surpluses would diminish the cost of storage and remove the need for export subsidies. Funds so released could be used to assist structural reform. The policy changes outlined here would then automatically help to relate contributions to resources and payments to the need for structural reform, depending on the size of the surplus agricultural population.

It will become easier to reach a more satisfactory general balance in payments and receipts when the Common Agricultural Policy ceases to be the preponderant part of Community activity. If the Community develops activities which benefit the most advanced industries and the latest technological methods, those countries which now make the greatest net contribution to help others to modernize antiquated agricultural structures will derive compensation from their larger share in projects concerning such key industries.

The important point is that, due to these mechanisms, the Community will reach a system in which contributions will be determined by each country's resources and in which funds will be allocated to countries in proportion to the burden of agricultural over-population, to regions whose development needs to be accelerated, and to the industries best equipped to attain overall technical progress.

This new method of sharing advantages and financial costs will strengthen the coherence of the Community by reconciling conflicting interests in the same manner as is done through the system of public finance of each country.

Appendix I

Great Britain and the Agricultural Common Market

The policy proposed in this Report, which is based on the Mansholt Plan, but which complements it and goes beyond it, corresponds to the interests of European agriculture and the position of the Community in the world. It has not been especially conceived to remove obstacles which stand in the way of Britain's adherence. However, as often happens, the search for objective solutions for one group of problems provides solutions for other problems at the same time. It will be apparent that many of the difficulties associated with the entrance of Britain into the Common Market would, if this policy were applied, be virtually eliminated.

The extension of the present system, without modification, to an enlarged Community raises one objection of principle. As it is, the logic of using the proceeds of import levies for paying subsidies on exports is dubious, although the value of the Community's imports is more or less equivalent to that of its exports. If Britain were included in the Community, imports would greatly outweigh exports. It is clear that in this situation imports cannot be regarded as being in any way linked to, or responsible for, exports. As things are it is difficult to justify a net payment by Italy to the agricultural funds of the Community. It is even more difficult to see why Britain, because it is the largest import market and at the same time possesses the most rational agricultural structure, should bear a disproportionate part of the costs of agricultural exports.

The solutions outlined here would modify considerably the repercussions which a Common Agricultural Policy would have on the British balance of payments. The rate of import levies would be progressively reduced, as would the prices paid for food bought from other member countries. Britain, on the other hand, would no longer derive supplies from a world market in which the governments in exporting countries compete with one another in their sales and thereby reduce the costs of their competitors in importing or processing. However, it will be a question of returning to a more normal situation in which imports are paid for at their true cost price; it will not imply the arbitrary imposition of abnormal burdens.

The contributions which Britain would have to make to the Community would, in any case, be an integral part of the whole. Contributions to Community funds based on the proportion of the gross national product would progressively exceed levies on agricultural imports. On that criterion, Britain's gross burden would be analogous to that of France, but less than that of Germany. Britain would receive considerably less Community support for its agriculture, since its active farming population is already close to a minimum level but, as structural reform proceeds, this imbalance should diminish. Further there ought to be some compensation resulting from transfers by the Community to promote advanced technological projects.

It is in the Community's own interest that common policies should place no excessive burden on the balance of payments of any member country. A deficit on external account imposes a slow-down in the rate of economic growth of the member country and this has adverse repercussions on the economy of the Community as a whole.

As far as the effect on the level of consumer prices is concerned, the British White Paper on *Britain and the European Communities* (Cmnd. 4289), presents a summary series of calculations. This indicates that the cost of living for the British consumer would rise at a rate of 1 per cent per year over five years as a result of the application of the current Common Market agricultural system.

The orders of magnitude are as follows:

As a result of increasing agricultural prices from existing to present EEC levels in the UK (largely determined by imports), the price of agricultural goods would rise by some 45 per cent. About half the cost of food is accounted for by the wholesale price of agricultural products, the rest covers processing and distribution. Thus the increase in food prices to the consumer would be about 22·5 per cent, plus any increases which result in distribution or processing margins. Food accounts for some 25 per cent of total consumer expenditure, so the impact on the cost of living would be of the order of 5·6 per cent $\left(\dfrac{25 \times 22\cdot5}{100}\right)$. If this were spread over a transitional period of five years, we arrive at the 1 per cent per annum increase in costs quoted above.

If Community prices evolve according to the proposals made here, the effect on the cost of living will be very much less. The prices will in that case never reach the excessive levels now found on the Continent. There would therefore be no serious obstacle on that account and any remaining price adjustment could be offset by some reduction in the prevailing rate of inflation in Britain, which for some years has not been below 5 per cent a year.

The system of 'deficiency payments' would disappear. British farmers would have to rely on market prices instead of 'deficiency payments' which have enabled them to compete with imported products. It is not easy to anticipate the net effect on British public finances of the contribution which would be required to the Common Agricultural Policy. However, prices and financial charges should remain within tolerable limits.

The Community, for its part, would benefit by the system proposed here. If its present price system were extended to Britain, the markets which its farmers hope to have gained in Britain would not really exist. No doubt more fruit and vegetables would enter Britain from the Community, as a result of the reduction or elimination of the high customs duties which now protect horticulture. However, the high level of cereal prices would lead to a rapid expansion of cereal production in Britain which would greatly aggravate the existing burden of surpluses. It also seems likely that Britain would increase its production of milk, and reduce its consumption of dairy products, of which it is now a considerable importer. On the other hand the meat deficit of the enlarged Community might well be still greater than now.

If the proposals made in the Report are implemented, the transitional period which would in any case inevitably accompany Britain's entry into the Common Market, would assume a special justification. The system which Britain would be joining would not be identical with the one existing now, but rather with one which would emerge as a result of reforms in which she would participate as a fully fledged member of an enlarged Community.

From the Rome Treaty to the Common Agricultural Policy

It would be unfair to be ironic about the list of objectives stated in Section II of the Rome Treaty, by refusing to see in them anything but pious and partly contradictory wishes. In fact, at the outset, emphasis was put on the need for rationalization and greater productivity. These were seen to be prerequisites of a higher standard of living for those who work on the land. Stabilization was, of course, mentioned, but so was dependability of supplies. It appeared that the risk of a protectionist interpretation was not consistent with reassuring phrases about the advisability of reasonable consumer prices. At this stage the outlines of a common policy had barely taken form, but the idea of creating one or several special funds already existed. It was left to a conference to compare the agricultural policies of the member countries. This was held at Stresa from 3 July to 12 July 1958.

The transitional mechanisms provided for by the Treaty are worth stressing. One possibility was to enforce minimum prices so as to avoid a sudden rush of imports from one country to another after removal of quotas. This was carried out for fruit and vegetables, until a market organization for these products was established. Another provision contained the seeds of a possible scheme for bringing price levels into line by means of an effective economic procedure. The reasoning was as follows: the Common Market entails the progressive removal of discrimination between national producers and producers of other member countries. It followed that an importing country ought to guarantee suppliers situated in other member countries the same prices as those it guarantees to its own producers. It was understood, however, that, as with the suppression of customs duties, this principle could only be applied gradually. In this way pressures would have been created to lower the highest prices, leading to the establishment of common prices. The very high prices set by Germany and Italy, for the benefit of their own producers, could only be maintained on the basis of taxes on imports so long as they were purchased at depressed world prices. The implementation of this procedure required that long-term contracts be concluded between importers and exporters within the Community; these contracts would cover increasing quantities which would progressively constitute the major part of imports. The proposed contracts would also have included a clause on prices which would have progressively raised prices paid to other members so as to align them with the prices paid to producers of the importing country. One can appreciate the political wisdom of this kind of arrangement. It avoided requiring the six Governments of a newly-formed Community to make joint decisions about fixing agricultural prices. This is difficult to do even within a single country. Instead, tension was created within each country between the interests of agriculture and the demands of economic equilibrium, between the Minister of Agriculture and the Minister of Finance.

This provision remained a dead letter and now belongs to the past. When the first formal decisions were made, establishing levies on imports to be maintained so far as trade with the outside world was concerned but to be reduced in trade with other member countries, they formed the basic requirement for the entry into the second phase of the transition period. It was expressly understood that these decisions were to replace the provisions of Section II of the Treaty.

In August 1962 the first regulations were laid down for cereals and certain products based on cereal feeds – pork, poultry and eggs. Some initial measures regarding fruit and vegetables were taken at the same time.

Regulations for rice, milk and dairy products and beef did not come into being until November 1964, for olive oil and oil-seeds until the end of 1966, for sugar and beet until 1967. Moreover, application of these measures took some time. It was not until 1967 and 1968 that common prices were enforced for almost all products. Regulations for tobacco and wine were not introduced until very recently.

It is in connection with cereals and products based on them that the fundamental system of the policy is more fully defined. Each year the Council of Ministers sets a target price related to the area known to have the greatest deficit in cereals – Duisburg. Prices calculated for other regions are based on this target price, with transportation costs deducted. The target price sets the basis for the threshold price for imported cereals. This is calculated in such a way that cereals can only be sold by an importer at a price which is at least on a par with that of Duisburg. To this end an import levy, calculated each week, makes up the difference between the threshold price and the import price.

We now see how Community preference functions. The threshold price is the highest in the Community. The import levy makes up the difference between it and the lowest import prices. Thus, any less advantageous outside offer, or any offer outside the area which has the greatest shortage, is forced above the Community price.

It is also necessary to ensure that prices are maintained and surpluses rapidly removed if excessive quantities are produced within the Community. Member countries are bound to buy any cereals offered by producers at an intervention price, fixed at a variable percentage below the target price according to regions. Exports to third countries outside the Community are made possible by restitution payments which guarantee producers the internal Community prices, although their products are sold at much lower prices on the world market.

Somewhat different arrangements are used for pork. A sluice-gate price protects pig producers from cheap imports and additional protection may be incorporated in the import levy. This levy compensates for the high cost of cereal raw materials, available only at the price level established within the Community, and adds an element equal to 7 per cent of the average sluice-gate price, to ensure preference for Community products. Analogous measures are applied to poultry and eggs as well as milk and dairy products.

There are three other variants to be considered. Animal fats are for the most part imported by the Community. Protective intervention is provided for the production of rape seed and sunflower seeds. A special system exists for olive oil. Italy is the only substantial producer of this, but it supplies only a fraction of Community requirements. In order to avoid raising prices very sharply, financial aid may be given directly to producers. Imports from third countries are subject to customs duties consolidated in GATT. These duties are zero for the raw materials, oil-scale or oil-fruit, and also for oil-seed cake. On the other hand, they reach a substantial level for processed products, such as 3 per cent to 8 per cent for vegetable oils for technical and industrial use, 9 per cent to 15 per cent for alimentary purposes, 25 per cent for margarine. This means that the by-products benefit from considerable protection in relation to their added value.

For sugar and sugar beet, contrary to what happens with cereals and their by-products, the procedure begins with the processed product and relates support prices to the raw material in the area which has the highest surplus. On this basis prices for other areas are established. However, price support is accompanied by quota restrictions. A basic quantity is allocated to each country according to the reference position of 1961-66. Each member state allocates a maximum quota to each sugar manufacturer, based on a coefficent of its basic quota. The quantities thus allocated are the subject to a tax assessed on the producers so as to finance sales-outlets. Sales above the maximum quota must be sought directly outside the Community. Each year the Council establishes the quantities to be covered by the Community price guarantee. These are equal, not to internal consumption, but rather to 105 per cent of anticipated requirements for the current year.

In contrast with these protective systems which are made effective by constant readjustment, fruits and vegetables are protected only by a fixed tariff. Threshold prices and forms of intervention are less strictly defined. A distinction is made between a crisis and a grave crisis, depending on the level of price on the market in relation to two factors; a basic price considered to be desirable, and a purchase price which is much lower than this, at which intervention takes place.

Meat is protected by a customs duty and an import levy. Intervention consists of financial aid to private stockpiling organizations which are asked to buy when the prevailing price falls 7 per cent below the orientation price fixed by the Council. Wine, for which limited measures had been contemplated much earlier, is the latest product to be given a Community status. The principal producers are France and Italy. The first was anxious to limit production and support prices, the second left production a free hand, and allowed prices to balance supply and demand. The measures chosen eliminate import quotas and rely instead on a common external tariff; they prohibit financial aid for new vineyards; they also eliminate production controls and fix intervention prices.

This decision sums up all the others: the unconditional support of prices, while doing away with limits on production, is the Community's device for creating unsaleable surpluses.

Appendix III

Comments on the Tables

The set of tables presented here illustrates the basic data to which the text refers.

We begin with public expenditure in support of agriculture, both by the Community and by the member states in tables 1, 2 and 3. This shows the massive rise in expenditure required to maintain prices, while expenditure to encourage structural changes has been limited to only one tenth of the total charges met from Community Funds. Payments from FEOGA in respect of cereals, sugar and powdered milk are totally out of proportion to their contribution to aggregate agricultural output, as recorded in Table 9.

The origins of the surpluses and the difficulty of their complete elimination are made evident by Tables 4, 5, 6 and 7. Tables 4 and 5 deal with production, consumption and stocks of cereals, sugar and powdered milk. Table 6 records stocks of wheat, secondary cereals and butter, in the principal producing countries. Table 7 presents FAO projections of import requirements and export availabilities for principal products for 1975.

The higher prices which result from the Community's agricultural policy and which explain the pre-existing surpluses, appear in Table 8. This compares prices for the principal products within the EEC to those ruling outside the Community. Table 9 takes this further, restating the value of different items of output by applying to the volume of production different price assumptions.

Table 10 indicates the differences in retail prices between member countries. This exists in spite of a common wholesale price level which was one of the objectives of the agricultural policy.

Table 11 records the development of EEC trade in agricultural products. It is apparent that subsidized exports did not especially help to complement the food supply of developing countries. On the other hand these countries were particularly affected by European agricultural protectionism.

The three tables which follow are concerned with structural problems. Table 12 shows the development size of the working population in agriculture and the relatively more rapid decline in the number of wage earners than of farmers. Tables 13 and 14 summarize capital expenditures in support of agricultural production by countries, and illustrate various purposes for which they were used.

The inequalities of land and labour productivity between regions are shown in Table 15.

Tables 16 to 20 examine the distribution among member countries of payments and receipts from FEOGA. Table 16 shows the development of the guarantee section, payments, reimbursements and balances by country. France and the Netherlands are the most important beneficiaries. Table 17 establishes a balance sheet for the Guidance sector, i.e. that part of the fund which is concerned with structural reform. It also shows the working of the special section. This includes Community participation in subsidies paid by Germany to her producers, and in certain support of particular policies such as those for olive oil and durum wheat. Germany and Italy are beneficiaries from that part of Community expenditure but the sums involved are far smaller than those under the guarantee section.

To try and see the distribution of benefits and of costs' payments from the Guarantee section required to maintain prices through storage and export subsidies are compared with the value of agricultural production in each country. The Guidance section's payments are compared with the sizes of the agricultural population of each country. Finally, the foreign exchange implications of the European Fund are examined in terms of net contributions or net reimbursements in relation to the current balance of payments of each country. It is clear that the incidence of these transfers varies among countries and from year to year. Although it is sometimes very small at other times it can, by contrast, amount to a very important fraction of the total surplus or deficit, sufficient even to change the sign of the total balance.

Table 1 — Actual or estimated expenditure, eligible to FEOGA
In millions of U.S. $

Market Organization	1962/63 [1]	1963/64 [1]	1964/65 [1]	1965/66 [1]	1966/67 [2]	1967/68 [3]	1968/69 [3]	1969/70 [4]
Cereals	28	49	126	117	136	429·5	657·1	921
Dairy Products			22	103	132	319·8	380·2	1,204 [5]
Pork			8	11	15	40·5	44·4	50
Eggs	1	1	1	1	1	0·9	1·6	1
Poultry		1	2	2	3	3·4	4·7	5
Beef & Veal						6·2	14·0	27
Rice			1	1	1	6·5	10·4	17
Fats					79	129·8	207·0	285
Fruits & Vegetables						17·9	27·0	32
Sugar				4	3	67·6	195·4	221
Other						12·2	17·8	20
Total	29	51	160	239	370	1,034·3	1,559·6	2,783 [7]

1 Real expenditure.
2 Estimated in the 1967 budget.
3 Expenditure taken into account in the two half-yearly provisional payments.
4 Estimate for 1970.

5 Original proposal of the Commission; the figure was brought down by the Council to $850 million.
6 Reduced to $2,529 million by the Council's decision, see note 5.

Source
Zijlmans, 'Le Financement de la politique agricole commune', in *Revue du Marché Commun* November-December 1969, 569, and Commission of the European Communities, Directorate of the FEOGA, Doc. 19.776/VI/69-F add. 2, 11 February 1970.

Table 2 — FEOGA Expenditure – All sections 1968, 1969, and 1970
In millions of U.S. $

	1967/68 [1]	1968/69 [2]	1969/70 [3]
Guarantee Section	1,034·3	1,559·5	2,462·5
Orientation Section	285·0 [4]	285·0 [5]	285·0 [6]
Special Section	140·3 [4]	69·3 [5]	
	1,459·6	1,913·8	2,747·5

1 Budgetary estimates.
2 Expenditures taken into account for two half-yearly provisional payments.
3 Draft budget for 1970.

4 Orientation and Special Sections, expenditure for 1969.
5 Orientation and Special Sections, expenditure for 1970.
6 Orientation Section expenditure for 1971.

Source
European Economic Community, Direction du FEOGA, Doc. 19.776/VI/69-F add. 2, 11 February 1970, and *Draft Budget for 1969 and 1970.*

Table 3 — Public expenditure for agriculture in millions of U.S. $ in 1969[1]

	Market support[2]	Re-structuring[3]	Social measures[4]	Other measures[5]	Total
Germany	662·0	693·0	261·0	142·1	1,758·1
France	746·4	663·2	880·6	157·4	2,447·6
Italy	452·3	584·5	131·1	131·6	1,299·5
Netherlands	374·5	110·8	6·0	8·2	500·2
Belgium	144·5	35·5	40·5	8·1	228·6
Luxembourg	5·7	6·3	3·9	0·6	16·5
Total EEC	2,385·4	2,093·3	1,323·1	448·7	6,250·5
United Kingdom					680·0
United States					5,450·0

1 Estimated direct and transfer expenditures in favour of agriculture, excluding fishery, covered by budgetary and parafiscal resources in the six member states. These figures also include for Italy the budgets of the *Cassa del Mezzogiorno* of the autonomous regions and of the Green Plan, and for Germany the budgets of the ten Länder.

2 Expenditure integrally financed by FEOGA, Guarantee Section. The figures concerning Germany also include 102·2 millions of U.C. for cereal compensation. The figures concerning France include a sum of 47·9 million U.C. of parafiscal taxes earmarked for support expenditures. The figures concerning Luxemburg include 3·78 million U.C. for milk and cereal compensation.

3 The figures indicated include 94·9 millions of U.C. financed by the FEOGA, Orientation Section in 1968 (the breakdown of FEOGA expenditure for 1969 is not yet final).

4 1967 data. The figures in this column relate to social measures (family and old age allowances, medical care, injury compensation) for the benefit of farmers (heads of family and family aids) and financed by various means (transfers from the budget, earmarked contributions).

5 Other measures: price reductions on some inputs (fuel, fertilizer), veterinary and phytosanitary measures, quality and variety control, orientation, development and adjustment, natural disasters.

Sources
For the member States, data provided by the EEC. Agriculture Directorate; for the U.K. and the U.S.A., national budgets.

N.B. The figures for France seem to be largely underestimated in this calculation. According to the French budget of 1969, the outlay for agriculture was:

	1000 Millions of French Frs.	1000 Millions of U.S. $ a	b
Support (FORMA, cereals, etc.)	5·97	1·22	1·07
Social Expenditures (BAPSA, FASASA, FAR)	6·68	1·36	1·20
Investment	2·43	0·50	0·44
Other	2·37	0·48	0·43
Total	17·45	3·56	3·14

a Exchange rate of 4·90 Frs. to 1 dollar.
b Exchange rate of 5·55 Frs. to 1 dollar.

Table 4   Cereal and sugar production and consumption in the EEC Evolution from 1962/63 to 1967/68 in 1000 metric tons

	1962/63	1963/64	1964/65	1965/66	1966/67	1967/68
Ia All cereals						
Marketable Production	57,756	56,704	59,432	60,206	57,984	68,157
Initial Stock	10,879	13,238	11,772	10,309	11,685	10,197
Imports 2	15,128	16,873	16,541	20,459	19,963	22,688
Exports 2	5,476	7,362	9,244	9,574	8,071	12,444
Total Internal Consumption	65,049	67,678	68,192	69,715	71,364	74,795
Final Stock	13,238	11,772	10,309	11,685	10,197	14,153
1957/58 = 100						
Marketable Production	117	115	121	122	118	139
Imports 2	144	160	157	194	190	215
Exports 2	160	215	270	280	236	363
Total Internal Consumption	111	115	117	120	123	128
Final Stock	134	120	105	119	104	144
Ib Wheat						
Marketable Production	29,496	24,438	29,158	30,369	26,309	31,207
Initial Stock	6,348	8,162	6,141	5,587	6,754	5,446
Imports 2	3,478	4,111	3,548	4,245	4,280	4,976
Exports 2	3,786	3,794	5,669	5,838	4,479	6,278
Total Internal Consumption	27,373	26,783	27,591	27,609	27,418	27,741
Final Stock	8,162	6,141	5,587	6,754	5,446	7,611
1957/58 = 100						
Marketable Production	120	99	119	124	107	127
Imports 2	89	105	91	109	110	128
Exports 2	120	120	180	185	142	199
Total Internal Consumption	105	102	105	105	105	106
Final Stock	128	96	88	106	86	120
II White Sugar						
Marketable Production	4,550	5,347	6,263	5,714	5,589	6,211
Initial Stock (1·7)	2,676	1,825	2,143	3,139	2,837	2,698
Imports 2	810	1,307	1,121	710	1,001	668
Exports 2	920	767	795	849	653	486
Total Internal Consumption	5,291	5,569	5,593	5,877	6,076	6,515
Final Stock (30·6)	1,325	2,143	3,139	2,837	2,698	2,576
1957/58 = 100						
Marketable Production	105	123	145	132	129	144
Imports 2	79	128	110	70	98	66
Exports 2	111	93	96	102	79	59
Total Internal Consumption	123	130	130	137	142	152
Final Stock (30·6)	85	137	201	182	173	165

1 Excluding rice.   **2** Excluding intra-EEC trade.

Source
OSCE Statistiques Agricoles, 1968 No. 1 and 1969 No. 1.

Table 5 — Production and consumption of butter and skimmed powdered milk. Evolution in the EEC from 1965 to 1968 and estimates for 1969 and 1970

	1965	1966	variation %	1967	variation %	1968	variation %	1969	variation %	1970	variation %
I BUTTER											
Production	1,236	1,255	+ 1·5	1,315	+ 4·8	1.403	+ 6·7	1,355	− 3·4	1,375	+ 1·5
Consumption	1,174	1,178	+ 0·3	1,188	+ 0·8	1,171	− 1·5	1,205	+ 2·9	1,335	+10·8
Net Exports	24	63	+162·5	95	+50·8	101	+ 6·3	93	− 8·0	125	+34·4
Net Surpluses	38	14		32		131		57		−85	
Stocks at 31·12	122	136	+ 11·5	168	+23·5	299	+ 78·0	356	+19·1	281	− 21·1
II SKIMMED POWDERED MILK											
Production	677	833	+ 23·0	1,058	+27·0	1,306	+ 23·4	1,260	− 3·5	1,260	±0
Consumption	701	721	+ 2·8	981	+36·1	970	− 1·2	1,020	+ 5·1	1,180	+15·6
Net Exports	− 30	75		78	+ 4·0	222	+184·6	120	− 46·0	180	+50·8
Net Surpluses	6	37		−1		114		120		−100	
Stocks at 31·12	68	105	+ 54·4	104	−1·0	218	+109·6	338	+55·0	238	− 29·6

Source

European Economic Community: 'L'Equilibre des Marchés

Agricoles' (*Communication de la Commission au Conseil*) Brussels, 19 November 1969 (Com 69 (1200)) p. 19 and 20.

Table 6 — Inventories at end of production years
in millions of metric tons

	Average 1955/56 1957/58	Average 1963/64 1965/66	1966/67	1967/68	1968/69 Preliminary Figures
WHEAT	47·0	38·0	31·6	37·4	51·4
Argentina	1·4	2·0	0·3	1·4	1·0
Australia	1·3	0·6	2·3	1·4	6·0
Canada	17·8	12·6	15·7	18·2	20·6
France	0·9	2·3	1·7	1·8	2·8
United States	25·6	20·5	11·6	14·6	21·0
SECONDARY CEREALS	52·2	56·0	40·6	50·4	51·2
Argentina	0·6	0·3	0·6	1·4	1·2
Australia	0·0	0·4	0·9	0·8	1·0
Canada	5·6	4·8	4·9	4·4	5·9
United States	46·0	50·5	34·2	43·8	43·1

			1966	1967	1968 Preliminary Figures
BUTTER					
(in thousands of tons)			338	446	596
United States			15·0	73·0	53·0
EEC			154·0	196·0	338·0
United Kingdom			38·0	36·0	51·0
Other Countries			34·0	42·0	52·0
Western Europe			69·0	69·0	74·0
Canada			28·0	26·0	28·0

Source

FAO: *Reports on Products 1968 and Prospects 1969.*

Table 7

All grains (excluding rice)
Net import requirements (+) **and export availabilities** (—)
**from current production by region. Average for 1961-63
and projections for 1975**

	Base period 1961–63 average million tons	1975 Low assumption million tons	1975 High assumption million tons
DEVELOPING COUNTRIES			
Import requirements	17	41	23
Export availability	8	19	23
Balance 1	+ 9	+22	
DEVELOPED COUNTRIES			
Import requirements	34	43	46
Export availability	47	76	73
Balance 1	−13	−33	−27
COUNTRIES WITH CENTRAL PLANNING			
Import requirements	12	12	12
Export availability	4	7	13
Balance 1	+ 8	+ 5	− 1
WORLD BALANCE	+ 5	− 6	−28

1 Import requirements and export availabilities as shown in this table represent the difference between current production and current consumption of grains, the net country balances having been added up separately for exporting and importing countries. The indicated figures do not correspond to the real volume or projection of trade, but rather reflect the tendencies of supply and demand. Thus, the presence of a positive balance in the "import balance" of the base period of 1961-1963 reflects the decrease of world stocks during this period, while the appearance of a negative balance (of 6 or of 28 million tons according to the hypothesis retained) for 1975 reflects the tendency of production to exceed consumption during the coming years, if measures for the limitation of supply were not adopted in exporting countries.

Source
FAO, *Agricultural Commodities Projections for 1975 and 1985,* Vol. I, p. 92.

Table 7(b)

All meats: Balance for 1961-63 and Projections for 1975
Net requirement (+) or availability (—) in millions of tons

	1961–63		1975 Low assumption		1975 High assumption	
	Balance	consumption per head (kg per year)	Balance	consumption per head (kg per year)	Balance	consumption per head (kg per year)
DEVELOPING COUNTRIES	−603	9·4	+159·7	10·3	+2,621	11·5
e.g. Argentina and Uruguay	−730	102·7	−827	102·6	−924	102·8
DEVELOPED COUNTRIES	+696	55·2	+791	62·6	+1,239	64·9
e.g. North America	+647	96·2	+927	102·6	+939	104·7
Western Europe	+1,004	44·6	+1,041	51·3	+1,411	54·6
Australia – New Zealand	−999	104·9	−1,509	109·2	−1,607	111·1
COUNTRIES WITH CENTRAL PLANNING 1	−65	36·9	+590	45·3	+744	47·5
World Total 1	+29	26·0	+2,978	27·6	+6,404	29·3

1 Excluding China

Source
FAO, *Agricultural Commodities Projections for 1975 and 1985,* Vol. 2, p. 138.

Table 8   Price comparisons for some agricultural products 1968
U.S. $/100 kg

PRODUCTS	EEC *a*	United Kingdom *b*	EEC excess in %	Quotations in the principal producing countries	EEC excess in %
	1	2	3	4	5
Wheat	9·38	6·43	46	4·91 **1**	91
Rye	9·04	5·10	77	4·56 **1**	98
Barley	8·48	5·93	43	4·90 **2**	73
Oats	7·95	6·37	25	4·86 **1**	63
Maize	8·78			4·46 **1**	97
Beef and veal meat (live weight)	66·18	44·35	49	40·56 **3**	63
Pig meat (live weight)	66·17	45·19	46	44·04 **1**	50
Milk	9·30	8·56	9	6·41 **4**	45
Butter	181·72 **5**	70·87 **6**	156	70·87 **6**	156
Eggs	66·99	57·44	17	30·59 **3**	119
Sugar beet	1·58	1·53	3	1·43 **4**	10
Sugar	21·33 **7**	11·28 **8**	89	4·87 **9**	338

a Balanced average of prices received by the producers in the EEC countries, including subsidies.

b Average of prices received by the producers, including subsidies.

1 Chicago quotation.

2 Winnipeg quotation.

3 Copenhagen quotation.

4 Prices received by Danish producers.

5 Balanced average of wholesale prices in the EEC.

6 Import prices London/Retail prices New Zealand.

7 Intervention prices.

8 Commonwealth Sugar Agreement, contract prices.

9 London quotation, average of three months.

Sources

Statistisches Bundesamt Wiesbaden: Fachserie M, Preise, Löhne, Wirtschaftsrechnungen, Reihe 9, Preise im Ausland I Grosshandelspreise, (Grundstoffe Teil I) and Weltmarktpreise ausgewählter Waren. 1969; EEC: *Informations, Marchés agricoles, Valeurs unitaires* (special number) July 1970; Commission des Communautés Européennes: Rapport sur la situation de l'agriculture et des marchés agricoles, Com (69) 550, June 1969 (stencil).

Table 9   **(A) Value of production in the EEC. Estimates at various prices 1967-8.** In millions of dollars (£=US$ 2.40)

		Production in the ECC 1,000 metric tons	Prices ($/100kg) A	B	C	A mill. $	%	B mill. $	%	C mill. $	%
(1)	Wheat	31,158	9·81	6·07	5·84	3,062·8	12·0	1,891·3	9·5	1,818·4	10·5
(2)	Rye	4,013	8·73	5·10	4·81	350·3	1·4	204·7	1·0	193·1	1·1
(3)	Barley	15,877	8·30	5·70	5·02	1.317·8	5·1	905·0	4·5	796·4	4·6
(4)	Oats	8,031	7·77	6·16	5·56	624·0	2·4	494·7	2·5	446·5	2·6
(5)	Potatoes	40,865	3·31	3·50	3·14 1	1,352·6	5·3	1,430·3	7·2	1,283·2	7·4
(6)	Sugar Beet		1·72	1·56	1·35 1	837·0	3·2	759·1	3·8	656·9	3·8
(7)	Milk	72,476	9·54	8·60	7·03 1	6,914·2	27·1	6,232·9	31·2	5,095·1	29·4
(8)	Eggs	2,257	63·36	54·66	38·75	1,430·0	5·6	1.233·7	6·2	874·6	5·1
(9)	Pork	5,026	80·57 2	62·67 2	52·83 2	4.049·6	15·9	3,150·3	15·8	2,655·2	15·3
(10)	Beef & Veal	3,825	115·41 2	77·31 2	72·42 2	4,414·6	17·3	2,956·9	14·8	2,770·0	16·0
(11)	Poultry	1,517	72·33 2	47·61 2	46·87 2	1,097·2	4·3	722·2	3·6	710·9	4·1
	Total 1–11					25,450·1	100·0	19,981·1	100·0	17,300·3	100·0

(B) Value of production in The United Kingdom. Estimates at various prices, 1967. In millions of dollars

		Production in the U.K. 1,000 metric tons	Prices ($/100kg) A	B	C	A mill $	%	B mill. $	%	C mill. $	%
(1)	Wheat	3,902	9·81	6·07	5·84	383·6	6·9	236·8	5·5	227·7	6·1
(2)	Rye	12	8·73	5·10	4·81	1·0	0·0	0·6	0·0	0·6	0·0
(3)	Barley	9,214	8·30	5·70	5·02	764·8	13·8	525·2	12·2	462·2	12·5
(4)	Oats	1,386	7·77	6·16	5·56	107·7	1·9	85·4	2·0	77·1	2·1
(5)	Potatoes	7,200	3·31	3·50	3·14 1	238·3	4·3	252·0	5·9	226·1	6·1
(6)	Sugar Beet	6,883	1·72	1·56	1·35 1	118·4	2·1	107·4	2·5	92·9	2·5
(7)	Milk	13,065	9·54	8·60	7·03 1	1246·4	22·5	1123·6	26·1	918·5	24·8
(8)	Eggs	916	63·36	54·66	38·75	580·4	10·5	500·7	11·6	354·9	9·6
(9)	Pork	803	80·57 2	62·67 2	52·83 2	646·9	11·7	503·3	11·7	424·2	11·5
(10)	Beef & Veal	982	115·41 2	77·31 2	72·42 2	1133·3	20·5	759·1	17·6	711·1	19·2
(11)	Poultry	439	72·33 2	47·61 2	46·87 2	317·5	5·7	209·0	4·9	205·7	5·6
	Total 1–11					5538·3	100·0	4303·1	100·0	3701·1	100·0

A Calculated on prices received by producers in the EEC.
B Calculated on prices received by producers in the
   United Kingdom. Sterling prices converted to $ at the rate
   $2·40 = £1.
C Calculated on world market prices.
1 Prices received by Danish producers   **2** Carcass weight
Sources
Production: OECD, *Agricultural Statistics 1955-1968*, Paris

1969. Prices: *Prix des produits agricoles et des engrais en Europe en 1967/1968*. New York: United Nations (St./ECE/ AGRI/31); Memorandum sur la réforme de l'agriculture dans la Communauté Economique Européenne (Secrétariat Général de la Commission Dec. 1968); Statistiches Bundesamt, *Preise, Löhne Wirtchaftrechnungen, Reihe 9, Preise im Ausland I, Weltmarktpreise ausgewählter Waren*, Stuttgart-Mainz, Jan-Dec. 1969.

Table 10 — Retail prices of selected consumer goods, October 1968 in $

	United States 50 towns	France Paris	Germany	Italy Milan	Netherlands	Belgium Antwerp	United Kingdom 200 towns
Wheat Bread kg	0·50	0·26	0·39	0·33	0·26	0·25	0·23
Rice kg	0·49	0·36/0·47	0·48	0·41	0·43	0·66	0·41
Macaroni kg	0·49	0·47	0·52	0·42		0·65	
BEEF kg							
Sirloin boneless	2·66	3·53	2·38	3·23	3·59	3·71	2·04
Brisket boneless	1·42	1·20	1·51	..	..	1·41	0·86
PORK							
Loin chops bone-in	2·34	1·72	1·90	2·46	2·05	2·30	1·58
Shoulder boneless	..	..	0·96	..	1·85	..	1·33
Ham kg cooked, sliced boneless	1·54	3·47	3·13	6·39 1	2·15	3·35	2·56
Veal leg bone-in	3·91	3·34	1·87	4·49 2	..	..	..
Margarine kg	0·61	0·74	0·63	1·14	0·48	0·56	0·46
Peanut oil litre	0·75	0·53	0·49	0·58	0·53	..	..
Whole milk litre	0·29	0·18	..	0·23	0·17	0·16	0·18
Butter kg	1·85	2·18/2·31	1·94	2·50	1·90	2·09	0·85
Eggs piece	0·05	0·06	0·06	0·07	0·04	0·05	0·04
Potatoes kg	0·16	0·06	0·07	0·14	0·08	0·07	0·08
Apples kg	0·65	0·30	0·24	0·36	2·20	..	0·45
Oranges kg	0·65	0·44	0·40	..	0·38	..	0·35
Sugar kg	0·27	0·28	0·31	0·39	0·35	0·38	0·19
Coffee kg	1·69	2·29	3·95	3·81	2·05	2·67	2·55

1 Raw ham.   2 Boneless.
.. not available

Source
Bulletin of Labour Statistics, 1969, 2nd Quarter, ILO, Geneva.

Table 11

EEC: Exports and imports of food products and livestock (C.T.C.I.O.) 1963-1969

A Exports (f.o.b.)

	1963		1964		1965		1966		1967		1968		1969		Average rate of increase 1963/69
	Mill. $	Part in total exp.	Mill. $	Part in total exp.	Mill. $	Part in total exp.	Mill. $	Part in total exp.	Mill. $	Part in total exp.	Mill. $	Part in total exp.	Mill. $	Part in total exp.	
Total exports	3,330	100	3,677	100	4,306	100	4,419	100	4,822	100	5,528	100	6,652	100	+12·3
Intra EEC	1,684	50·6	1,905	51·8	2,395	55·6	2,534	57·3	2,851	59·1	3,467	62·7	4,512	67·9	+18·1
United States	115	3·5	117	3·2	129	3·0	161	3·6	181	3·8	194	3·5	190	2·9	+ 9·0
EFTA	686	20·6	730	19·8	796	18·5	752	17·0	826	17·1	790	14·3	840	12·6	+ 3·5
Eastern Europe	131	3·9	144	3·9	163	3·8	172	3·9	86	1·8	132	2·4	122	1·8	+ 4·0
Developing countries	546	16·4	695	16·4	633	14·7	612	13·9	678	14·1	705	12·8	739	11·1	+ 5·2
Other countries	168	5·0	186	5·1	190	4·4	188	4·3	200	4·1	240	4·3	249	3·7	+ 6·9

B Imports (c.i.f.)

	1963		1964		1965		1966		1967		1968		1969		Average rate of increase 1963/69
	Mill. $	Part in total exp.	Mill. $	Part in total exp.	Mill. $	Part in total exp.	Mill. $	Part in total exp.	Mill. $	Part in total exp.	Mill. $	Part in total exp.	Mill. $	Part in total exp.	
Total imports	6,352	100	6,988	100	8,028	100	8,469	100	8,525	100	9,017	100	10,511	100	+ 8·7
Intra EEC	1,672	26·3	1,921	27·5	2,388	29·7	2,554	30·2	2,814	33·0	3,406	37·8	4,471	42·5	+18·1
United States	738	11·6	820	11·7	996	12·4	1,126	13·3	872	10·2	919	10·2	861	8·2	+ 3·6
EFTA	623	9·8	631	9·1	681	8·5	642	7·6	663	7·8	591	6·5	647	6·2	+ 0·8
Eastern Europe	329	5·2	295	4·2	397	5·0	451	5·3	499	5·8	460	5·1	577	5·5	+10·9
Developing countries	2,311	36·9	2,551	36·5	2,723	33·9	2,819	33·3	2,835	33·3	2,784	30·9	3,051	29·0	+ 4·7
Other countries	679	10·4	770	11·0	843	10·5	877	10·3	842	9·9	857	9·5	904	8·6	+ 4·9

Source
OECD: *Foreign Trade Statistics. Series B. Commodity Trade*
Analysis by main regions 1963-1969.

Table 12

Composition of the labour force employed in agriculture 1 1960 and 1968 in thousands and in percentages

	Employers and Self-employed	%	Unpaid family workers	%	Wage-earners	%	Total	%
GERMANY								
1960	1,159	32·0	1,931	53·3	533	14·7	3,623	100
1968	873	33·2	1,453	55·2	304	11·6	2,630	100
Index (1960 = 100)		75·0		74·0		57·0		73
FRANCE								
1960			3,240	77·3	949	22·7	4,189	100
1968			2,467	79·1	654	20·9	3,121	100
Index (1960 = 100)				76·0		69·0		75
ITALY								
1960	2,070	47·0	1,033	23·5	1,300	29·5	4,403	100
1968	1,512	51·7	429	14·7	984	33·6	2,925	100
Index (1960 = 100)		73·0		42·0		76·0		66
NETHERLANDS								
1960			345	74·2	120	25·8	465	100
1968	193	54·8	74	21·0	85	24·2	352	100
Index (1960 = 100)				77·0		71·0		76
BELGIUM								
1960	154	71·0	41	18·9	22	10·1	217	100
1968	120	78·9	18	11·9	14	9·2	152	100
Index (1960 = 100)		77·9		44·0		64·0		70
UNITED KINGDOM								
1960	396	38·5	..		632	61·5	1,028	100
1968	345	45·0	..		422	55·0	767	100
Index (1960 = 100)		87·0				67·0		75
UNITED STATES								
1960	..		..		..		5,458	
1968	1,985	52·0	550	14·4	1,281	33·6	3,817	100
Index (1960 = 100)		..		..		..		70

.. not available.   **1** Annual average estimates.

Source

OECD: *Labour Force Statistics 1957-1968*, Paris 1970.

Table 13

Gross fixed capital formation in agriculture (a) in percentage of the gross agricultural product at factor cost and at current prices (%)

	1957/1958	1965/1966
Germany	19·6	31·9
France *b*	14·3	15·1
Italy	13·9	14·6
Netherlands	8·3	15·2
Belgium	11·9	12·2
United States *c*	17·8	21·1
United Kingdom	14·3	17·1
Japan	11·3	17·8

a Including – except where otherwise stated – forestry and fishery.

b Excluding fishery.
c Excluding investment.

Source
OECD, *Capital and Finance in Agriculture, Statistical Annexe.*
March 1970 (Unpublished document).

Table 14

Composition of gross fixed capital formation in agriculture: 1965-66 percentage shares at current prices

	Farm buildings	Land improvement	Machinery
United States	21		79
United Kingdom	38		62
Belgium **1**	16	3	62
France	19		81
Germany	18	(45) *a*	37
Italy	54		46
Japan	30	(28) *a*	42

a Estimates assuming the difference between the sum of the investment in building and machinery and the total (given by National Accounts in this case) is the amount for land improvement.

1 Besides the items mentioned, investment in research equipment and the legal costs of real estate transfers are considered part of GFAF: these amount to 3% and 16% respectively of the total.

Source
OECD: *Capital and Finance in Agriculture, Statistical Annexe.*
March 1970 (Unpublished document).

191

Table 15

Regional inequalities in productivity: examples from Germany, France and Italy in 1960

	Final Production per work unit (in $ – 1953)	Final Production per hectare of cultivated agricultural surface (in $ – 1953)	Number of hectares of agricultural surface used per work unit
GERMANY			
Schleswig–Holstein and Hamburg	3·513	374	9·39
North Rhine–Westphalia	2·539	444	5·71
Rhineland–Palatinate	1·553	441	4·25
Bavaria	1·941	337	5·77
FRANCE			
Nord–Pas de Calais–Somme	3·155	400·5	8·7
Ardennes–Meuse–Meurthe et Moselle-Moselle	2·650	167·0	17·4
Manche–Calvados–Orne	1·510	237·5	7·0
Allier–Puy de Dôme–Cantal– Loire–Haute Loire	1·427	151·3	0·4
Tarn–Dordogne–Lot– Aveyron–Lozère	1·326	157·6	9·2
ITALY			
Lombardy	1·746	432·0	3·98
Emilia	1·469	446·3	3·24
Tuscany	250	227·4	4·04
Calabria	646	161·5	3·87

Source

European Economic Community, *Evolution de la productivité dans le CEE,* June 1969.

Table 16

FEOGA guarantee section balance (1962/63 – 1965/66: final accounts)
in millions of U.S. $

	1962/63 a	1962/63 b	1962/63 c	1963/64 a	1963/64 b	1963/64 c	1964/65 a	1964/65 b	1964/65 c	1965/66 a	1965/66 b	1965/66 c	Total a	Total b	Total c
Germany	8·0	1·3	−6·2	14·3	2·6	−11·7	46·8	6·9	−39·9	75·6	18·6	−57·0	144·7	29·4	−115·3
France	8·0	24·4	+16·4	13·2	45·5	+32·3	38·7	124·0	+85·3	77·7	139·1	+61·4	137·6	333·0	+195·4
Italy	8·0	1·8	−6·7	14·2	0·7	−13·5	44·8	2·1	−42·7	43·0	4·9	−38·1	110·0	9·5	−100·5
Netherlands	2·3	0·9	−1·4	4·8	1·5	−3·3	15·8	25·0	+9·2	22·8	62·3	+39·5	45·7	89·7	+44·0
Belgium	2·3	0·3	−2·0	4·1	0·4	−3·7	13·4	1·8	−11·6	19·0	13·6	−5·4	38·8	16·1	−22·7
Luxemburg	0·1		−0·1	0·1		−0·1	0·3		−0·3	0·5	0·1	−0·4	1·0	0·1	−0·9
EEC	28·7	28·7		50·7	50·7		159·8	159·8		238·6	238·6		477·8	477·9	

a Contribution of member States of FEOGA.
b FEOGA reimbursements to member States.
c Balances.

Sources
H. Zijlmans, 'Le financement de la politique agricole commune.'
Revue du Marché Commun. Nov.-Dec. 1969, pp. 568-69.

Table 16 (continued)

FEOGA guarantee section balance (1966/67 – 1968/69: provisional accounts)
in millions of U.S. $

	1966/67 a	1966/67 b	1966/67 c	1967/68 a	1967/68 b	1967/68 c	1968/69 a	1968/69 b	1968/69 c	Total a	Total b	Total c
Germany	114·2	27·3	−86·9	309·9	127·9	−182·0	460·3	288·8	−171·5	884·4	444·0	−440·4
France	108·4	154·1	+45·7	184·9	402·4	+217·5	344·3	632·7	+288·4	637·6	1189·2	+551·6
Italy	81·5	96·1	+14·6	294·0	192·3	−101·7	411·4	234·3	−177·1	786·9	522·7	−264·2
Netherlands	36·1	75·0	+38·9	160·1	219·7	+59·6	210·1	290·2	+80·1	406·3	584·9	+178·6
Belgium	29·4	17·8	−11·6	83·9	91·6	+7·7	131·1	112·0	−19·1	244·4	221·4	−23·0
Luxemburg	0·8	0·1	−0·7	1·5	0·4	−1·1	2·5	1·7	−0·4	4·8	2·2	−2·6
EEC	370·4	370·4		1034·3	1034·3		1559·5	1559·5		2964·4	2964·2	

a Contributions to FEOGA from member states.
b Repayments to FEOGA from member states.
c Balances.

Sources
For 1966/67 and 1967/68. Zijlmans. 'Le financement de la politique agricole commune'; for 1968/69.
Bulletin des Communautés européennes. July 1970.

Table 17 — Orientation and special sections: balance of member states in U.S. $ 1964 – 1967 and 1968

	Orientation Section 1964–1967	Orientation and Special Sections 1968		
		Orientation	Special	Total
Germany	−21·4	−10·3	+81·7	+71·4
France	−24·7	−13·8	−58·3	−72·1
Italy	+58·9	+30·2	+ 6·7	+36·9
Netherlands	− 7·8	− 4·3	−16·4	−20·7
Belgium	− 6·2	− 2·4	−16·4	−18·8
Luxemburg	+ 1·2	+ 0·6	+ 2·7	+ 3·3

Source

Zijlmans, 'Le financement de la politique agricole commune'
and European Economic Community, Directorate of the
FEOGA, document quoted.

Table 18 — FEOGA, guarantee section: ratio of reimbursements to the value of agricultural production 1

COUNTRIES	1965/66		1966/67		1967/68		1968/69		1965/66–1967/68	
	Reimb. in million US $	in % ag. prodn. 1965	Reimb. in million US $	in % ag. prodn. 1966	Reimb. in million US $	in % ag. prodn. 1967	Reimb. in million US $	in % ag. prodn. 1968	Reimb. in million US $	in % ag. prodn. 1965–68
Germany	18·6	0·36	27·3	0·38	127·9	2·41	288·8	5·17	115·6	2·16
Belgium	13·6	1·49	17·8	2·05	91·6	10·18	112·0	11·43	58·7	6·45
France	139·1	1·91	154·1	2·06	402·4	5·00	632·7	7·68	332·0	4·28
Italy	4·9	0·07	96·1	1·34	192·3	2·46	234·3	3·19	131·9	1·80
Luxemburg	0·1	0·25	0·1	0·25	0·3	0·75	1·7	4·25	0·5	1·25
Netherlands	63·3	4·43	75·0	5·43	219·7	14·94	290·2	18·36	162·0	11·09
EEC	239·6	1·09	370·4	1·66	1,034·2	4·58	1,559·7	6·56	800·7	3·54

1 Value added at factor cost.

Sources

Reimbursements 1965/66-1967/68: H. Zijlmans, 'Le finance-
ment de la politique agricole commune'. *Revue du Marché*
Commun, Nov.-Dec. 1969, pp. 568-69. For 1968/69.
Bulletin des Communautés européennes, July 1970; GDP;
OSCE, National Accounts 1969.

Table 19 — FEOGA, guarantee section: reimbursements per head of agricultural population 1965-1968

COUNTRIES	1965 Reimb. in 1000 US $	1965 per pers. occupied in agr. (US $)	1966 Reimb. in 1000 US $	1966 per pers. occupied in agr. (US $)	1967 Reimb. in 1000 US $	1967 per pers. occupied in agr. (US $)	1968 Reimb. in 1000 US $	1968 per pers. occupied in agr. US($)	1965–1968 Reimb. in 1000 US $	1965–1968 per pers. occupied in agr. 1965–68 (US $)
Germany	4·969	1·7	11·600	4·0	8·051	2·9	27·694	10·5	13·078	4·7
Belgium	755	3·3	3·279	15·2	2·169	10·4	7·320	36·4	3·380	15·8
France	3·692	1·0	8·924	2·6	7·098	2·2	22·567	7·3	10·570	3·2
Italy	5·866	1·2	26·771	5·7	60·403	13·3	57·188	13·4	37·577	8·2
Luxemburg	275	14·5	899	49·9	157	8·7	826	48·6	539	29·9
Netherlands	1·577	4·0	3·112	8·3	2·162	5·9	7·665	21·8	3·629	9·8
EEC	17·134	1·4	54·585	4·7	80·040	7·2	123·260	11·7	68·773	6·1

Sources

'Le Fonds Européen d'Orientation et de Garantie Agricole et son Action depuis 1962' (Extracted from *Bulletin des Communautés Européennes* July 1970) ; OSCE : *Statistiques Générales,* No. 7, 1969.

Table 20 — FEOGA: All sections. Member states' net contributions or reimbursements compared to their current balance of payments 1964/65 – 1968/69 in millions of U.S. $

	1964/65 Net Contributions (—) or net Reimbursements (+)	1964/65 Balance of payments: balance of current operations	1964/65 a as % of b	1965/66 Net Contributions (—) or net Reimbursements (+)	1965/66 Balance of payments: balance of current operations	1965/66 a as % of b	1966/67 Net Contributions (—) or net Reimbursements (+)	1966/67 Balance of payments: balance of current operations	1966/67 a as % of b
	a	b	c	a	b	c	a	b	c
Germany	−44·4	−1,101·5	4·0	− 73·8	−1,287·8	5·7	−75·3	+1,855·3	4·1
France	+81·0	+ 371·0	21·8	+42·3	+ 472·0	9·0	+20·7	− 407·0	5·1
Italy	−31·1	+2,211·0 1	1·4	+ 7·1	+2,127·0 2	0·3	+41·0	+1,599·0 3	2·6
Netherlands	+ 7·0	+ 131·0	5·3	+34·2	− 174·0	19·7	+24·8	− 12·0	206·7
Belgium	−13·0	+ 152·0 1	8·2	− 9·4	− 96·0 2	9·4	−11·2	+ 76·0	14·7
Luxemburg	+ 0·5			− 0·4					

	1967/68 Net Contributions (—) or net Reimbursements (+) a	1967/68 Balance of payments: balance of current operations b	1967/68 a as % of b c	1968/69 Net Contributions (—) or net Reimbursements (+) a	1968/69 Balance of payments: balance of current operations b	1968/69 a as % of b c
Germany	− 54·8	+2,435·0	2·3	− 71·4	+2,477·0	2·9
France	+104·9	+ 9·0	65·5	+171·4	−2,759·0	6·2
Italy	− 69·6	+2,204·0	3·2	−122·6	+2,801·0	4·4
Netherlands	+ 28·2	+ 75·0	37·6	+ 46·0	+ 22·0	20·9
Belgium	− 10·6	+ 98·0	8·9	− 25·4	− 51·0	45·9
Luxemburg	+ 1·9			+ 2·0		

1 Balance of current operations 1965.
2 Balance of current operations 1966.
3 Balance of current operations 1967.

Sources

Statistisches Jahrbuch über Ernährung, Landwirtschaft und Forsten der Bundesrepublik Deutschland 1970, Bundesministerium für Ernährung, Landwirtschaft und Forsten, Hamburg and Berlin 1970. I.M.F.: *International Financial Statistics* No. 12 Dec. 1968, No. 12 Dec. 1969 No. 8 Aug. 1970.

List of Abbreviations used in the Tables

ILO	International Labour Organization
EEC	European Economic Community
FAO	Food and Agricultural Organization
FEOGA	European Fund for Agricultural Orientation and Guarantee
IMF	International Monetary Fund
OCDE	Organization for Economic Cooperation and Development
OSCE	Statistical Office of the European Communities
GNP	Gross National Product
GDP	Gross Domestic Product
UC	Unit of account (=US)

Appendix IV

Individual reservations

from: Dr HANS-BRODER KROHN

'The preparatory discussions of this Report in which I participated concerned the report itself, and covered neither the topics dealt with in Appendixes I and II nor the tables.

Furthermore, the Group did not examine the methods and the elements upon which is based the reference, page 9, to a 11 to 13 thousand million dollar charge which is assumed by the economy of the European Community in favour of agriculture.'

from: Prof Dr HANS WILBRANDT

'I shall forgo making comments on questions of minor importance. I feel I ought, however, to say a few words about some problems which I consider essential. The following paragraphs are in part an expression of dissent, in part a mere difference in emphasis.

(1) *With regard to basic problems.*

1a. – The agricultural problems of Europe are – each page of the Report confirms this – highly complex. If one did not take mutually interdependent factors into account, the solution of one or other particular problem would simply raise many others. Methods acceptable to all partners can hardly bring about ideal solutions: it is easier to elaborate theoretical solutions than to apply practical ones. We must strike the optimum balance from a set of pluses and minuses.

1b. – In so far as European agriculture will achieve increased efficiency thanks to the implementation of future agricultural policy, it will be entitled as an equal partner in the economy to an adequate per capita income for future farmers. If we want the agricultural population to co-operate fully with the creation of an efficient agriculture within European industrial society it is necessary, in case of a conflict of objectives, to accord to this postulate, which the Report fully recognizes, the priority it deserves.

1c. – A level of agricultural prices whose relationship to world prices would be determined by a margin of protection which, on the average, would not exceed by more than two or three times that enjoyed by manufacturing industry, is a good guideline for reaching the long-term goal of improving the efficiency of the economy as a whole. The degree and speed of the realization depend, nonetheless, on the extent and tempo of improvement in productivity and efficiency which future agricultural policy will determine for the great number of European farms. The question to what extent the lowering of prices represents an appropriate instrument and, hence, the condition for an improvement in productivity; or, on the contrary, whether lowering of prices can only result from such improvement, will be debated indefinitely.

In any case, we cannot set aside the idea of price normalization, within the context of the long-term structural programmes aimed at satisfying postulate 1b, and during which the labour force leaving agriculture would be offered employment in other sectors, while areas used until now in an uneconomic fashion would be put to optimal economic use.

1d. – The Report expresses at various points the fear that an insufficient price reduction would damage the competitive capacity of European industry. This does not seem justified by past experience, and will be even less so in the future in that, in spite of increased needs in absolute terms, the share of food in consumers' expenditure will decrease as per capita income increases.

1e. – A drastic and sudden price reduction instigating acts of despair, a massive exodus of labour unable easily to find employment in other sectors, and the abandonment of land perfectly suitable for economic production, would be more of a disservice than a service to a good cause.

1f. – I believe the optimistic evaluation of the economic and fiscal effects (see p. 33 and following pages) of short- and long-term measures proposed in the Report is premature. A valid judgement cannot be established until there has been a statistical examination of the problem on the basis of data which is not yet available. In any case, the interesting and thought-provoking proposals of the Report deserve full consideration at a time when a new conception is about to emerge. Nevertheless, the overall assessment of economic gain should be based less on the increase or decrease of the burden on the tax payer, consumer or producer of agricultural products, than on a comparison of the improvement in productivity resulting from structural changes within and without the agricultural sector and the sums expended to that end.

1g. – Considerations of world market reform take a step into the future and establish a direction. We must expect that the decisions on European agricultural policy will have to be taken without waiting for fundamental changes in the world market.

(2) *With regard to the redirection procedure.*

2a. – In the process of deciding on the means which will enable the implementation of the desired redirection, other considerations come into play. I consider the possible margin of nominal price reduction of agricultural products – even if the transition be eased by income support – to be very limited. It can hardly be otherwise in view of the budgetary and administrative realities of domestic policy and social preoccupations, not to mention the tendency, hard to ignore, which the member countries will continue to show, towards mutual concessions on price increases. Given the continual increase of the general level of European prices, it is possible that a stabilization of agricultural prices at their present level would stimulate reorientation to a greater extent than the Report indicates. Even so there, too, the margin is limited.

2b. – The fact that, during recent years, the surpluses in respect of some products (above all butter and sugar) have diminished, mainly as a consequence of less abundant crops and of losses incurred in the selling off of stocks, is deceptive; it would be a mistake to deduce a flattening-out of the production curve. Powerful factors are still at work, and will continue to be so, at least in the near future, in the direction of an increase in production. Among them should be noted:

– Technical progress which will undoubtedly continue at a rapid rate and which will continue to provide progressive farmers with new means of increasing production.

– The relationship, which will continue to act as a production incentive, between the prices of products used in agriculture, and which contribute to an increased production, and the prices paid to farmers, even if these are moderately reduced.

– 'Opportunity costs', the effects of which, already felt after the decrease in the proportion of the labour force occupied in agriculture and the rise in industrial productivity, will be increasingly manifest in a development of agricultural income parallel to that of other incomes. This is particularly true for the still very large number of small farms in which the manpower employed represents an irreducible minimum. In this case, a compensation for the decrease in income resulting from a price reduction and, if possible, an improvement in such income, could only be ensured through an increased production effort.

Taking these facts into account, I doubt whether a lowering of the level of agricultural prices, which could in any case only be moderate, would in the short run reinforce, to the extent which the Report assumes, the effect of the measures foreseen in the Mansholt Plan; that is, to adapt the supply to a European demand which can hardly be enlarged. The impact of these curbs will not be fully felt until there is a continuous improvement in agricultural structures.

2c. – Under these conditions, it is right to emphasize particularly the urgency of the other measures indicated in the Mansholt Plan as well as in this Report, designed to adapt agriculture to present and future requirements, however costly this may be during the transitory period.

2d. – One of the first imperatives of the new European agricultural policy is to limit production in order to avoid the accumulation of new surpluses. The liquidation of surpluses not only involves a waste of millions, but is also likely to divert aid to developing countries into paths which do not efficiently favour growth.

2e. – The more limited the influence which the price policy is able to exert on a voluntary limitation of agricultural production, the more urgent the question of how to achieve such a goal in the short run. Without ignoring the pitfalls (emphasized, perhaps, too strongly, in my opinion, in the Report, p. 34) of fixing quotas for agricultural products I deem it indispensable that we consider the possibility of supplementing structural policy, the effects of which on the volume of production will only be felt in the long run, by other measures, of more immediate effect, and limited to a few years; I mean negotiable production quotas which would be eliminated as soon as the changes designed to curb production achieved their full impact.

Note by Professor Kaldor and Mr J S Marsh

The analysis presented in the Report and its emphasis on the need to reduce the agricultural prices of the Community has our full support. In our view it is essential that this should afford no greater protection than that accorded by the Community to other sectors of the economy. The proposals made in the Report would, if fully implemented, give effect to this principle.

Protection limited to this level would avoid much of the damage that the present CAP does to world trade. Genuine low cost producers would continue to have access to the Community market. There would be no dumping of EEC surpluses on the world market. The consequent improvement in world trade would help not only agricultural exporters, but all countries, including the EEC, which participate in international trade.

On the other hand, any higher pattern of prices would not only impede the evolution of a satisfactory agricultural structure within the Community, but perpetuate an arrangement whereby some member countries pay a continuing and growing subsidy for the support of others. As the Report makes clear, the principles which now govern the contributions to, and the receipts from, the Community Fund cannot be justified either on the criterion of ability to pay or that of need.

It seems to us that the recommendations of this Report as regards the gradual replacement of price support by income support are essential if the Community is to be enlarged by the accession of Britain and other members of EFTA. Their adoption would avoid most of the disruption of traditional trading links between Britain and the Commonwealth, it would greatly reduce the burden of import levies and of the cost of food bought from other EEC members and thus relieve pressure on the British balance of payments. Finally, the recommended level of prices, together with the measures for structural reform, would justify the net contribution which Britain would be asked to make to an enlarged Community, as an aid to the solution of the pressing problem of low incomes in EEC agriculture, rather than as a means of perpetuating the present obsolete pattern of farm production in the EEC.

We agree that the adjustment to the proposed price level cannot be made immediately but we believe that it should be brought into effect in stages, over a period laid down in advance, in the same way in which the Community has implemented many of its other policies; and that the transitional arrangements for Britain and the other new members should be harmonized with these arrangements, so that the new members should be able to adapt their own agricultural policies in the direction of the ultimate level of protection to be accorded to agriculture, and should not be asked to adopt the present level of prices.

The question of British membership of the EEC involves, of course, numerous other issues apart from agricultural policy. As it stands, however, the Common Agricultural Policy represents a formidable obstacle to accession by Britain. Should the Community prove unwilling to accept the policy of gradually lowering the level of agricultural prices to a point which represents no more than the *ad valorem* level of protection on industrial goods or, alternatively, to offer terms to Britain (and other new members) which avoided the serious consequences of the imposition of an agricultural policy unjustified on economic grounds, we would not feel that it would be in the interest of Britain to enter into the European Economic Community.